CIA

Also by Andrew Tully

WHEN THEY BURNED THE WHITE HOUSE

A RACE OF REBELS

TREASURY AGENT

ERA OF ELEGANCE

CIA

THE INSIDE STORY

By Andrew Tully

WILLIAM MORROW AND COMPANY

NEW YORK

1962

In a few cases, fictitious names have been used and operational methods have been disguised—for obvious reasons of security.

—AT

Fifth Printing, May 1962

Library of Congress Catalog Card Number 62-8549

To Barbara Witchell Tully

Table of Contents

CIA

Knowledge is never too dear.
                        –Sir Francis Walsingham

1. *CIA—What and Why?*

ON A FINE SUMMER'S DAY in 1954, the manager of a state-owned button manufacturing plant in Communist Berlin picked up the phone and called a supplier across town. When a voice answered on the other end of the line, plump, rosy-cheeked Otto Bauer was all business.

"I have authority to negotiate with you, Herr Hauptman" said Otto Bauer. "If you could bring your samples over again we could discuss the matter further."

An hour later Bauer and Hauptman were deep in their negotiations. Bauer was backed up by his accountant and a plastics expert, whom he had called into his office when Hauptman arrived. The discussion continued for nearly two hours, concerned mostly with prices and delivery deadlines. But when Hauptman left Bauer's office he had a contract in his pocket and a covering letter from Bauer touching on the main points of the deal.

Hauptman took the covering letter home with him that night. There, in his locked study, he pored over the single-spaced text until one o'clock in the morning. By midnight he believed he had found what he was looking for, but he spent another hour checking and rechecking. At the end, the message he deciphered from the covering letter meant nothing to him, but that did not matter because it would have meaning elsewhere.

1

Elsewhere, in this case, meant a grimy little cloak-and-suit wholesaler's office in Marseille, France. There, a few days later, the manager of the business received a letter from Hauptman offering him an advantageous price on certain raw materials. And in a week's time that letter lay on the desk of Allen Welsh Dulles, the then director of the United States Central Intelligence Agency, marked "AWD's eyes only." The message pinpointed for America's huge espionage apparatus the location just outside Berlin of a terminus of telephone cables serving East German military and civilian officials—a conglomeration of wiring which could handle simultaneously 432 calls.

Otto Bauer, Hans Hauptman and the Marseille cloak-and-suiter are agents of the CIA, although these are not their names, and none of them has anything to do with the button or wholesale clothing business. Bauer is worthy of particular notice, because he has been an Allied spy practically all of his adult life. He has been a German citizen since the mid-Twenties, when he was assigned by British intelligence to Berlin and furnished with capital to start a small manufacturing business. In line with his instructions, he made no attempt to contact his superiors until more than five years after his arrival in Germany. But from then through the years of World War II, Otto Bauer fed the British with an unceasing supply of information—on the collapse of the Weimar Republic, on Hitler's rise to power, on the invasion of Poland, on German war plans. It is not known, except to CIA and British intelligence, why he transferred to the American payroll, but he apparently did so shortly after V-E Day. At any rate, from his vantage point as a Communist East German businessman—which gives him quasi-official status—Otto Bauer has been trickling information back to Washington for more than fifteen years.

The telephone cable terminus bit was quite a trickle, and CIA went to work on it at once. Because in espionage nothing is taken for granted, there first was a check on the information that took nearly three months to complete. Finally, the information checked out by means of a simple process. "Somebody" in the Soviet Zone merely "dug a hole in the ground." The terminus was there, all right, waiting to be exploited.

However, this was an opportunity that could not be exploited on the spot. American agents presumably could get to the cables for tapping, but it was impossible to provide the physical facilities for recording these phone conversations in the Communist Zone. Obviously, the cables had to be got to from West Berlin.

The situation was surveyed, in person and by maps. The telephone terminus was five feet underground, below the village of Alt-Glienicke on the Soviet side, and approximately six hundred yards from the American Zone border village of Rudow. In other words, the terminus was a tantalizing six football fields away from official American ears. Yet, somehow those lines had to be tapped because by doing so the CIA would be privy not only to Communist military conversations but to messages to and from Moscow.

By late 1954, prodded by Allen Dulles, America's German organization had gone into business—the business of tunnel building. Other ideas had been discussed and discarded. There was only one way to reach that terminus and that was to build a road to it, underground.

CIA will not tell how long it took to dig the tunnel. For that matter, there has been no official acknowledgment of it. But it seems to have been completed in less than four months—a triumph of engineering with all modern conveniences. In Rudow, nudging the border, a new United States Air Force radar station was erected. Several other buildings, all with guard towers, were planted around the radar station. Then the digging started.

Beginning in the huge and airy basement of the radar station, the impromptu sand hogs burrowed twenty feet down, on a slight incline, scooping out an underground highway beneath the asphalt-paved Schoenefeld road which connects Rudow with Alt-Glienicke and continues on to the airport used by the Soviet army and the East German civilian air fleet. Thousands of tons of clay were hauled up into the radar station basement or diverted to the other buildings and then trucked away in huge boxes plastered with a variety of innocuous labels that would seem innocent to the Communist spies who infested the neighborhood.

The work went on for five weeks without even a scare. Then one day workmen grubbing deep under the Schoenefeld were startled suddenly to hear ominous noises overhead. Somebody up there was digging, and it could not be anybody who liked Americans because by this time the tunnel was well into Communist territory. By telephone the word was passed hurriedly to headquarters in the radar station. Meanwhile, work came to a standstill, while the men stood around, sweating and nervous.

Above ground, a phone call was put in to a man in West Berlin who was a double agent—a spy who "worked" for the East German government and furnished his Communist bosses with phony information while using his position to steal official secrets for the Allies. He was told to find out what the digging was about on the Schoenefeld road.

The agent drove across the border and into Alt-Glienicke to buy a special kind of sausage unobtainable in the American Zone. He loitered long enough to drink a couple of bottles of beer, and on his way back he exchanged a few phrases of rough humor with some workmen toiling in a trench along the side of the road. It was nearly dark when he telephoned his contact in the American Zone. The workmen on the Schoenefeld road, he reported, were "replacing some water pipes." Work on the tunnel was resumed immediately.

That was the only time work on the tunnel was interrupted, which seemed incredible when finally the job was finished. For, with typical American efficiency and thoroughness, the Yanks had built a burrow with overtones of elegance. The tunnel was six feet in diameter, made of bolted sections of corrugated iron lined on the sides with sand bags. It was completely air-conditioned and had electric pumps to take care of rain-water seepage. It contained switchboards, electric current boosters, 432 amplifier units to handle every one of the lines in the terminus simultaneously if necessary, and a system of elaborate listening and recording devices to tape messages.

Tapping wires protected by thick layers of lead ran through a wooden partition and up a steep passageway and then through two steel doors and into the East German terminus. These wires were attached to the Communist cables without disturbing service for even a second, a ticklish job that had to be done just that way lest the Communist authorities become suspicious. Impulses running through long-distance wires were detoured and the amplifier units gave them a boost via a distributor unit to the radar station, where there were 432 magnetophone recorders to take down the Red messages.

For almost a year American authorities used this tunnel to listen in on conversations between East German military officers, East German and Soviet authorities and messages to and from Moscow. Millions of words were recorded and transcribed, digested, and filed carefully away for cross-checking. In Washington, scores of persons at CIA headquarters were kept busy for months analyzing and filing these messages, and dispatching their gist to proper authorities.

Then, on April 22, 1956, the tunnel was discovered by a squad of Soviet signal troops. The discovery came during a routine check of the terminus by a young non-com who found a "stray wire." The soldier also was puzzled by the steel door bearing the inscription, in Russian, NO ADMITTANCE

BY ORDER OF THE COMMANDING OFFICER. This inscription, of course, had been lettered on the door by the American tunnel diggers to give the Reds pause even after they discovered the wire tap.

After some confusion and some hot words through channels, permission finally was received to investigate the mysterious door, and the Soviet troops broke it down to reveal the tunnel. Meanwhile, however, an alarm had been sounded the moment the first Soviet hand touched the wire-tapping apparatus and the tunnel had been cleared of all personnel.

Immediately, the Soviet Union dispatched a note to Washington demanding punishment for those persons who had dug the tunnel "to engage in subterranean espionage." The Communist press charged that the wire tapping violated the sovereign rights of the German Democratic Republic, and claimed that Mrs. Eleanor Lansing Dulles, the State Department German expert and sister of Allen Dulles, had visited the tunnel on two occasions "to check its efficiency."

But, curiously, both the Soviet and East German press heaped praise on the project. They described it as "bold . . . daring . . . audacious . . . skillful . . . and difficult." And shortly the Soviet opened the tunnel to visitors as a tourist attraction, with guides to explain the intricacies of its wire-tapping operations. It was closed to the public June 9, 1956, with the announcement that forty thousand members of "worker delegations from East Germany and the Soviet Union" had seen this triumph of American espionage.

The Communist tourists had a right to be impressed by what they saw. In a field where elaborateness of operation is common, the Berlin spy tunnel was one of the modern wonders of espionage. Whatever its cost, it was worth it, for it furnished the United States with bales of secret information. It also almost surely saved some lives—the lives of foreign agents for the United States who changed their mode of operations because of messages passing through that tunnel.

The Berlin tunnel, however proud an achievement, is only one short chapter in the story of the Central Intelligence Agency. That story has other proud chapters, and, within the limitations imposed by the American system, CIA is equipped intellectually, financially and operationally to add more successes to its record. But every balance sheet has its debit side and, unfortunately for the nation, the CIA has not always performed as brilliantly as it did in the matter of the Berlin tunnel. It has committed blunders in both judgment and operations since its founding in 1946 as the Central Intelligence Group, and sometimes its mistakes have been dangerous enough to threaten world peace. Taking a long, hard look at the CIA is a sobering experience because it is a reminder that in these tense days an espionage organization as big and as powerful—and as rich—as CIA can exert a considerable influence on American foreign policy.

Indeed, over the past decade, there has been considerable confusion in the mind of the average American as to whether CIA was actually *making* foreign policy as well as acting as a kind of scout for and instrument of that policy. This is because there has been confusion in Washington over CIA's role. That role has grown with the years and with the opportunities presented by a world in turmoil—opportunities which CIA has seized and manipulated largely because no other agency stepped in to do so. Broadly speaking, CIA operates *within the confines* of policy in a given area of the world, but decisions on day-to-day operations have been left to the judgment of its director and often to the man in charge on the scene, and under these circumstances CIA sometimes has overstepped the boundaries of its responsibilities and powers.

Most Americans find spying distasteful, if not immoral. As a nation we are not old enough to have acquired the detached viewpoint of, say, the British, who have lived with espionage for so many centuries that they are able to keep it locked up in a special closet reserved for things "one doesn't think about" or discuss with the neighbors. And so, in the furor that has enveloped CIA in recent months, some Americans have awakened to wonder what the CIA is all about and where it came from, and—especially after the Cuban disaster of April, 1961—if CIA is worth the tariff it imposes on the citizen's pocketbook.

Respectable or not, espionage is almost as old as man himself and over the centuries it has been a valuable instrument in the hands of military leaders and ambitious rulers. Moses discovered its value when, according to the Bible, he sent his agents "to spy out the land of Canaan." The noted Chinese military philosopher, Sun Tzu, also gave intelligence high credit. He wrote in the Sixth Century, B. C., that "what enables the wise sovereign and the good general to strike and conquer and achieve things beyond the reach of ordinary men is foreknowledge." The Mongols who overran Europe in the Thirteenth Century depended on a well-knit intelligence service to gather an abundance of information which Michael Prawdin in his *The Mongol Empire* reported included even "the family connexions of the ruler." Meanwhile, "Europe knew nothing about the Mongols." As Europe was emerging from the darkness of the Middle Ages, Queen Elizabeth I enjoyed the services of a really top-notch intelligence operator, Sir Francis Walsingham. State Secretary Walsingham's motto was "knowledge is never too dear," and he spent a considerable portion of his private fortune to finance an espionage network which included an elaborate system of codes and ciphers.

It is reasonable to explain the birth of the Central Intelligence Agency in simple terms. CIA exists because of Pearl Harbor. That surprise Japanese attack which all but destroyed our Pacific fleet was not only a shock to the average citizen; it carried a lesson with it to governmental authorities that a nation of America's power and wealth and responsibilities should never have been caught with its guard down. Investigation revealed there had been ample warning that the Japanese were up to something, reams of information picked up here and there that should have alerted Army and Navy commanders in the Pacific that we were in danger. But for the most part this intelligence, gathered by military informants, had lain unused because there was no single, central organization equipped to analyze it and see to its speedy dispatch to those concerned. In the crisis of war, Franklin D. Roosevelt created the country's first national spy agency, the Office of Strategic Services, but after the war the OSS was abolished by Harry S. Truman, largely because it was unwanted by the government lobbyists around him. That is, its demise was demanded by both the military intelligence services and J. Edgar Hoover's FBI, all of whom insisted that in peacetime the OSS would merely constitute a costly duplicating agency.

But whatever its faults, OSS at least had been a *central* point from which intelligence could be transmitted to the White House. Shortly after Harry Truman abolished it, he discovered that the conflicting intelligence reports flowing across his desk left him confused and irritable—and monumentally uninformed. Characteristically, he announced one morning that he wanted, as soon as possible, "somebody, some outfit, that can make sense out of all this stuff."

More formally, Truman sat down on January 22, 1946, and dictated identical letters to Secretary of State James F. Byrnes, Secretary of War Robert P. Patterson, Secretary of the Navy James V. Forrestal, and his military advisor, Admiral William D. Leahy. These men were instructed by the President to constitute themselves as the "National Intelligence Authority," which was to plan, develop and co-ordinate "all Federal foreign intelligence activities." Shortly, members of the Authority assigned personnel and funds from their departments to form the Central Intelligence Group to assist the Authority in its task. To head the group, Truman appointed Rear Admiral Sidney W. Souers as Director of Central Intelligence. In short, the Central Intelligence Group was the operating arm of the National Intelligence Authority, and Admiral Souers, in effect, was the nation's first boss spy.

Admiral Souers, however, operated under wraps, with the Secretaries of State, War and Navy constantly looking over his shoulder and directing, if sometimes rather loosely, his activities. Admiral Souers was not an equal among equals, but a subordinate, and his major assignment was to collate and digest for the President's eye the fruits of all intelligence activities. This apparently satisfied Truman, who wanted only a method by which he could be kept informed, but it was unsatisfactory to many people, who believed a central spy agency should have more independence and more elbow room. One of these people was Allen Dulles, who had served with considerable distinction in espionage activities during both World Wars.

While agitation was growing for such an organization, the Central Intelligence Group continued to operate under a succession of directors. General Hoyt S. Vandenberg of the then Army Air Corps succeeded Admiral Souers in June of 1946, and Vandenberg was succeeded in May, 1947, by Rear Admiral Roscoe H. Hillenkoetter. It was while Hillenkoetter was in office that Congress ordered the unification of the defense establishment, abolished the Central Intelligence Group and replaced it with the present Central Intelligence Agency which would function under the National Security Council.

Among those who testified as to the kind of organization CIA should be, Allen Dulles made the most sweeping proposals. He urged that CIA should control its own personnel;

that its chief should have complete authority to pick his own assistants; that the agency should have its own budget, supplemented by funds from the Department of State and the Defense Department; that CIA should have exclusive supervision over intelligence operations and access to all intelligence relating to foreign countries; that it should be the "recognized agency" for dealing with central intelligence agencies of other countries, and that "official secrets" legislation be enacted to protect and punish CIA's personnel in the matter of breaches of security.

Dulles, and many others, wanted the CIA to be headed by a civilian, if possible, and he opposed making it "merely a co-ordinating agency for the military intelligence services." He wanted CIA to be *the central* espionage organization in the United States. However, he pressed an important limitation. CIA, he said, should be confined to weighing facts and drawing conclusions from those facts, in order that other agencies concerned with determining policy and engaging in operations would have at their command an organization untainted by any connection with making policy. "The Central Intelligence Agency should have nothing to do with policy," said Dulles. "It should try to get at the hard facts on which others must determine policy."

Perhaps the trouble CIA has got into is due to the fact that neither Dulles nor Congress pressed this limitation which Dulles proposed with such vigor. For the National Security Act of 1947 contained a vague passage which was to prove titillating to an organization dedicated to espionage. Specifically, the Act assigned three duties to CIA: to advise the National Security Council on intelligence activities; to correlate and evaluate intelligence related to the national security, and to perform "services of common concern for the benefit of existing intelligence agencies."

But the confusion arises from the last sentence in Section 102 of the Act. This provides that CIA shall perform "other functions and duties" as directed by the National Security Council. It is this clause which has caused CIA's critics to complain that Congress, in effect, has given our spies a blank check to topple governments, and otherwise to interfere, benignly or not, in the internal affairs of other countries. This is indeed a powerful clause, but it is not quite a blank check. For these "other functions and duties" by law may not be engaged in without the direction of the National Security Council, whose membership includes the President, the Vice President, the Secretary of State, the Secretary of Defense and the Director of the Office of Civil and Defense Mobilization.

Moreover, since its inception the CIA has been subjected to periodic if sometimes casual supervision by other specially appointed bodies. The first such body operated during the early days of CIA and consisted of the Under Secretaries of State and Defense and the Director of CIA. This group reviewed all proposed projects of the agency, decided whether to approve or disapprove them, reported its judgments to the National Security Council and kept key members of Congress informally advised of CIA operations. The committee apparently worked well, if only because during its lifetime there were no disastrous failures involving CIA, but for some reason lost in the realm of government maneuvering and lassitude the committee was discontinued. Had it continued to operate, CIA might not have come under the lash of the late Senator Joe McCarthy during the early Fifties when the Wisconsin legislator caused one of his sensations by charging that the agency had been infiltrated by Communists. Dulles issued one of his rare public statements, calling the senator's charges false, and the Eisenhower Administration shrewdly by-passed a threatened McCarthy investigation of CIA by the announcement that a special task force of the Hoover government reorganization commission would examine the agency. This survey, directed by General Mark W. Clark, recommended the establishment of a joint Congressional watchdog committee to supervise CIA, and the appointment of a Presidential committee to "periodically examine the work of the government foreign intelligence agencies."

The proposed Congressional committee, then and since, has never been able to muster any considerable support on Capitol Hill, although backed vigorously by such able legislators as Montana's Democratic Mike Mansfield. To those who argued that the joint Congressional committee on atomic energy has been most successful, opponents of a CIA watchdog group pointed out that both the Armed Services and Appropriations Committees of the House and Senate had subcommittees to supervise CIA operations through regular conferences on appropriations and projects.

However, President Eisenhower did create, in 1956, a Presidential watchdog group called the President's Board of Consultants on Foreign Intelligence Activities, headed by Dr. James R. Killian, Jr., chairman of the corporation of the Massachusetts Institute of Technology. Killian served until 1958, when he left to return to Boston, and upon his resignation the board went into hibernation and for all practical purposes ceased to be a functioning body in the sense prescribed by General Clark's recommendations. One explanation is that President Eisenhower was "too busy to be bothered with it."

This was too bad because the board might have averted President Kennedy's first major disaster—the Cuban invasion fiasco—which most critics agree was due in considerable degree to the lack of an independent judgment of CIA's intelligence estimates. At any rate, shortly after the Cuban adventure, President Kennedy recalled Dr. Killian and reactivated the board, renaming it the President's Foreign Intelligence Advisory Board. It is a continuing body, as visualized by the Hoover Commission, and reports to the President every six months on the competence and "batting average" of CIA.

Seeking more immediate results, President Kennedy appointed a special committee to find out what was wrong with CIA and to recommend what steps should be taken to avoid another Cuba. The committee was composed of General Maxwell D. Taylor, later named military advisor to Kennedy, Attorney General Robert Kennedy, Allen Dulles and the then Chief of Naval Operations Admiral Arleigh Burke. After two months of labors, the committee made two major recommendations: 1. That CIA should have no operational role in future major actions similar to the Cuban adventure, but should continue its small-scale, covert activities. 2. That a new post of Director of National Intelligence be created, this official to serve immediately under the President at the National Security Council level, and to supervise the independent evaluation of all intelligence collected by both CIA and the military services.

The recommendations took cognizance of the two major criticisms of CIA's operations: that Dulles was wedded to his own intelligence estimates even when intelligence gathered by other organizations offered contradictory evidence; and that CIA was not equipped with the necessary knowledge to engage in military ventures. The idea behind the proposals was to reduce the status of the CIA director as the nation's last-word authority on the evaluation of espionage reports and as a kind of commander in chief of the department of dirty tricks.

President Kennedy accepted the recommendation reducing CIA's role in major military actions; he would have done so anyway after the Cuban business. But when he named former Atomic Energy Commission Chairman John Alex McCone to succeed Allen Dulles there was no mention of any super spy master who would look over McCone's shoulder. At the time, in late September, 1961, the word from the White House was that Kennedy felt fully competent to evaluate intelligence estimates, with the assistance of General Taylor. There was little doubt that under the new setup CIA no longer would be the free-wheeling outfit it had become under Dwight D. Eisenhower and with the encouragement of the late Secretary of State John Foster Dulles.

Nevertheless, over the years CIA and its Director have been given other powers that not only set it apart from other government agencies but made of it a little principality which, in effect, wrote its own laws. The Director was authorized to hire and fire without regard to Civil Service restraint, to spend money in any amount on his personal voucher, and to withhold publication of "titles, salaries or numbers of personnel employed by the Agency." In other words, nobody but a few people in the top echelon of the government could know how many employees CIA had or what their salaries were. Even in Congress, those legislators who pass on CIA appropriations often are unaware when they vote on funds for other government departments that these actually are a part of CIA's budget, concealed for security purposes.

This camouflaging of funds, of course, is the main reason why it has been impossible for anyone outside the tight little circle at the governmental top to find out how much CIA spends in a given year. The *New York Times*, which is not given to hyperbole, has estimated it as high as one billion dollars a year; others have set it at about five hundred million. Thus, in theory, the Director of CIA can write a check for many millions of dollars without explaining what he wants it for except in general terms to the President and a selected few. As Harry Howe Ransom says in his book, *Central Intelligence and National Security*, "this is truly an extraordinary power for the head of any Executive agency."

However, Congress has enacted legislation to prevent CIA from becoming a kind of American Gestapo. It has specified that the agency shall have no police, subpoena, law enforcement powers or internal security functions. This safeguard has been bolstered by the provision that whereas all other agencies are required to report their intelligence findings to CIA, the FBI is not. When CIA wants a specific piece of information, it can get it from the FBI if the request is made in writing, but the FBI does not keep the agency informed as a matter of routine. Congress always has been determined that CIA should not casually meddle in the affairs of the private citizen.

Admiral Hillenkoetter was the first director of the then new Central Intelligence Agency, serving from September, 1947, when it was born, until October, 1950. General Walter Bedell Smith, Chief of Staff to General Eisenhower during World War II, was director from October, 1950, until February, 1953, when Allen Dulles took over. Thus, Dulles ran the show for nearly nine eventful years before being replaced by John McCone in the fall of 1961. In the intervening years, CIA has come a long way from the pious days after World War I when Henry L. Stimson disbanded the State Department's "Black Chamber" of code experts because "gentlemen don't read other people's mail."

2. CIA—How?

MEMBERS OF IRON CURTAIN EMBASSIES, on Sunday afternoon drives in the Virginia countryside, must be fascinated by the profusion of green and white signs directing them to the new headquarters of the Central Intelligence Agency. The headquarters is situated on one hundred and forty acres in the bucolic township of Langley, twenty minutes by car from both the White House and the Pentagon, and, for an organization dedicated to secrecy, it can only be described as an attention-getter. To be sure, the building is almost entirely surrounded by trees, but a mere glimpse is enough to impress both the casual and the interested.

It is, first of all, big even by Washington standards—covering nine acres. From north to south, the building extends a maximum of nine hundred and twenty-six feet, and the depth, including a cafeteria, goes back four hundred and seventy-five feet. It contains one million square feet of working space, plus corridors and service areas totaling an additional six hundred thousand square feet. Ground and first floors constitute an oblong base with curved outer walls and corners enclosing three landscaped courts, and from this base rise five connected towers housing the second through the seventh floors. There is a five-foot setback at the second floor and a ten-foot setback at the seventh floor to relieve the architectural monotony, and continuous glass windows form the exterior walls of these two floors. The building is constructed of reinforced concrete with a quartz aggregate finish which, while predominantly white, contains enough color to relieve the drab concrete shade. Two penthouses, each thirty-two feet high, fifty-five feet wide and two hundred and eighty-two feet long, house elevator machinery, fan rooms for air conditioners and other mechanical and electrical equipment.

The entire building, of course, is air-conditioned against Washington's soppingly hot summers. The cafeteria seats more than one thousand persons at one time, in two dining rooms. In addition, there are two small table-service dining rooms, and snack bars are located throughout the building, two to a floor. There is also an auditorium seating five hundred people, a reinforced concrete dome-shaped structure with a small stage with a disappearing curved screen for film projection. There are more than two miles of roads on the site, and two parking lots covering twenty-one acres with a capacity for three thousand cars. An escalator serves the ground and first floors and there are four banks of four elevators each, serving all floors, plus two freight elevators. In the rear of the building there are two large loading docks for incoming and outgoing mail, supplies and equipment. Alarm systems throughout the building are wired to a central control room.

This businesslike Taj Mahal of bureaucratic architecture —next to the Pentagon the capital's biggest building—cost the taxpayers a little more than forty-six million dollars; still it is not large enough to house all of CIA's employees in Washington. The number of employees is a secret, but most estimates put it at around 10,000, which is almost as many as the number of employees in the State Department. Persons curious to know why enough new space was not provided to accommodate all CIA's employees are referred to the odd economics of the government. It is explained that Allen Dulles asked fifty-six million dollars for the job, that the Bureau of the Budget cut it to fifty million, and Congress reduced it to forty-six.

Thus a part of CIA's force still is housed in the battered old former United States Public Health Service complex at 2430 E Street in the gashouse section of Washington known as Foggy Bottom. This is a grouping of four masonry buildings and a dozen temporary structures known as "The Hill," which border on an unused brewery and sit squalidly amid tangled underbrush, enclosed by a fence with topping of barbed wire. From this complex, formerly CIA headquarters, little green buses ferry passengers and messages to the Pentagon, the White House and the new headquarters in Langley.

At Langley headquarters any person may drive through the gates, even though he be a well-known member of the Soviet Embassy spy apparatus. But the security line is drawn as the visitor crosses the threshold to the huge building. There armed guards take over, ask the visitor's business and require him to write down on a special form his name, address and citizenship and the name of the person he has come to see. A personal escort then takes the visitor to the office where he is expected and, when his business is done, the escort walks him back to the guard at the entrance. Along his route, the visitor will see signs which advise how classified wastepaper must be prepared and the hours when it is picked up. On the same wall will be a bulletin board, advertising cars for sale and apartments for rent by CIA employees. The swarthy man with the mustache hurrying down a corridor may be one of the one hundred aliens a year—usually defected Communist spies—which the CIA is allowed to bring into the country if the Director finds their entry "in the interest of national security, or essential to the furtherance of the national intelligence mission."

Inside the headquarters, employees entering and leaving must show huge plastic passes, no matter how many times they come and go; different kinds of passes permit access to different areas. At office hours any morning, the youth with the crewcut may be a U-2 pilot reporting for special instructions, the man behind him an expert in electronics, the young woman with the streak of gray in her hair one of the world's foremost authorities on the Swahili language. Entry to some of the doors down the long corridors is barred by combination locks; in the offices behind those doors experts are monitoring thousands of hours of foreign broadcasts every week or compiling data on the latest Soviet missile program. Among the men there is apt to be a sameness of appearance, a tall, trim, youthful look associated with the so-called "Ivy League." Although CIA reaches out with catholic hands for its recruits, the upper echelons of its force are largely from eastern universities.

Despite the Ivy League emphasis, mysterious and furtive figures continue to serve our intelligence networks undercover in foreign countries. But these days most of the triumphs achieved by these spies are the result of patient, plodding and often maddeningly tedious research in which perhaps hundreds of CIA agents play a role. The case of the bent coat hanger is a prime example of the kind of research and dogged persistence that pays off in the end at the Washington headquarters of the CIA. This research job was successful because somebody working for CIA at an airport in Vienna was interested in trash.

A Russian commercial Aeroflot liner had just landed, and the ground crew went aboard to clean up the plane for its return flight. As the plane was being spruced up, a man in a dark suit approached the airport garbage concessionaire and slipped him a bill. Shortly thereafter the concessionaire picked up the trash from the Soviet plane, loaded it into his truck and hauled it to his station. There the man in the dark blue suit turned up to claim the box in which the Soviet litter had been dumped. He put the box in the back seat of his car and drove home. Then, with the door locked, he went through the trash: torn magazines, paper napkins, an empty bottle, a crust from a sandwich, a broken plate—and a bent coat hanger.

The man wrapped the coat hanger carefully in brown paper, tied it with strong cord and walked over to a railroad station. There he deposited his package in a locker. It was picked up by another man a few hours later.

In Washington, a few days later, the coat hanger was sent along to one of the little offices off a wide corridor at CIA headquarters. The men who signed a receipt for it were delighted. They had been working for months to put together information on a new Soviet long-range bomber. They had found out a number of things about the plane, but had been unable to get anything on its range or bomb load. They did know, however, that shavings from the machinings of the wing were remelted and used to make a special kind of coat hanger.

This, at last, was the coat hanger. By spectroanalysis and chemical tests, experts were able to learn the kind of metal alloy used to make the hanger. With that formula at hand, CIA knew what the bomber wing was made of, and from there it took only a few more steps to figure out both the range and the bomb load of that particular plane.

The information wrested from an analysis of that coat hanger was the work of CIA agents who are in the new tradition of international espionage. Spying now is as much the scientist's job as it is the character equipped with "cloak and dagger." CIA is packed with rugged individuals who are experts at judo, but it would be lost without its metallurgists, its chemists, its industrial engineers, its lawyers, its psychologists and its nuclear scientists. It also has its political experts and its experts on geography, and of course CIA has perhaps the greatest collection of language experts in the world. Most of these speak at least four languages fluently; one agent is fluent in twenty-three languages and dialects and there are many who speak a dozen. Recruits joining CIA to specialize in languages first have to convince a board they are capable of learning a given language such as, say, Mandarin. Then they study the language at CIA expense, but on their own time—during lunch hours and evenings. When an agent becomes proficient in a language, he is paid a $500 bonus, but each year he must pass a stiff proficiency test to maintain his rating. It is comforting here to state the obvious: Most beginners must learn Russian as a basic intelligence requirement. They do so by sitting in cubicles for hours, headsets clamped over their ears, listening to tape recordings, while CIA observers keep tab on their reactions and their mental alertness. Within six to eight weeks, the student usually can read such publications as *Pravda* and *Izvestia* and can carry on a simple conversation in Russian.

CIA's recruiting program is as painstaking as its examination of a Soviet coat hanger. It was instituted by General Smith during his tenure as director and was the result of a frustration suffered by him as a youthful lieutenant just home from World War I. Smith wanted to make a career in G-2, the intelligence branch of the Army, and he naïvely made application at the nearest Army post. There he was informed that in peacetime the collection of intelligence was a responsibility largely assigned to military attaches at our embassies abroad, who were expected to wine and dine their prospects and generally mingle socially with people who might be expected to possess information the United States wanted.

"How much private income do you have?" Smith was asked.

"Why none," Smith replied, a trifle abashed. "I have to live on my salary."

"Then you're out, Lieutenant," he was told. "You can't afford to be in intelligence."

When he became director of CIA, Smith therefore determined to open the door—carefully—to the best people he could find, regardless of their private income. He realized that CIA could not be content with rich men's sons looking merely for a respectable job, but must try to corral the best brains in the country, persuade them to work at salaries which did not exceed $14,000 a year, and instill in them the kind of esprit de corps which would keep them on the job in spite of inevitable disappointments and frustrations.

For his regular operating personnel, therefore, Smith looked to the colleges and universities and developed a system of "observance" that processes prospects even before they know they are being looked over. That is, former G-2, OSS and CIA officers, now members of school faculties, regularly look over their junior classes for prospective CIA material. Then, in the senior year, those who have passed "observation" are interviewed by CIA representatives, and those who are chosen take special aptitude tests devised by the Educational Testing Service at Princeton University and are surveyed by CIA assessment teams who check on everything from the student's personality (Do people like him?) to his behavior in the dentist's chair (Is he a wincer?).

CIA rarely bothers with any student who is not in the upper 10 per cent of his class, and it is an exceptional year when more than 100 college graduates make it into the agency. For example one graduate who led his class and was a three-sport star was discarded after he had passed a long series of tests. The reason: "He doesn't like to be kidded." Prospects are told that their starting salary probably will not exceed $5000 unless they are critically needed specialists, and that they will be lucky to reach the top of $14,000. Still, the CIA has far more applicants than its screening process will accept. Out of every 1000 persons who apply for jobs, only a handful wind up getting them. Eighty per cent are screened out immediately, largely because of insufficient education or obviously unfavorable background. The remaining 20 per cent are turned over to security officers for investigation. Eleven per cent of this 20 per cent are eliminated, in the words of the agency, "because they drink too much, talk too much, or have relatives behind the Iron Curtain who may make the applicants subject to foreign pressure." Of this 11 per cent, four per cent are screened out for serious security reasons; they are individuals who have contacts that render them undesirable for service in a highly sensitive agency.

All employees also must take a polygraph, or lie detector, test, and among the questions asked are always these two: "Have you had any homosexual relations?" and "Have you given any official information to anyone?" CIA does not regard the lie detector as a device to catch people lying, rather, as one CIA official said, "It makes people tell the truth. It's a kind of compulsion with them." Unfortunately, some perfectly honest people break down from the nervous strain of taking the test, and these are rejected as emotionally unstable. Curiously, in a nation accused of having deteriorated into physical wrecks, far fewer candidates fail CIA's physical training tests than mental examinations. Little is known about this phase of CIA's preparation of its recruits for a spying career, but it has been compared to Marine boot training and one CIA official, a veteran Marine, claims he now would find a Marine combat course anticlimactic after passing the CIA test.

CIA employees are divided into two categories—the "blacks" and the "whites." The blacks are the real cloak-and-dagger spies; the whites are the so-called "overt" employees some of whom may admit that they work for CIA and who labor largely on research. White employees often are assigned to go back to school—to take special courses in foreign economics, postgraduate courses in international law or training in various sciences in order to be able to assay Russian technical journals. All over the world, too, CIA has its white workers, working or traveling under their own names as scientists, students, economists, engineers, hotel clerks and housewives. Most white employees are stationed in Washington, where they work on the mass of detail which flows into CIA headquarters every day. These overt employees may not tell anyone, including wives and husbands, what work they are doing even if it currently consists of nothing more interesting than reading a new Soviet history book; moreover the work is so compartmentalized that a CIA employee rarely knows what the person in the next office is doing. For that matter, every bit of information is classified even among the CIA force. It may be divulged to an individual only on a "need to know" basis; that is, nobody is told anything unless that information is needed in the job he is doing. In many cases, a piece of intelligence, put together from smaller pieces gathered all over the world, is known only to the Director.

Yet it is a fact that about 80 per cent of all information about what is going on in Communist countries is obtained openly. Much of this comes from United States diplomats and military attaches stationed abroad, especially in Iron Curtain countries. Reports of meetings of medical associations and scientific organizations are carefully checked, because all over the world doctors and scientists love to chat about their work, and a stray word here and there often will tell the CIA a great deal. CIA also buys every Communist publication it can lay its hands on; more than 200,000 pieces of literature are delivered to CIA headquarters every month. There, in the hands of experts on every conceivable subject, these bland publications sometimes are more revealing than a microfilm report smuggled out of Moscow. A new road map or a railroad timetable or a provincial newspaper is seized upon with glee by technicians who can find something significant in the change in the name of a Polish town or the abandonment of a branch rail line. In Prague, a Czech-American CIA researcher can strike intelligence gold by spending months in the perusal of the latest telephone directory. There he may find the names of newly arrived Russians and may search in vain for old familiar Czech names who have departed the city—or, perhaps, this vale of tears. Plans for a new mechanization program in the Czech Army were passed on to Washington by an agent whose "research" started when he discovered the name of a Russian general, known to be an expert in tank warfare, in a local newspaper.

To help its researchers speed their work, and to aid accuracy, CIA has what the Senate Committee on Government Operations described as "the most comprehensive information system now in operation." Among the features of this system are a specialized miniature photograph laboratory, scores of facsimile printing devices, punch cards extending to more than 40 million, and machine-translation computers that are capable of rendering Russian texts into English at the rate of 30,000 words per hour. CIA's records—one of the reasons for its huge headquarters building—probably are the world's most comprehensive of their kind. They contain everything from the physical description of an obscure Bulgarian provincial official ("speaks with lisp, wart on lobe of left ear") to data on the quality of farm machinery in Kiev. In a period of eighteen months, the CIA accurately recorded six changes in the color of the hair of the mistress of a collective farm official near Stalingrad. The collection of this information was incidental, picked up in the course of keeping the data up-to-date on the agricultural bureaucrat, but CIA rarely throws anything away. It was filed simply because in espionage you never know what kind of information will be valuable at some later date.

Somewhere on the CIA staff there is a nuclear scientist who knows as much about his business as anyone else in the world. There are doctors and surgeons who can diagnose the illness of a Soviet official from afar, from personal knowledge and from the comments of the official's own team of physicians.

One expert specializes in Chinese boatbuilding, another in Chinese agricultural methods, a third in the Soviet school system. There are experts who know what is wrong with the concrete the Chinese Reds are using at a given time. There are industrial engineers who can prepare an inch-thick report on Soviet production methods merely by examining the buttons the Russians are making. There are experts in factory markings who can look at a dockside photograph taken anywhere in the world and, by reading the labels on the crates, tell what is in the box, where it was made and where it is being shipped.

Give one of the pretty girls in CIA headquarters the name of a Pole living in East Berlin who is posing as a representative of a Polish state-owned agricultural machinery factory and within hours she will expose him as a former soldier in Hitler's German army who defected to the Russians, went to work for the Soviet secret police, plays the horses, has been married twice and now lives with a redheaded Rumanian girl, and probably has been assigned to ferret out "deviationists" in the East German heavy-industry program. While the pretty girl is digging up this information, the man in the next office, an expert on Islamic law, will be preparing a memo concerning an incident in Iraq.

Such experts in the "white" division retain their identity. That is, they live normal lives as themselves, keeping regular office hours and going home every night to wives and families in Washington suburbs. But to become an agent in the "black" or espionage branch, a man or woman must undergo a transformation, in effect, into another person. They not only take new names, but they must learn how to protect these new identities.

An operative being drilled for assignment to an Iron Curtain country first is supplied with a cover story. That is, he receives a new name, a new birthplace, a new set of relatives complete with snapshots, and a new educational background

—all in the country to which he has been assigned. Time after time, the agent is required to recite his story down to the last detail. Often he is routed from a sound sleep in the middle of the night and asked a question like "Why did your Aunt Olga marry the second time?" He learns that European tailors sew buttons on with a cross-stitch, while American tailors use a parallel stitch. He learns how to eat continental style, since it would be suicide, in a Sofia restaurant, to transfer his fork from his left to his right hand before lifting it to his mouth. He must know the schedules for the commuting trains in East Berlin and the kind of beer preferred by construction workers in the Soviet Zone.

Nowhere in the world are identity papers more important than in the Soviet Union and in its satellite countries. Thus the agent is taught the art of forgery, known nicely in CIA as "authentication." If his assignment calls for it, he must be able to forge passports, visas, working permits and ration books. He must have a working knowledge of the use of microfilm and special inks, and he must carry a complicated code in his head. And, since his value is based on communicating his information to his superiors, he must maintain—and sometimes establish—a "drop" system whereby his intelligence eventually will move out of the country. For moments of extreme danger, he carries pills so that if he is captured and his captors resort to torture to extract information from him he can end it all. No operative is told to commit suicide in such a situation, but it is one of the facts of espionage life that the CIA has to be happier if he does.

CIA takes its agents where it can find them and places them where they can do CIA the most good, and sometimes these agents cause CIA embarrassment and anguish. There was the man with the long name in Germany, for instance, who turned out to be a Soviet agent during the moments when he was not spying for CIA. This was Georgi Vladimirovich Khorumzhil, alias Georg Muller, of Frankfurt. In October, 1953, the New York *Daily News* reported that Muller was "being questioned around the clock by the CIA in an effort to learn how much he told the Russians about their cloak and dagger activities." The Frankfurt *Abendpost* charged Muller was responsible for the disappearance of "many enthusiastic young persons who had sworn to fight against the Soviet Union." These were Iron Curtain refugees who came through the anti-Communist research center where Muller worked as a top official, and whose names Muller allegedly gave to Soviet counterintelligence.

Then, in September, 1955, two American war veterans revealed they had worked as Soviet spies in West Germany for six months in a self-conceived plot to "serve our country by infiltrating Soviet intelligence." They accused CIA of "gross malfeasance" because it refused to hire them as double agents when they volunteered. The men, Theo K. Hollie, twenty-eight, of Los Angeles, and Gregory J. Lima, thirty, of New York City, said the Russians paid them $6000 for spy missions ranging from a report on the United States Military Intelligence School at Oberammergau, Germany, to a visit to Belgium's largest munitions plant at Liége. After these missions, they said, they went to CIA headquarters in West Germany in May, 1955, and proposed that CIA hire them. They claimed CIA first tentatively promised to finance the double-agent project, but then disowned them and failed to pay about $1000 in debts they had incurred on CIA's instructions.

Sometimes, too, it would seem, would-be agents decline the honor. In August, 1960, a young Chicago business executive named Obert Berlin said CIA had asked him to do some spying during a tour of the Soviet Union. Berlin, a twenty-eight-year-old vice president of a sales company, told the *Chicago American* that the agency approached him in June, 1958, but that he refused to handle the assignment because of the risks involved and because he did not think it was right for a tourist to engage in espionage. The reason he was talking, Berlin said, was that the United States government had just protested the ejection of some American tourists from Russia after the Soviet Union accused them of being spies. CIA, of course, had no comment, but one of those spokesmen did allow that "It is our business to seek information wherever we can get it, just as the Russians try to get information. And it is a lot easier for them to get it." What he meant, of course, is that only a Russian who is tired of living would refuse to accept his country's invitation to spy.

Stories both weird and shocking are told about CIA. One of these was the charge made in July, 1953, by Lieutenant General Pedro A. Del Valle, a retired Marine, who allegedly told a Washington newspaper CIA attempted to enlist him in a plot to "get" General Douglas MacArthur, then Supreme Commander in the Far East. According to the newspaper's account, General Del Valle identified General Walter Bedell Smith, then CIA director, as the man who sought to have him work to downgrade MacArthur. He said the plan was "highly regarded" by the Joint Chiefs of Staff, and that he was asked to come to Washington to discuss it.

In Washington, General Del Valle told the now defunct *Washington Times-Herald,* he was closeted with General Smith. "My reaction was prompt and violent, and I left at once. I told Smith that as a good American I could never be party to an attack on the best soldier statesman we had ever produced. Allen Dulles caught me on the way out and tried to wheedle me into staying with them. They even sent a colonel to New York to try to persuade me to play their game. My refusal was final."

Another case of allegedly highhanded tactics by CIA came out in December, 1952, when a Japanese writer, Wataru Kaji, told a Judiciary sub-committee of the Japanese Diet that he was held and grilled for seven months by CIA after Japanese sovereignty had been restored. Kaji said CIA wanted him to return to China as a spy, and quoted CIA agents as telling him, "We want you to do something like you used to do in China during the war."

In this case, as in all the others, CIA found itself in headlines without being able to do much to defend itself, since it never either confirms or denies reports for public consumption. But from time to time it gets involved with newsmakers and has a hard time of it, as it did in the case of Professor Owen Lattimore, a Far East expert at Johns Hopkins University, who had been charged with being a Communist agent and who had denied it under oath.

A travel agent in Seattle was alleged to have told a CIA agent that Lattimore had made reservations for a secret trip to Moscow. CIA passed the tip along to the State Department, which acted swiftly. It issued secret instructions to all customs officials to watch for Lattimore and prevent his leaving the country. At the same time, State asked the FBI to check the Seattle tip.

In June, 1952, the ban on Lattimore's travels leaked out. A few days later, the FBI disclosed that it had completed its investigation and the information against Lattimore was "wholly unfounded." The Seattle informant, the FBI said, had confessed that his story was false. President Truman asked for and received a full report. The Justice Department convened a grand jury in Seattle to investigate. The travel agent, Henry A. Jarvinen, thirty-two, allegedly admitted he had fabricated the whole story against Lattimore, and said he was drinking when he told it to the CIA man. The grand jury indicted him for giving false information to the government. The State Department issued a public apology to Lattimore.

At Jarvinen's Seattle trial in October, 1952, Federal Judge William J. Lindberg cited two CIA agents, Wayne Richardson and Miller Holland, for contempt when they refused to testify. They said they could not talk on orders of their superior, General Smith. The government offered to drop one charge against Jarvinen if the court would drop the contempt charges. Judge Lindberg refused and went on to find Jarvinen not guilty.

Nobody in the know is supposed to talk about CIA operations, but sometimes one does and the public has to decide for itself whether the person knows what he is talking about, since the CIA remains mute. Thus CIA ignored a story when it was dropped by Charles Edmundson, a former official of the United States Information Agency in Korea, who had been dismissed in January, 1957, for criticizing President Eisenhower's Middle East program.

Edmundson, appearing on the television program, "College Press Conference," declared that the United States had refused to let American newsmen go to Communist China because they might discover that some Americans held prisoner there were United States intelligence agents. He named two of them as "Fecteau and Downey," names that had a familiar ring since among ten Americans known to be held by Red Chinese at that time were Richard Henry Fecteau of Lynn, Massachusetts, and John Downey of New Britain, Connecticut. Both were listed as civilian employees of the United States Army.

One of CIA's functions, authorized or not, which has reddened the necks of its critics is its "third force" operation, the top-secret activity of aiding freedom forces in their attempts to fan revolt or to sabotage a government. In one satellite, for instance, factory workers were griping about Communist pay cuts. A CIA agent trained in the technique of labor organizations infiltrated the workers' ranks and promoted work slowdowns. Frequently, CIA will provide the latest in explosives to resistance movements and throw in some expert training on their use; the result is another blown-up railroad bridge or the derailing of a train. CIA operatives can take a piece of sticky plastic explosive and, applying it to a rail trestle, predict to within one or two wooden ties how much of the bridge will be destroyed.

This is all risky business, of course, and not calculated to bring serenity of mind to the average operative. Even among the overt employees of CIA, the strain is often so great that the toughest of them succumb to nervous breakdowns. When this happens, a CIA-screened psychiatrist is called in to straighten out the patient. When agents are ill or hurt, they are treated by CIA-approved doctors and nurses. For, after all, a person in a coma or under the influence of drugs might say the wrong thing—and thereby endanger the security of the United States. Besieged by such pressures twenty-four hours a day over a long and grim decade, the top spy of them all would have been excused had he shown signs of wilting, or at least, of weariness. Yet the strain was never apparent in the demeanor of the man who became known as Mister CIA —Allen Welsh Dulles.

3. Dulles of CIA

"IT DOESN'T MATTER who takes Allen's place at CIA," a friend remarked during the furor over the Cuban invasion fiasco in April, 1961. "He's given CIA his imprint. It will be a long time before CIA will be anything but Allen Dulles' baby."

Even allowing for the prejudice of friendship, the comment had considerable validity. For Allen Welsh Dulles, whatever his faults, will go down in the history books as the nation's first career spy, a man whose cloak-and-dagger service spanned two World Wars and whose national tour of duty was climaxed by direction of his country's battle of intelligence with the Communist conspiracy. The Central Intelligence Agency was still in infancy when Allen Dulles became its director in February, 1953; for better or for worse, he has made it what it is today.

Dulles' critics have been many and vigorous, but most of them have acknowledged in retrospect that he was the sophisticate CIA needed when it was being whipped into shape. At that time, Dulles did indeed rate among the world's cognoscenti in the field of espionage, with a fund of knowledge gained as a young intelligence agent in Switzerland during World War I, as an older and much more important OSS operative in the same country in World War II, and as one of the men who helped organize CIA in the early postwar years when Soviet imperialism came harshly to the surface.

34

Dulles has always admitted that this knowledge came hard, beginning with an incident that reddened his face in Switzerland toward the closing months of World War I. An intermediary invited him to meet and chat with an odd little journalist with a spade beard and piercing eye whose political ideologies were most radical. Somehow young Dulles never found the time for the appointment and eventually the journalist departed Switzerland to keep a date with a revolution in Russia. His name was Nicolai Lenin.

Over the years, as a result, Dulles was always a little more receptive to meeting odd characters with unconventional political theories. "You never know where or when lightning will strike," he says.

It was not until his tour of duty with the OSS in World War II that Allen Dulles came into national prominence. The citation accompanying the Medal for Merit presented to him by President Truman on July 18, 1946, succinctly tells the story of Dulles' successes as Chief of the German Mission and Senior Strategic Services official in Switzerland: "Mr. Dulles, within a year, effectively built up an intelligence network employing hundreds of informants and operatives, reaching into Germany, Yugoslavia, Czechoslovakia, Bulgaria, Hungary, Spain, Portugal and North Africa, and completely covering France, Italy and Austria . . .

"Particularly notable achievements by Mr. Dulles were first reports, as early as May, 1943, of the existence of a German experimental laboratory at Peenemünde for the testing of a rocket bomb . . . his report on rocket bomb installations in the Pas de Calais, and his reports on damage inflicted by the Allied Air Forces as a result of raids on Berlin and other German, Italian and Balkan cities, which were forwarded within two or three days of the operations."

Dulles enjoyed similar, if backhanded, praise from the Cold War enemy. Soviet propagandists described him as the nation's "master spy," and the Soviet pamphleteer, Ilya

Ehrenburg, paid tribute to Dulles' single-minded approach. "If the spy, Allen Dulles, should arrive in Heaven through somebody's absent-mindedness," Ehrenburg wrote in *Pravda,* "he would begin to blow up the clouds, mine the stars and slaughter the angels."

In reaching such a pinnacle, Allen Dulles probably has often reflected that in his case, at least, environment was everything, for he was born into a family with an intense preoccupation with international affairs. He was born in Watertown, New York, on April 7, 1893. His father, Allen Macy Dulles, was a Presbyterian minister; his mother, Edith Foster, was the daughter of General John Watson Foster, Secretary of State in the Republican Administration of Benjamin Harrison. By the time Allen Dulles was ready to try on the world for size, his uncle, Robert Lansing, had become Secretary of State under Woodrow Wilson.

A child of considerable precociousness, Allen early showed a most satisfactory reaction to the influence of Grandfather Foster, who was a frequent and genial host in Washington to Allen and his older brother, John Foster. At the Foster dining table, the conversation often grew heated as guests discussed the pros and cons of the Boer War and Allen became a champion of the Boers. He felt so strongly about their cause that, at the age of eight, he wrote a book which paid them lavish tribute and which gave the British the rough side of his pen. His proud grandfather arranged for the book to be published, complete with misspellings and grammatical errors, and it was reviewed by the *New York Times* and sold several thousand copies in behalf of the Boer relief fund.

"England goes around fighting all the little countries," Allen Dulles wrote. "But she never dares to fight either China or Russia." He wound up the book with "I hope the Boers win this war because the Boers are in the right and the british in the wrong." Dulles later explained that he used a small "b" for British because he wanted to show his dislike of them.

Allen Dulles graduated from Princeton with Phi Beta Kappa honors in 1914 and forthwith shipped to India to teach English for a year in a missionary school. He returned to Princeton, picked up his Master of Arts degree, then joined John Foster in the diplomatic service then being directed by Uncle Robert Lansing. He went first to Vienna as an undersecretary in the American Embassy, and when war broke out and Austria-Hungary took its place beside Germany he was transferred to Switzerland to gather political intelligence from Southeastern Europe. What *Time* magazine later would call "the first of the grandiose plots which were to become his trademark" was hatched in Berne when Dulles took part in secret negotiations designed to salvage the Hapsburg Empire. However, Emperor Charles abdicated and the monarchy collapsed of its own weight.

After Berne, Dulles attended the Versailles peace conference as assistant head of the Department of Current Political and Economic Correspondence—a kind of combined secretarial-messenger service for all communications to the American delegation. His boss was Ellis Dressel, a leading American expert on German affairs and one of the first diplomats of his time to seek a German-American rapprochement as a defense against the new Bolshevism. Dulles made several trips to Germany with Dressel in 1918 and 1919 and saw a great deal of German industrialists and generals who were enthusiastic for the idea of organizing a European army to fight the Bolsheviks. During that period Dulles showed he was soaking up the theories of his environment by writing a memorandum entitled "Lithuania and Poland, the Last Barrier between Germany and the Bolsheviks."

After a tour of duty in Constantinople, Dulles returned to the United States and found the woman he was to marry. He met Clover Todd during a holiday in the Thousand Islands and told his mother he wanted to marry her. Miss Todd accepted his suit, so Allen Dulles went to New York for an audience with the girl's father, a professor at Columbia University.

Professor Todd liked young Dulles, but as a pedagogue he was unsure of the intellectual qualifications of his daughter's suitor. "Who *is* this Allen Dulles?" he asked his wife that night, and then hurried to the university library to find out if the young man had ever contributed anything to the world of letters. Sure enough, there it was in the card catalogue: Dulles, Allen W. *The Boer War*. The couple was married three months later.

Young Dulles was doing well in the State Department. At twenty-nine he was chief of the Division of Near Eastern Affairs and he was a delegate to the Arms Traffic and Preparatory Disarmament Conferences in Geneva. Between times he earned his law degree by attending night school at George Washington University. Now, State offered him the post of counselor to the American legation in Peiping. It was a promotion but it carried no increase in Dulles' $8000 salary, so he resigned. He needed more money to support his family and he knew where he could make that money. He became a private citizen for the first time in his adult life, joining the powerful New York international law firm of Sullivan and Cromwell, in which John Foster Dulles was a partner. Still, he kept a hand in public service. He was legal advisor to the American delegations to the Three Power Naval Conference in 1927 and to the Geneva Disarmament Conference of 1932 and 1933. He became a director and then president of the Council of Foreign Relations.

Happily for a man who fought one intelligence war against the Germans and would fight another, Dulles' chores with Sullivan and Cromwell involved him intimately in the financial-legal affairs of Europe's industrial and banking community. During the crucial decade preceding World War II, he struck up scores of business acquaintanceships with leading

European industrialists—including those in Hitler Germany. Thus he was able to observe at first hand the alliance between Hitler and Germany's industrial power which brought the infamous little house painter to national power and then kept him there. Sullivan and Cromwell was one of the world's leading international law firms, and in his role as a partner in that firm, Allen Dulles had a private window through which to watch the surge of events in Hitler Germany.

This was more important to the United States than is realized these days when the atmosphere which led to World War II is obscured in the haze of history. For, to a large extent, Hitler had cut off his people from normal contacts with the peoples of other nations. Cultural and scientific societies and other similar organizations found their German branches suddenly dissolved. Contacts made in the course of business by law firms and their clients were important sources of information. And, obviously, Dulles' experience during this decade gave him a peculiar insight into the ways of the Nazi élite, for when Pearl Harbor exploded into the nation's consciousness, he was almost immediately tapped for national service. He had developed a friendship during his Washington days with an Assistant Attorney General named William J. (Wild Bill) Donovan, and when Donovan was picked to head the Office of Strategic Services (OSS), he hired Allen Dulles to set up shop in his old espionage neighborhood in Berne. With his contacts inside Germany, Dulles was a logical choice.

By February, 1943, these contacts were bearing fruit in a series of fascinating conferences between Dulles and Prince Maximilian Hohenlohe, a high-level agent in Himmler's SS. Hohenlohe, who used the cover name of Herr Pauls, was in Switzerland to try to sell Dulles on separate peace settlements with the West in order to preserve Hitler's Reich, but with Himmler as the new Fuehrer. Military cliques already were plotting Hitler's assassination and Himmler, if assured of American co-operation in supporting his seizure of power, apparently was prepared to give the assassins the go-ahead.

The meetings had the flavor of a reunion, since Dulles and Hohenlohe had met before, in Vienna in 1916 and in the 1920's in New York. A version of the talks is contained in papers found in the files of Department VI of the SS Reich Security Office which found their way into the hands of a leftist British Parliament member, Bob Edwards. Edwards used portions of the texts of these letters in a 1961 pamphlet, *A Study of a Master Spy* (Allen Dulles).

Hohenlohe reported that Dulles said "he was fed up with listening all the time to outdated politicians, emigrés and prejudiced Jews. In his view, a peace had to be made in Europe in the preservation of which all concerned would have a real interest. There must not again be a division into victor and vanquished, that is, contented and discontented; never again must nations like Germany be driven by want and injustice to desperate experiments and heroism. The German state must continue to exist as a factor of order and progress; there could be no question of its partition or the separation of Austria . . . To the Czech question (Dulles) seemed to attach little importance, at the same time he felt it necessary to support a cordon sanitaire against Bolshevism and pan-Slavism through the eastward enlargement of Poland and the preservation of Rumania and a strong Hungary."

This Nazi version indicates Himmler had found a sympathetic ear in the spy Dulles. Hohenlohe reported that Dulles "seemed quite to recognize" that Germany should be Europe's industrial leader and "of Russia he spoke with scant sympathy. He does not reject National Socialism in its basic ideas and deeds so much as the 'inwardly unbalanced, inferiority-complex-ridden Prussian militarism.'" Dulles further was quoted as saying that "with all respect to the historical importance of Adolf Hitler and his work, it was hardly conceivable that the Anglo-Saxons' worked-up public opinion could accept Hitler as unchallenged master of Greater Germany."

Some critics have seen in these documents evidence that

Dulles somehow was betraying the ideals of the Allied fighting men, who were sworn to achieve the unconditional surrender of Hitler Germany. But the maneuvers of a "master spy" are not quite that simple to analyze. Dulles' job was to find out what one strong segment of German leadership was thinking, and one of the ways to do this was to feign sympathy for their goals. It may not be moral to lie to anyone, even an SS officer, but that is one of the necessary evils of espionage. If Dulles could persuade Himmler that he would have American support in his plotting, Himmler's own hands might hasten the fall of the Hitler regime and the collapse of its armies. It was important to nurture the seeds of dissension in the enemy's camp.

In any case, Dulles continued to do business with the Nazi plotters—and to keep the United States informed of the progress of the assassination program. His chief contact was the German vice-consul in Zurich, Hans Gisevius, whom he met by prearrangement during a blackout. Gisevius was a member of Hitler's counterintelligence service, the Abwehr, but his vital role was as an anti-Nazi double agent and a leader in the assassination conspiracy.

Dulles had his doubts about Gisevius, but the latter soon removed them by producing confidential Abwehr transcripts of Dulles' communications with Washington, proof that the OSS code had been broken. Happily, Dulles had used another cryptographic system to transmit messages concerned with the Hitler plot, a switch that offered Gisevius as much relief as it did Dulles. From there in, Gisevius kept Dulles informed of each new development in the several plots against Hitler's life, and several hours before the event, Washington had a detailed report on the mechanics of the near miss on July 20, 1944, when a Nazi officer planted a bomb in Hitler's conference room in East Prussia.

Dulles' headquarters in Berne was an apartment in a medieval house complete with courtyard and creaking gate. His door bore the sign: Allen W. Dulles, Special Assistant to the United States Minister. To that door one night came a man known as George Wood, a top employee in the German Foreign Office in Berlin, and in the next two years Wood brought with him through that door more than two thousand Nazi documents in microfilm.

Among other things, Wood's papers told Dulles of a secret radio transmitter in the German Embassy in Dublin which was used to direct submarine raids on Allied shipping. On at least one occasion, Wood's reports helped Dulles to arrange for the rerouting of a large American convoy which would have been trapped by a submarine pack had it taken the original route. It was Wood who tipped Dulles off about the mysterious Nazi spy named Cicero, who was valet to the British Ambassador in Turkey, Sir Hughe Knatchbull-Hugessen. Through other contacts, notably an SS-Obergruppenfuehrer, Karl Wolff, Dulles was able to embark on clandestine negotiations which brought about the surrender of German troops in Italy—an achievement which saved thousands of Allied lives.

The British have been inclined to pooh-pooh the credit given Dulles for his reports on the German rocket base at Peenemünde. Winston Churchill, for instance, wrote that German experiments with rockets at Peenemünde were known even before the war and in 1939 "references to long-range weapons of various kinds began to appear in our Intelligence reports." But the fact remains that Dulles was on top of the project from the very beginning and his detailed reports enabled the Allies to bomb Peenemünde and set the program back six months.

In any event, by the time President Truman decided to set up a central intelligence organization after World War II, Dulles was recognized as pre-eminent in his field. He served on a committee in 1948 which examined the new-born CIA and recommended a host of administrative changes, and when

General Walter Bedell Smith succeeded Admiral Roscoe H. Hillenkoetter as director of CIA in 1950, he telephoned Allen Dulles.

Smith's opening remark was characteristic of this blunt man. "Now that you've written this damn report," he said, "it's up to you to put it into effect."

Dulles joined CIA as Smith's top assistant in November, 1950, and three years later he moved up to the directorship shortly after President Eisenhower took office and appointed General Smith to the post of Under Secretary of State. It was a tribute to Dulles' competence that he was slated to succeed Smith whether the Democrats or the Republicans won the 1952 election.

This veteran spy master was a personality switch from the acidulous and monosyllabic Smith. A big, broad-shouldered man with tousled white hair, a soaring forehead and an ample gray mustache, Allen Dulles looked, and talked, more like a prep-school headmaster than a secret wholesaler in plots and counterplots. When asked about him, his friends always found time to remark on Dulles' charm, which is considerable and which always places a visitor at his ease. Unlike the commanders of intelligence troops in the rest of the world, Dulles has always been gregarious and he has attended as many Washington parties as any top official in the town.

Dulles admits he goes to parties because he enjoys them, but there was a serious side to this after-hours activity. Since the day he missed a date with Nicolai Lenin, he has always tried to see as many people as he could and he has always looked on Washington's gossip-filled cocktail routs as a built-in opportunity for mingling with the folks. "Parties help you to judge people, and that is very important," he explained.

After the failure of the Cuban invasion, Dulles came under heavy fire and there were reports that he would be dismissed. By early July a White House spokesman reported that Dulles would be gone "within a month—the hunt is on for a successor." But when President Kennedy reappointed Dulles in November, 1960, Dulles had told him that he did not want to stay on for longer than another year; he did want to see CIA established in its new headquarters in Langley, Virginia. So President Kennedy decided to permit Dulles to follow his schedule and resign late in 1961; besides, the interval gave Kennedy several important months to decide on a successor.

There is every indication that Dulles feels he has served his purpose during his tenure at CIA. His goal, he always told interviewers, was that of building the organization into a tightly knit and efficient spy shop. "What interested me," he said on one occasion, "was the idea of building up a new kind of structure in the American government, creating a good intelligence organization and giving it its momentum, its start."

And in the midst of the fuss over the Cuban fiasco, Dulles refused to be downcast by the attacks on his stewardship. "I couldn't have had a job more concerned with trying to unmask and defeat the objectives of Communism," he told a reporter from *Newsweek*. "If I can make a contribution here, I would like to leave the United States a better intelligence system." Over those years of international acrimony, Allen Dulles had done just that. Unfortunately, however, the Cuban adventure had splashed a CIA blunder on front pages all over the world, and shortly it was to have unfortunate repercussions across the Atlantic—in Algeria.

4. *Suspicious Ally*

THE SCENE WAS the ornate suite in the Quai d'Orsay of Maurice Couve de Murville, Foreign Minister of the Republic of France, onetime Ambassador to the United States. On stage were M. de Murville and Pierre Salinger, Press Secretary to the President of the United States, onetime reporter and newspaper editor.

SALINGER: Monsieur de Murville, do you have any evidence at all that the United States Central Intelligence Agency was involved in the revolt of French generals in Algeria?

DE MURVILLE: No, we have no evidence.

SALINGER: Then I suggest that you stop peddling the story.

Pierre Salinger was furious personally, and by proxy for President Kennedy, over rumors of CIA meddling in the Algerian crisis which not only had not been denounced by official France but which had been passed around by supposedly responsible French officials. The gossip was that CIA had become convinced that the Communists would take over in Algeria if General Charles de Gaulle carried out his intent to give the country independence and so had given aid and comfort to the revolting generals in their abortive putsch. Before the dust settled and CIA's role was made clear, this is what had happened:

On April 22, 1961, within hours after the outbreak of the

mutiny, rumors began to circulate in Europe, and notably in France, that CIA had played a part in encouraging the revolt. At the time CIA was very much in the international news because of its role in the disastrous "invasion" of Cuba by an anti-Castro force that same month. The rumors stressed the logic of CIA's involvement by noting that General Maurice Challe, leader of the revolt, had been close to American military circles during a term of service with the NATO forces.

The rumor first appeared in print, as a fact, in the Rome daily newspaper, *Il Paese,* a fellow-traveling journal edited by Mario Malloni, a member of the Communist-front organization, the World Peace Council. *Il Paese* purports to be an independent newspaper, but it regularly serves Communist ends as an outlet for disguised Soviet propaganda. It consistently releases and replays anti-American, anti-Western and pro-Soviet bloc stories which are either distorted or wholly false. Said *Il Paese:*

"It is not by chance that some people in Paris are accusing the American secret service headed by Allen Dulles of having participated in the plot of the four 'ultra' generals . . . Franco, Salazar, Allen Dulles are the figures who hide themselves behind the pronunciamentos of the 'ultras'; they are the pillars of an international conspiracy that, basing itself on the Iberian dictatorships, on the residue of the most fierce and blind colonialism, on the intrigues of the CIA . . . reacts furiously to the advance of progress and democracy . . ."

On the next day, *Pravda* published in Moscow a long article about the generals' revolt, in which it said that the mutiny was encouraged by NATO, the Pentagon and the CIA. Richard Helms, assistant director of CIA, explained to a Senate Internal Security Subcommittee that there was a reason why *Pravda* was a day behind *Il Paese* in circulating the story. "Instead of having the story originate in Moscow, where everybody would pinpoint it, they planted the story first in Italy," Helms testified.

Pravda reported that "Taking part in the war against the Algerian people is not only the France of the arms manufacturers . . . The war in Algeria is a war of NATO. This was openly and cynically stated by American General Norstad, Commander in Chief of the Armed Forces of the Atlantic Bloc. U.S. reactionary quarters are helping the French colonialists . . . The traces of the plotters lead to Madrid and Lisbon, these hotbeds of fascism preserved intact with the money of American reactionaries and with direct assistance of top NATO circles. The traces from Spain and Portugal lead across the ocean to the Pentagon and the Central Intelligence Agency of the U.S. . . ."

Pravda's article was repeated that same day in a Tass dispatch prepared in English and transmitted from Moscow to Europe. On April 25 and 26, Radio Moscow relayed the story to the Middle East in Arabic. By April 27, the Communist *London Daily Worker* was carrying a front-page story headlined: U. S. SPY AGENCY ENCOURAGED REVOLT, COUNTED ON BIG RISING—WHY ALGIERS PLOT FAILED. This version apportioned blame for the revolt about equally between the government of President de Gaulle and CIA. The Parisian Communist daily, *l'Humanité,* printed much the same story, but this issue was confiscated by the French government.

Much more damning, however, was a version with a new twist which appeared in a non-Communist Paris newspaper. It was written by Geneviève Tabouis, a journalist described by Helms in his testimony to the Senate Subcommittee as "markedly anti-American and pro (Communist) bloc." Madame Tabouis assured her readers that "the fact that the effort of Challe was encouraged, if not supported, by the most Atlantic of American services, is from now on a secret everyone knows." In a subsequent column, she reported that CIA "caps" all other American services—that is, that it was the supreme authority, and added, "The result is false estimates of national and local conditions, as in the Algiers group. . . ."

All this was unofficial stuff, of course, but the French government long before had slipped into the act in back-door fashion. When the first rumors of CIA's involvement in the revolt were being passed around on April 22, some of them were launched cautiously "by minor officials at the Elysée Palace itself," according to Crosby S. Noyes in the *Washington Star*. Noyes went on: "At least a half dozen foreign newsmen were given privately to understand that the generals' plot was backed by strongly anti-Communist elements in the United States Government and military services. The leader of the revolt, General Maurice Challe, was reported to have received assurances that any move to keep Algeria under permanent French domination and out of Communist hands would be in the interests of the United States. There also was a strong implication that a change in the NATO policies of General de Gaulle would be welcome as one of the results of a successful coup d'état."

Paul Ghali of the *Chicago Daily News* got the French Army into the act, too. He reported that "a determined campaign of anti-Americanism" had been started "within Army circles here in the French capital. These circles made it known that they had 'irrefutable' documents proving that CIA agents in Paris and Algiers promised General Challe full U. S. support if the coup succeeded. Simultaneously, the Polish Ambassador in Paris, Stanislaw Gajewski, volunteered the same information with even more precision to colleagues and social acquaintances."

Certainly the Soviet propaganda machine was having a field day. But now the gossip was taken up by respected and responsible French newspapers which could not, by any stretch of the imagination, be included in the normally anti-American fringe of French opinion. The story was considered important enough to be the subject of the lead editorial in *Le Monde*, the most respected and influential newspaper in France:

"It now seems established that some American agents more or less encouraged Maurice Challe, whose experience in NATO should have put him on guard against the dealings of these irresponsible people and their Spanish and German colleagues. Kennedy obviously had nothing to do with this affair. To make this plain he considered it necessary to offer aid to General de Gaulle, well-intentioned certainly but inopportune."

The United States Embassy issued a denial labeling the editorial as "completely absurd and unfounded," but the French seemed to want to believe the gossip, possibly as an explanation of why respected officers like Challe had been drawn into such a senseless adventure. Columnist Marquis Childs noted that some people at the top were, at the least, suspicious.

Childs wrote: "As one of the highest officials of France put it: 'Of course your government, neither your State Department nor your President, had anything to do with this. But when you have so many hundreds of agents in every part of the world it is not to be wondered at that some of them should have got in touch with the generals in Algiers.' "

And *l'Express* devoted two full pages to "Challe and the CIA" in a report the content of which obviously bore the imprint of high officialdom. Among other things, *l'Express* affirmed that "Knowing the sobriety, the prudence and ambition of General Challe, all of his close friends are convinced today that he was encouraged by his companions (at NATO). In the course of the final conversations which he had in Paris certain American agents must have told him 'succeed quickly —in less than forty-eight hours—in a technical coup d'état and we will support you.' "

This was the situation when Pierre Salinger arrived in Paris on May 2 to make arrangements for President Kennedy's forthcoming visit to De Gaulle. Before he left Washington, Salinger telephoned CIA Director Allen Dulles and asked for a briefing on the Algerian generals' revolt—"since I'm sure to be mixed up in it." A few hours later CIA's Richard Helms showed up at the White House with a bulky folder and gave Salinger a fill-in.

Helms denied categorically that CIA at any time had sided with the rebel generals. He admitted that CIA, as a matter of course, had conversations with people around the generals on a kind of fact-finding mission, but said there was no contact with the generals themselves, no promises were made to anybody, and there was no discussion of possible American attitude if changes were to be made in France's Algerian policy.

In Paris Salinger immediately tackled Pierre Baraduc, Chief of the Press Section of the Foreign Office. To Salinger, it was obvious the rumors of CIA involvement in the revolt were coming from official sources.

"Why are you putting out this story?" Salinger asked Baraduc, his voice sharp with irritation.

"I'm not putting it out," Baraduc replied. "It seems to have sprung from nowhere. But you have to admit the story sounds logical. It seems to me President Kennedy should investigate and see if it is true."

"What do you want him to investigate?" Salinger asked. "No charge has been made, no evidence has been submitted. There's nothing to investigate. It looks to me as if somebody is trying to place the President at a disadvantage for his meeting with President de Gaulle."

The next day General James M. Gavin, United States Ambassador to France, attended a luncheon of the French-American Press Association. Also on hand was Pierre Baraduc. Salinger was not present.

All went well until Ambassador Gavin stood up to answer questions from the guests. One of the guests was Sam White, an Australian and Paris correspondent for the irreverent London *Evening Standard*. White, a man of blunt and simple Anglo-Saxon words, handed Ambassador Gavin a bomb-shell of a question: "Now that the rumor that the CIA played a part in the Algerian mutiny has received the blessing of the Quai d'Orsay, what steps does the American Ambassador propose to take to kill it?"

Gasps arose from the head table, and Baraduc leaped to his feet, his face crimson with anger. Baraduc said the question was outrageous and issued the ultimatum that "either White leaves or I do." General Gavin persuaded Baraduc to stay in the same room with White and then told his questioner that no steps were contemplated to kill the rumor; Gavin gave the impression he wasn't very concerned about it.

But by this time there apparently was considerable concern in the higher echelons of France's government. Baraduc arranged a meeting between Salinger and Foreign Minister de Murville which lasted half an hour.

De Murville began the conversation by commenting that the scene at the press luncheon had been "lamentable." Salinger nodded. "Possibly," he said, "but it was inevitable, since certain people in the French government seem to have planted the story."

De Murville denied that such was the case, but, as Baraduc had done, he suggested that President Kennedy should be asked to conduct an investigation of CIA's possible involvement.

"What do you want us to investigate?" Salinger asked.

De Murville did not answer the question directly, but mentioned that CIA had been sticking its nose into internal affairs all over the world.

"That may be true," Salinger replied, "but CIA does not operate in a vacuum. It's responsible to the President. It doesn't operate without any direction from the top."

"I'm afraid the CIA has been rather irresponsible," De Murville replied.

"Perhaps in the past," Salinger said. "I wouldn't know, so

I couldn't go along with you. But it's not irresponsible now. If it hadn't been for the Cuban affair this matter would never have come up."

Salinger then asked De Murville if he had any evidence that CIA was involved in the generals' revolt and, when De Murville said he did not, Salinger suggested that the French stop putting out the story. The next day De Murville appeared before the Foreign Affairs Committee of the Chamber of Deputies to testify that there was no evidence of CIA's complicity.

Obviously, however, CIA made whatever contacts it could in the controversy raging over De Gaulle's Algerian policies. For instance, there was the top-secret luncheon in Washington on December 7, 1960. The luncheon was given by the French intelligence chief in Washington and the principal guests were Jacques Soustelle, the onetime passionate De Gaullist who turned against the general because of his Algerian policy, and Richard M. Bissell Jr., director of CIA's operations section. The luncheon lasted well into late afternoon and Soustelle spent most of the time bending Bissell's ear. As operations director of CIA, Bissell was in charge of aerial missions, guerilla warfare and propaganda. CIA, of course, is always bound to acquire as much intelligence as it can about dissenting groups all over the world, whether they be in friendly countries or not. It is not the kind of thing CIA likes to talk about, but Walter Lippmann has reported that it was known that CIA agents meddled in France's internal affairs during the French debate on the nuclear arms program.

CIA was aware of the violent dissatisfaction of the rebellious generals with the De Gaulle program in Algeria, and its agents went to work to discover whether this dissatisfaction was great enough to cause them to rebel. Their conclusion was that if the generals became convinced no other course would stop De Gaulle, then they would stage a revolt in an attempt to take the Algerian question out of De Gaulle's hands. In gathering this intelligence, which required contact with people who knew the generals and probably with the generals themselves, there is every reason to believe that some irresponsible CIA men went too far. That is, the evidence indicates there were CIA operatives who let their own politics show and by doing so led the Challe rebels to believe that the United States looked with favor on their adventure.

Here again, CIA's critics could draw up their favorite indictment that America's super-secret intelligence organization was overly eager to get mixed up in policy-making operations. The indictment, perhaps, should be drawn up only against those operatives, naïve and politically ignorant, who could not resist taking a detour from pure intelligence to dabble in king-making. But, the responsibility for keeping such people in hand rests at the top. When that responsibility is not exerted strenuously Moscow has a propaganda carnival, as it did with the revolt of the French generals.

CIA has a noble end in view—the defeat of the international Communist conspiracy. But with such a goal, the nagging question has always been whether CIA could keep its intelligence impartial, that is, whether it could restrain itself from reporting dangerous conclusions merely because those conclusions coincided with the urgent necessity of battling Communism. If some CIA agent had sold himself on the view that De Gaulle's Algerian policies would lead to a Communist takeover there, he might have been tempted to indulge in words and actions that would give aid and comfort to those opposed to the De Gaulle policies. Even if this had been secret American policy, no intelligence agent would have had a right to state it without orders from on high and certainly no agent was empowered to make any commitments in the name of the President.

The type of situation posed by the French generals' revolt was foreseen by those who hesitated to concur when the

United States organized its first centralized intelligence agency after World War II. Notably, the arrangement was questioned by Admiral Ernest J. King in March, 1945, when the Secretary of the Navy asked him what he thought about the proposed CIA.

King admitted he saw the logic in such an organization, but suggested it had inherent dangers. He said he did not like the possibility that a central intelligence agency might acquire power beyond anything intended. This, he said, raised the question of whether such an organization "might not threaten our form of government."

A few years later, when CIA was a reality, a Yale professor named Sherman Kent, who had been an intelligence officer in World War II, expressed concern over what he called "the disadvantage of getting intelligence too close to policy." In his book, *Strategic Intelligence for American World Policy*, he said that "This does not necessarily mean officially accepted United States policy, but something far less exalted. What I am talking about is often expressed by the words 'slant,' 'line,' 'position,' or 'view.' Almost any man or group of men confronted with the duty of getting something planned or getting something done will sooner or later hit upon what they consider a single most desirable course of action. Usually it is sooner; sometimes, under duress, it is a snap judgment off the top of the head. I cannot escape the belief that under the circumstances outlined, intelligence will find itself right in the middle of policy, and that upon occasions it will be the unabashed apologist for a given policy rather than its impartial and objective analyst."

At the time of the French fuss, the British were figuratively saying, "I told you so." In the light of their four hundred years' experience in the spying business, the British have always doubted the wisdom of combining under one roof the functions of gathering intelligence and covert action against those who were the subject of espionage. This, they claim, prevents an objective analysis because the people charged with doing something about the information at hand are the same people who obtained that information. To avoid this schizophrenia, Britain's Military Intelligence 5 has always been separate from the Special Operations Executive, which acts on M. I. 5's information.

CIA's job, and quite properly, is to gather all the information available about a given situation abroad—*without getting involved.* This is an impossible feat in many cases, such as in Iran where as we shall see some CIA action was needed to forestall what the policy makers concluded would be catastrophe. In the revolt of the French generals, it was CIA's responsibility to know what was going on; in cases where it appears CIA has failed to live up to this responsibility its critics, especially in Congress, are quick to bellow their outrage. In the classic tradition of Government's relationship with its espionage organization, then, CIA is damned if it does and damned if it doesn't.

An example of how CIA gets blame from all sides was the Turkish generals' revolt which overthrew the pro-Western but harshly repressive government of Premier Adnan Menderes in May, 1960. Some news dispatches reported that the revolt "was a complete surprise to high ranking officials of the State Department in Washington." This reddened the necks of one segment of CIA's critics. Other reports, however, were that CIA virtually master-minded the generals' plot. This brought brickbats from those who consistently protest what they call CIA's "meddling" in the internal affairs of foreign nations.

The facts were that CIA had discovered and dutifully reported to Washington that the Turkish Army was restive under Menderes' repressive government. A week before the uprising, CIA was able to state that a coup was "imminent." Its only failure was in dismissing General Cemel Gursel, chief of the Turkish ground forces, as a "non-political general"—only a few days before General Gursel emerged as leader of the revolt.

From the viewpoint of international politics, the Turkish government of Premier Menderes and President Celal Bayer was just what Washington had wanted. Menderes and Bayer had come to power in a genuinely free election in 1950, and both had the popular appeal that accrued to lieutenants of the late revered Mustapha Kemal Attaturk, father of modern Turkey. They used American aid to build Turkey into perhaps the West's strongest bastion against the Communist threat. They permitted United States and NATO bases on Turkish soil and contemptuously turned aside Soviet protests. Turkey's 470,000-man army constituted the biggest force contributed to NATO by any member; it sent troops to the Korean War in greater numbers than any nations except the United States and Great Britain.

But Menderes was determined to make over his country economically overnight. He spent money so freely on new dams and factories that soon Turkey had one of the world's most unstable currencies. At one point its credit rating was so poor that even the Turkish Central Bank refused to honor government orders to release foreign exchange. The increasing problems which plagued Menderes made him more autocratic and more sensitive to criticism. He smothered the press and opposition under a blanket of repressive legislation. Respected journalists and professors were jailed for criticizing his regime, and ministers who tried to discuss cabinet decisions were expelled from office.

CIA operatives reported to Washington that tensions were rising in Turkey. The Turkish people were up in arms about the cruel measures Menderes had taken to suppress a students' strike on April 28, and about Menderes' vendetta against the highly respected General Ismet Inonu, Bayer's predecessor as President and crown prince to the adored Kemal Attaturk. The immediate cause of the students' revolt had been the action taken by Menderes' tame Parliament in suspending all party political activity for three months. Menderes' Democratic party accused Inonu's Republicans of "destructive and illegal activities."

The events which led to Menderes' overthrow began when Menderes ordered the Army to prevent an address by General Inonu at a political rally scheduled for Kayseri, outside of Ankara. The Army was hesitant; Inonu was almost a legendary figure in Turkey. But Inonu took the approach of the activist he had always been. Delayed in reaching Kayseri, he decided simply to walk through the soldiers' lines. The troops opened ranks and saluted him with cries of "Ismet Pasha!" "Ismet Pasha!"

Menderes ordered an inquiry and disciplined many of the soldiers involved. Among them was General Gursel, who was sent on indefinite leave pending retirement in June. Gursel was typical of the traditions of the Army he headed. He had always preached that soldiers should stick to their trade and not meddle in politics. When he was ordered on leave, he warned his troops in a farewell speech: "At this moment, especially, you must know how to keep aloof from the bad effects of the political climate of the country. Stay out of politics!" Casually noting his departure, most intelligence observers assumed that Gursel would retreat into oblivion.

But CIA had underestimated Gursel—a "non-political general" of sixty-five who was virtually unknown even to Turkish diplomats in Washington and to American Embassy personnel in Ankara. Once out of uniform, he considered himself freed of his oath to support the government and to stay out of politics. Almost immediately he took over the little organization of dissident Army officers which was plotting against Menderes.

Thus, although CIA expected an imminent coup, its leadership was a surprise. The takeover began at midnight on May 27 and was over by four o'clock in the morning. Armored brigades and thousands of tough, well-trained infantry troops were posted in key cities all over Turkey. Menderes was captured as his limousine sped along the road from Eskisehir to Kutahya, an area where he had been on a speaking tour to test sentiment among his loyal peasants. Gursel took over with a "committee" of thirty senior Army officers, with himself as Premier. "I tried to reason with the politicians, but they were blinded by ambition," Gursel explained. "They would not listen and wanted to go on by force. We had to act."

CIA's reports to Washington had concluded that a coup was inevitable; that Menderes' days were numbered. Obviously, it had had contacts with dissident Army elements, although it had failed to uncover General Gursel's leading role in the revolt. It was CIA's foreknowledge of the plot, however, that led some critics to reopen the charges of "meddling," thus awarding CIA more blame, or credit, than was merited. The cry arose that CIA had no warrant from the people of the United States to dicker with any group planning the overthrow of a friendly government. Yet there was no way CIA could get the information it wanted without making contact with the rebels.

CIA's problem in both the Turkish coup and the revolt of the French generals in Algeria was that it was vulnerable on past performance. In the French revolt, there is good reason to believe that President Kennedy was almost as upset at CIA's international image as he was with the French Foreign Office's pusillanimous dabbling in dangerous gossip. The Presidential concern was not necessarily caused by any CIA agent who might have compromised the United States, but by the reputation CIA had earned over the years which made it suspect every time there was an international crisis. The history of CIA, in effect, is the story of how that reputation grew and flourished all over the world—in operations from Germany to Formosa, from Hungary to the Congo, from Guatemala to Japan.

5. From Guatemala to Japan

ALLEN DULLES had a ready answer whenever someone questioned CIA's judgment in the matter of taking sides in the internal affairs of a foreign country. When the person pointed out that CIA seldom looked deeper than to determine whether a would-be leader was anti-Communist, Dulles came as close as he could to turning snappish.

"We support our friends," he always said. "Do you suggest that we support our enemies?"

Dulles' critics did not see things as quite so black and white. They complained that it was not enough for a foreign government or a leadership to be inimical to the Kremlin, that government also should be an advocate of the necessary social reforms that would buttress its country against Communist infiltration. Our support in some cases, according to Walter Lippmann, "has been exactly what Mr. K's dogma calls for." That is, "that Communism should be the only alternative to the status quo with its immemorial poverty and privilege."

As a case in point, some of Dulles' critics grumble that CIA's efforts in Guatemala during the 1954 overthrow of the fellow-traveling Jacobo Arbenz Guzman have shown a scant profit. In a long article in *The Nation* in June, 1961, Fred J. Cook complained that Arbenz' successor, Colonel Carlos Castillo Armas, never did make good on his promises of social and democratic reforms. Cook wrote that "Half of the arable land in the nation of four million persons still remains in the hands of 1100 families. The economy of the country is dominated by three large American corporations, topped by United Fruit. Workers in the vineyards of United Fruit staged a strike in 1955 trying to get their wages of $1.80 a day raised to $3. They lost. And Guatemala is still a distressed country . . ."

It is also true that the rich and the well-to-do in Guatemala have successfully balked all attempts to make them bear a fair share of the tax burden. Seven years after Guatemala's liberation from Communism, in the summer of 1961, the country was still without an income tax for the simple reason that the members of Congress were almost all professional men or men of property and they were not interested in taxing themselves. The real estate tax structure is a farce; the owner of a Guatemalan plantation with an assessed valuation of $100,000 pays a real estate tax of only $300 a year. President Miguel Ydigoras Fuentes makes more money than the President of the United States; he draws a salary of $72,000, plus another $72,000 for "expenses," and the salary is tax-free. The President of the United States pays a heavy tax on his $100,000 salary.

It is not necessary to dispute any of today's facts of life in Guatemala because the point is not what happened after Arbenz was overthrown but that in 1954 Guatemala had acquired the first Communist government in the Western Hemisphere and that the United States was deeply concerned with seeing that regime liquidated. This concern was expressed publicly with considerable vigor. It led shortly to one of CIA's most dramatic triumphs.

The Guatemala story shows CIA at its very best—in the gathering of information world-wide, in the communication of that information to headquarters and in its speedy evaluation for the guidance of policy makers. In other cases, there is little doubt that CIA has violated its mandate by trespassing on policy making, but in the Guatemala case—except for necessary inferences—it merely told its story to the National Security Council and from there the Defense Department took over.

This was the situation as CIA's fact-finding apparatus began to move: Colonel Castillo, an anti-Communist former officer in the Guatemalan Army, was in exile in Honduras where he was trying to obtain arms for a little army of refugees from the Arbenz regime. Honduras and El Salvador were nervously eying apparent moves by Arbenz to invade their territories. There was concern felt that, should Arbenz gather added strength in these countries, he might even make a thrust at the Panama Canal.

The first person on stage as this secret drama unfolded was a tall and angular German businessman, newly arrived in Stettin, a port city on the Oder River in Communist Poland, to take over a small machine-tool factory. During the balmy spring days of April the businessman had made it a habit to pack his lunch in a paper bag and stroll with it to a bucolic hill top overlooking the wharves. Like so many Germans he was a nature lover, and he had with him a pair of field glasses with which he observed the birds in the nearby trees. From time to time he casually let his glasses sweep along the riverfront piers, where freighters were being loaded for passage into the Baltic Sea and beyond.

One April afternoon, in his little office, the German businessman dictated a long and statistic-filled letter to his blonde secretary. Addressed to a French automobile parts concern, it was a stiff missive creaking with precise specifications and references to favorable discounts. It offered presses for the stamping out of motorcar fenders, machines that had the official guarantee of the Ministry of Machine Industry of the Polish People's Republic and, besides, were cheaper than the British could offer. After signing the letter, the businessman gave it back to his secretary so she could carry it to the commissar for approval. Casually, the commissar attached his stamp, and the letter went out that evening.

The commissar should not have been quite so casual, although it is doubtful even a careful scrutiny could have discovered anything wrong with the letter. But had the commissar known that the "German businessman" and his secretary were both CIA agents he at least would have impounded the letter for a few days until the experts had had a chance to look at it.

Now, however, the letter was enroute to the Paris address, which was a CIA drop. There it was received by another CIA agent, a legitimate and astute businessman who that year would increase the profits of his auto-parts company by 12 per cent. But he forgot business for a while to carry the letter personally to a shabby building in the Montmartre hung with the sign SALON DE PHOTOGRAPHIE. In the back room of the studio after the auto-parts man had left, a CIA microfilm expert took over. Using a magnifying glass under powerful lights, the expert scraped at each period on the typewritten page with a tiny instrument with a razorlike edge. Shortly he was rewarded—one little black dot slid off the paper.

Underneath that black period was what the technician had been looking for—a tiny circle of microfilm barely larger than the point of a pin. It had been pasted to the paper at the end of a sentence and then disguised by the ink from the secretary's typewriter as she pressed the period key. The agent removed the minute dot of film with a pair of tweezers and carried the film to the photographic enlarger. A short time later he had the finished product in his hand—a square of photographic paper the size of a salad plate with the letters in the blownup message as large as those in a typewritten letter.

The message was in code and was indecipherable to the microfilm expert, which was standard operating procedure since CIA's right hand seldom lets the left know what it is doing. It was a cryptogram for which the key rested in the Washington office of CIA Director Dulles, and the key was in the twenty-second prayer of David in the Book of Psalms which begins, "My God, my God, why hast Thou forsaken me?" Hence, the microfilm expert's next chore was to deliver the message to still another CIA agent, a radio operator, who forthwith transmitted the unintelligible scramble to Washington by short-wave radio with the coded address: "For AWD's eyes only." This meant it was for the personal and sole attention of Director Dulles.

In Washington, Dulles had the cryptogram decoded by a cryptographic machine and transcribed on a sheet of typewriter paper with one carbon. (The carbon immediately was destroyed and when the secretary left that night, her typewriter would be locked up to preserve the secrets that might be found imbedded in the typewriter ribbon.) Dulles called in the supervising agent on the "German-businessman-in-Stettin" project and together they digested the message.

It was startling stuff. It said that the freighter *Alfhem*, flying the flag of Sweden, had tied up at the dock at Stettin where more than 15,000 crates and boxes had been lowered into her hold. The cargo had arrived by rail from Czechoslovakia and it consisted of munitions from the Communist Skoda arms works. There were unconfirmed reports that the cargo was headed for a port in the Western Hemisphere.

Radio messages went out to a corps of agents in Europe and Africa, and back came their replies. From Stockholm the word was that the *Alfhem* was owned by the Swedish shipping line, Angbats A. B., which had chartered the vessel to a shipping agent in London, E. E. Dean. From London the message was that the terms of the charter stipulated that Dean should recharter the freighter to Alfred Christianson in Stockholm. Again from Stockholm came the information that Christianson claimed the *Alfhem* was carrying optical laboratory equipment and optical glass for the French West African port of Dakar.

CIA kept on the job. From Dakar a few days later came word that the *Alfhem,* two days out of Dakar, had received orders to change course for Trujillo, Honduras. Two days out of Trujillo a Caribbean agent reported that the *Alfhem*'s captain had been ordered to change course and proceed to the Guatemalan port of Puerto Barrios. Seldom has a shipping agent shown so much solicitude for a cargo of optical equipment and glass.

At Puerto Barrios, security was as tight as any secret police officer could make it. Yet the next day CIA headquarters had a message from Guatemala City: The 15,000 unmarked crates and boxes contained about 2000 tons of small arms, small-arms ammunition and light artillery pieces.

To CIA the message was clear. With those arms, Arbenz could stroll through Honduras and El Salvador and probably dominate all of Central America. And a shipment of the arms from Czechoslovakia meant that the Soviet Union, disregarding the Monroe Doctrine, was taking a hand to secure a Communist toehold in Latin America. Dulles called an emergency session of the Intelligence Advisory Committee, composed of the heads of the Army, Navy and Air Force intelligence, the intelligence officers of the Joint Chiefs of Staff, the State Department and Atomic Energy Commission, and a representative of the FBI. Together, the conferees agreed on a quick evaluation of this new development—that with these arms in his possession, Arbenz was almost surely bent on embarking on aggressive war.

The next day Dulles laid the estimate before the National Security Council. He made no specific recommendation, but he warned that some action was urgent and there was an implication that the United States should go—as a supplier of arms—to the military defense of Arbenz' neighbors. Also, Dulles reminded the NSC that Colonel Castillo had a band of Guatemalan refugees in the Honduras jungles waiting for weapons.

Two days later, on May seventeenth, Secretary of State John Foster Dulles announced that the United States had positive information on the Communist arms shipment to Guatemala. This shipment, he said, was viewed by the United States with grave concern because of its size and because it had come from an Iron Curtain country. No more was said. But in the next week the Department of Defense dispatched two Air Force Globemasters—huge cargo planes—to Honduras and Nicaragua. Each plane carried more than twenty-five tons of rifles, pistols, machine guns and ammunition.

Most of these arms found their way to the headquarters of Colonel Castillo. When distribution had been accomplished, each of Castillo's men was equipped with a burp gun, a pistol and machete. Meanwhile three old Air Force B-26 bombers which were not in use fell into Colonel Castillo's hands. Then, as Castillo sent his troops across the Honduran-Guatemalan border, the ancient bombers soared aloft and flew on to buzz Guatemala City and drop a few bombs for punctuation.

Castillo issued an ultimatum to Arbenz to capitulate. Arbenz replied with a defiant roar—but that was about all he had left. Intimidated by the B-26's, Arbenz' tiny air force (three P-38 fighters from World War II) defected almost immediately. The Guatemalan Army, predominantly anti-Communist though otherwise without admirable political qualities, suddenly was seized by the fear that Arbenz would use the 2000 tons of munitions to arm his Red-dominated labor unions. Everybody from colonels down to buck privates "conferred," then everybody refused to fight. Arbenz fled and an anti-Communist junta took over.

Despite the sincere social consciousness of people like *The Nation's* Mr. Cook, it is hard to find fault with the CIA's performance in the Guatemala incident. The United States properly abhorred the idea of a Communist regime in the Western Hemisphere and felt it should do something to help the Guatemalans rid themselves of it. When the Communists shipped arms to Arbenz and thus involved the international Communist conspiracy in the internal affairs of a Latin American country, it was the CIA which furnished the United States policy makers with the vital intelligence that provided a most valid excuse for intervention. In this case, Allen Dulles did not have to press any policy on the policy makers; his intelligence was so accurately disturbing that there was only one thing the country could do.

Guatemala was also a place where good intelligence was used wisely, which has not always been the case in the operation of American foreign policy. Failure to act properly on information gathered at firsthand has always been a cause for complaint by those who furnish it. For intelligence of itself is not enough, no matter how good it is necessary for the policy makers to understand these cold facts and to know how to use them. As General Jimmy Doolittle told the Senate Committee on Armed Services in 1957: "The acquisition of intelligence is one thing; the interpretation of intelligence is another; and the use of that intelligence is a third." In the case of Guatemala all three things were done with success.

A Hoover Commission task force which investigated American intelligence services in 1955 came up with probably the best definition of intelligence. It is, said the Commission, "all the things which should be known in advance of initiating a course of action." It is for this reason that, almost since its inception, the Central Intelligence Agency has played a primary role in the deliberations of the nation's top policy-planning organization, the National Security Council.

Regularly, usually once a week, the National Security Council meets at the White House to discuss the state of the nation as it is concerned with international affairs. Almost always, the first speaker is the Director of Central Intelligence, who presents a summary of his agency's latest findings, especially as it concerns the subject under discussion. He is there because policy cannot be made without a fill-in from him on the latest developments in a world which does not take the United States government into its confidence.

Most frequently, the CIA is required by the demands of the policy makers not only to present facts as it knows them today, but to look into the future and predict what the facts will be next week, or next month. For instance, the United States may be planning a brand-new grant of military aid to a nation bordering the Soviet Union. What will be the Kremlin's immediate reaction to this grant? Even if it is angrily aggressive, will time soften its attitude? Will the Soviet take a hard line generally in the next three or four months? How is the Soviet progressing in its development of new weapons and what are the capabilities of those weapons? Is the latest Soviet softening on disarmament to be trusted? Is unrest in the satellite countries serious enough to require a considerable part of the Kremlin's attention during the next ninety days?

No intelligence service, however efficient and well-manned, can be expected to offer guarantees with its answers to questions like these. Usually all CIA can do is to put forward *probabilities* based on the best information available, evaluated by the most competent experts it can lay its hands on. The Hoover Commission's definition of intelligence is the definition of the ideal intelligence; CIA and all the other information seekers toiling for the United States strive for that ideal but seldom achieve it.

Yet it is a fact that never before in the history of any nation has a government had the benefit of intelligence so carefully gathered and evaluated. It is as dependable as modern methods and dogged, painstaking toil can make it. Its only weakness—an Achilles heel of considerable infirmity in some cases—is the human element that goes into its evaluation. For, after all, nothing but a crystal ball would enable human beings to look into the mind of, say, Nikita Khrushchev, and decide what he is going to do. And so the President and his top planners have to be content with an incompleteness of product which yet gives them a resoundingly good idea of the probabilities. Then the decision must be made, often the kind of decision which, in the words of Admiral Arthur Radford, is "the action an executive must take when he has information so incomplete that the answer does not suggest itself."

Even when intelligence is available, the action taken on it may seem to disregard that information since policy making is woven of many more threads than mere reports on the situation in a given area. The President may be forced by the exigencies of national morality to make decisions contrary to the information furnished him by CIA. President Eisenhower had to do just that when he condemned the Israeli-British-French invasion of Egypt in 1956, despite CIA's warnings that it could cause a permanent rift between us and our allies and its assurances that, given time, the invaders would succeed and eliminate Nasser as an international fever blister. Thus also the decision was made to go ahead with former Vice President Richard M. Nixon's goodwill trip to Latin America, although CIA had what it called "good information" on the vigor of anti-Americanism south of the border.

"We knew there would be demonstrations," said Allen Dulles. "But you can't predict when a mob will go berserk. We had to take some chances; you can't cancel a trip like that except for extraordinary reasons—you can't let people blackmail you."

Moreover, later investigations revealed that even the most violent of the agitators in Peru and Venezuela had no intention of going any farther than a campaign of loud-mouthed heckling. Nixon, in effect, brought the violence on himself by the good manners he showed on his first stops in Uruguay and Argentina, by his straightforward speeches and the grace with which he and Mrs. Nixon communicated with the masses. His statesmanship made the Communists desperate, and so they had to resort to sticks and stones and spit to try to prove their point. Even when this happened, the situation could have been handled but for the failure of local police to function in Lima and Caracas. They simply failed in their job; fearful of Communist reprisals, they refused to operate.

Throughout the Vice President's trip, CIA and other intelligence agencies operated with considerable success. In Bogota, Colombia, CIA agents eavesdropped on a meeting of Communist leaders who were drawing up plans to assassinate Nixon. As a result, all the chief conspirators were rounded up by Bogota police the night before Nixon's visit and not so much as a coffee bean was thrown at him.

Working together, CIA and the Secret Service also uncovered two other assassination plots, both in Caracas. Nixon was unperturbed by these reports; he saw them as merely more of the same kind of thing he had been hearing since he assumed office in 1953. Venezuelan security officers were confident they could handle the situation, but no one knows what would have happened had Nixon not changed his schedule and route after the attacks on his party at the airport and on the way into the city. If CIA failed anywhere in the pure intelligence field it was in failing to understand the psychology of the green and untried Caracas police force. Most of the experienced policemen had been killed or sacked during the revolution, and the Communists made the most of this by a subtle campaign of reminding the new cops what had happened to their predecessors for getting tough with mobs.

When President Eisenhower's trip to Japan was canceled in

June, 1960, it was a case of CIA benefiting from the experience of the Nixon trip. At least a month before the President's departure for the Far East, CIA was all but convinced that his visit to Japan would have to be canceled. Eastern European agents were reporting a determined campaign by the Kremlin to whip up a hostile attitude toward Eisenhower in Tokyo. Khrushchev's agents had descended on Tokyo en masse and were conferring day and night with their Japanese Communist counterparts on ways to keep Eisenhower out of Japan. One report said that the Socialist chairman, Inejiro Asanuma, "is very worried. The Communist Party is advocating violence."

Eisenhower knew all this, thanks to CIA, but he insisted on going ahead with plans for the visit to Japan. Allen Dulles privately dragged his feet, however. He told the author a few weeks before Eisenhower left that "We may have to take him off that plane at the last minute."

In Manila on June 16th, it was announced that the President was dropping Tokyo from his itinerary. United Press International reported that "violent left-wing demonstrations forced the pro-Western Japanese government to seek a postponement of President Eisenhower's visit, and the President accepted with regret." What actually happened was that, at CIA's insistence, United States Ambassador Douglas MacArthur II had been ordered to pay a visit to Prime Minister Nobusuke Kishi and tell him that the Japanese government would have to disinvite the President because of the political situation in Japan. The violent Communist demonstration which greeted White House Press Secretary James C. Hagerty and Appointment Secretary Thomas E. Stephens on their arrival in Tokyo on June 10th had made up CIA's mind.

Eisenhower was furious at this turn of events, especially since it followed on the heels of Khrushchev's cancellation of his invitation to the President to visit the Soviet Union. But Allen Dulles was adamant, and he was backed up by

U. E. Baughman, chief of the Secret Service. They told the President if he went to Japan, he was almost sure to come to physical harm, and there was a good chance he would be assassinated.

In Japan, unlike Guatemala, the nation's intelligence organization did more than infer what action should be taken; it shouted the answer in a voice clearly audible to the policy makers, and then took a hand in carrying out the answer. But in most cases, the proper aim of the intelligence expert is merely to supply the policy maker with the facts. These may not produce or even suggest the proper decision but, possessed of these facts, the policy maker's chances of making the correct move are considerably enhanced.

6. Coup in Iraq

CIA's ACTIVITIES in Guatemala and Japan were excellent examples of the proper collection, evaluation and use of intelligence, but unfortunately CIA is not always so efficient. For example, the Kuwait crisis in the summer of 1961 was a prime example of what befalls the free world in due course when CIA fails to find out what the free world's enemies are up to. For the key to the Kuwait crisis was a violent event which occurred in neighboring Iraq three years previously on July 14, 1958, and which caught the United States by surprise.

That event, of course, was the overthrow of the pro-western government of Iraq's King Faisal by a brigadier general named Abdul Karim el-Kassem. Kassem was helped to power by the Communists and thereafter used the Reds at his convenience to help keep that power. By June, 1961, Kassem was sure enough of himself to tell the world that the small sheikdom of Kuwait was the property of Iraq.

Most Americans had never heard of Kuwait, a tiny nation about the size of Connecticut at the head of the Persian Gulf. It has a population of only 310,000. But its oil reserves, estimated at sixty-two billion barrels, are twice those of the United States and represent 20 per cent of all known oil reserves in the world. Kuwait therefore is not only important to the Arab world but to the world of imperial communism.

In 1899, when the sheikdom was threatened by a Turkish occupation, the British signed a treaty with Kuwait which gave them control over the country's foreign relations. The reason was Kuwait's oil, of course; by 1961, Britain was getting 40 per cent of its oil from Kuwait, and had heavy oil investments in the nearby sheikdoms of Bahrein and Qatar. By June, 1961, the world movement toward independence and against imperialism caught up with the British in Kuwait. They terminated their "obsolete and inappropriate" 1899 protectorate treaty with the sheikdom, and signed another pact which put Kuwait on its own in foreign affairs. However, the new treaty contained a clause which promised British military aid if Kuwait requested it, thus maintaining protection of British oil interests in the Persian Gulf area.

Two weeks later, Premier Kassem of Iraq stepped onto the stage. He announced Iraq's claim to Kuwait on the grounds that the 1899 treaty had been forged and that the sheikdom was an "integral part" of Iraq. Great Britain immediately dispatched more than 4,000 troops to Kuwait, plus several warships, while Kuwait mobilized its 2,400-man army. Kassem, with 60,000 troops at his disposal, cooled down somewhat; he indicated he never had intended to seize Kuwait by force and said he would continue to press Iraq's claim to the sheikdom through diplomatic channels. Kassem's move had not found the expected support among Iraq's Arab neighbors. This was probably due to the fact that President Gamal Abdel Nasser of the United Arab Republic and Kassem have been rivals for leadership in the Arab world, and Nasser was quick to support Kuwait's sovereignty. Lebanon and Jordan were noncommittal. Yet the Kuwait conflict came at a time of relative calm in the Middle East, and during a period of encouraging coolness in relations between Nasser and the Kremlin. Kassem's move gave the Soviet Union opportunities for fresh propaganda maneuvers in the area. And Kassem was on the scene largely because he had caught the United States with its spies asleep three years before.

The overthrow of King Faisal by Kassem's troops in 1958 caused considerable consternation on Capitol Hill. Iraq, as a member of the pro-Western Baghdad Pact, was considered safely tucked into bed with the free world and suddenly it had been taken over by a man who seemed likely to carry on a long flirtation with the Communists. On July 22, 1958, the Senate Foreign Relations Committee irritably decided to call officials of the Central Intelligence Agency for questioning as to why the Kassem revolt had found the United States unprepared.

The committee could well be puzzled. Under Secretary of State Christian Herter had spent a full day before its members and had shed little light on what had happened. Chairman J. William Fulbright, Democrat of Arkansas, complained to reporters that Herter had told him nothing he "didn't already know from the morning papers." Fulbright therefore offered the motion to summon Director Allen Dulles and other CIA officials for questioning. The late Senator William Langer, maverick Republican from North Dakota, followed this up by introducing a resolution calling for a "thorough investigation" of CIA. Langer said it was imperative to prevent "even more devastating damage . . . in the security of our nation and the world."

On the other hand, Allen Dulles had a right to a feeling of wistfulness. For there had been two plots to overthrow Middle Eastern governments, and CIA had nipped one of them. As information developed, the Iraqi revolt, which led to the assassination of King Faisal, Crown Prince Abdul Illah (his uncle), and Premier Nuri es Said, had been closely linked to one scheduled to break out simultaneously in neighboring Jordan, governed by Faisal's blood cousin, King Hussein. With the help of CIA and the American Embassy, Hussein had thwarted the Jordan plot by the mass arrest of more than

60 army officers and top noncoms—less than a week before Kassem's coup. Jordan and Iraq only recently had united as the Arab Federation, in response to the merger between Egypt and Syria into the United Arab Republic.

But, because it succeeded, it was the Iraqi coup that commanded the attention of the Congress and the free world. Kassem's victory threatened to open another crack in democracy's defenses.

Actually, CIA did have some fragmentary foreknowledge of Kassem's takeover. Some of the Army men arrested by Hussein in Jordan sought amnesty by telling of a similar plot in Iraq, but they did not know when the coup would occur. CIA dutifully passed this on to Baghdad, but admittedly did not press too hard to get to the specifics since Iraq was considered more of a British show as far as intelligence went. And of course, as it turned out, Kassem's move was not scheduled for any particular day; he merely took advantage of a situation to act.

The situation was this: On July 13, 1958, units of the Twentieth Brigade, commanded by General Kassem, were ordered by Premier Nuri to proceed to Jordan to reinforce the 12,000 Iraqi troops already there. They were to pass through Baghdad on the nights of July 13 and 14. Always before, Nuri had been careful to ration or limit live ammunition issued to units of which he was unsure. On this occasion, however, the brigade was given a full issue—and thus was in condition to strike.

Instead of issuing orders to his men that they were to go to Jordan, Kassem marshaled other forces and told them to join him in Baghdad that night. Word also went to other revolutionaries in other parts of the country. Kassem knew that King Faisal and Crown Prince Abdul Illah, his uncle, were preparing to leave for a Baghdad Pact meeting in Istanbul. He figured, rightly, that there would be a relaxation of Army watchfulness in the midst of these preparations.

At five o'clock on the morning of July 14, a company of Kassem's infantry supported by a tank and several antitank guns mounted on jeeps surrounded the Royal Palace. At the same time, other army units surrounded the home of Premier Nuri, a pro-Westerner but one of the Arab world's cruelest men, and took positions around the residences of other government ministers. Other units went to Baghdad Radio. Centurion tanks rumbled to strategic points throughout the city. General Rafiq Aref, the Army's Chief of Staff, was arrested.

The twenty-three-year-old Faisal was shaving when Kassem's troops surrounded the palace. An Iraqi Army captain demanded that the King come out and surrender. Instead, the King, with the Crown Prince at his side, began firing from second-floor windows. A soldier was wounded in the arm. The Army then brought up antitank guns and shelled the stucco-covered brick mansion, setting the interior afire. The royal family fled by a back door in an attempt to escape by car. Prevented from reaching the car, they walked up a gravel path toward the front of the house and toward the troops.

Members of the family were shot down on the lawn about twenty feet from the palace. Those killed included the King, the Crown Prince, the Crown Prince's mother and two sisters, a woman servant and the Crown Prince's aide-de-camp. Prince Abdul Illah's wife was wounded but later recovered. In a wild scene outside the palace, the Crown Prince's body was "given to the people," and was torn apart. The other victims were buried in unmarked graves.

Meanwhile, Radio Baghdad went on the air with this announcement: "This is Baghdad Radio, the voice of the Republic of Iraq." The announcement brought people into the streets and by seven o'clock there were thousands in cars, buses and afoot in all the streets around the palace, at Nuri's home and in front of the Defense Ministry. General Kassem ordered guards stationed at all foreign embassies, legations and consulates—about twenty men armed with light weapons were sent to the American and British Embassies. At the British Embassy, where a crowd of several thousand gathered, the mob began tearing down the statue of General Maud, the British officer who occupied Iraq after World War I, and a statue of King Faisal in a nearby park. The British comptroller, Colonel P. L. Graham, fired at the demonstrators. The mob then broke into the British compound, killed Colonel Graham and threatened the British Ambassador, Sir Michael White, his staff and servants. Iraqi troops took Sir Michael to the Baghdad Hotel for safety. The Embassy was sacked and burned.

Premier Nuri es Said escaped from his house on the Tigris River, the only side on which it was unguarded. He crossed the river in a small boat and took refuge in the house of a friend. But the rebels paid a servant 10,000 dinars ($28,000) to tell them where the ousted prime minister was hiding. He was found, disguised as a peasant woman, with a pistol hidden in the folds of his garments. He put up a good fight— killing two of his attackers—before he was captured. Later his body was torn apart and dragged through the streets.

Shortly, the Iraqi mob, led by Communists, took violent action against CIA, which had been prominent in the maze of espionage and counterespionage that preceded the revolt. Four members of a Jordanian mission, three Americans and seven Europeans were arrested at the Baghdad Hotel. They were herded into a truck and taken to Radio Baghdad, then rerouted to the Defense Ministry, where Kassem had his headquarters. On a side street, the truck was halted by the mob and the prisoners were hauled out and all but two, who escaped, were beaten to death. Among those killed was Eugene Burns of Sausalito, California, a former newspaperman who had founded an organization called the American Friends of the Far East. Burns had arrived in Iraq only a few days earlier, ostensibly on a trip to arrange for relief of needy

Arab children. But the Kassem regime claimed that Burns in fact was a CIA agent and for that reason was a marked man. Historically, of course, charitable organizations often have been a cover for intelligence operations.

In the face of this carnage, Washington seemed somewhat bewildered. Although Kassem had been a student in various American war colleges, no one in the Pentagon nor the CIA remembered him. Indeed, it was several days before anyone in Washington could establish the correct spelling of the man's name. Meanwhile, Kassem hammered on the theme that "imperialist" conspirators headed by CIA were plotting against his regime. Washington sent Assistant Secretary of State William Rountree to Baghdad to confer with Kassem. He was met with hostile demonstrations and signs, supplied by the Communists: "Rountree, Go Home."

Rountree accomplished very little in his Baghdad talks, but Kassem did give the United States encouragement by saying he would respect all treaties, including the vital Baghdad Pact which was the Middle East's first defense against communism. By this time CIA had caught its breath, however, and warned that Kassem could not be trusted. He had several avowed Communists in his official family: Wasfi Taher, his bodyguard; Loutfi Taher, the government censor; Selim Kakhry, boss of the radio and television stations; and Fadhil Mahdawi, president of the so-called "People's Court." Moreover, the Iraqi Reds on the first day of the revolt had maneuvered successfully to prevent the Kassem regime from joining Nasser's United Arab Republic.

In this maneuver the Reds played successfully on Kassem's egotism. The word from top Army officers around Kassem was that the goal of the revolt was to unite Iraq with the UAR, which bans all political parties, including the Communist. Nasser's pictures suddenly appeared all over Baghdad and it began to appear that he was the hero of the coup. Kassem hated the thought of playing second fiddle to Nasser and the Reds knew it. They persuaded him that he would need plenty of help to stay in power, to withstand the pressure from the pro-Nasser people. In exchange for his promise to legitimatize the Communist party, the Reds put on a series of demonstrations for Kassem, with the mobs carrying Kassem's picture instead of Nasser's.

Kassem started putting Communists or pro-Communists into important government jobs. The Reds persuaded the Army to let their followers have arms for their "People's Resistance Squads," and within weeks thousands of Communists were armed. As CIA had warned, Kassem renounced the Baghdad Pact; he already had withdrawn from Iraq's Arab Federation link with Jordan.

Kassem had plenty of troubles at first. His overthrow of Faisal's government was followed by a series of revolts on the part of various tribes, notably the warlike Kurds, who were angered by the assassination of Faisal. It would be comfortable to assume that CIA had a part in these harassments, but unfortunately Dulles' men were not operating with any real efficiency. Their only "intelligence" came from the vague reports of "travelers" encountered in Cairo and Beirut, Lebanon. But Kassem, like a good dictator, sought to turn the heat off himself and onto the Americans by linking the U. S., through CIA, with assorted plots to meddle in Middle Eastern affairs.

The principal "plot" in which the United States was alledged to have been involved was unfolded in August, 1958, during the trial of a former Iraqi army chief of staff, Major General Ghaza Daghistani, on charges of treason. Lieutenant Colonel Majid Amin, a known Communist and military prosecutor for the Kassem regime, told the court that the Western powers and Israel—a "must" in all Arab conspiracies —had conspired with the old Iraqi monarchy through slain Premier Nuri to destroy the independence of Syria and put Iraqi Crown Prince Abdul Illah on Syria's throne. Lieutenant

General Rafiq Aref, who had been arrested on the first day of the Kassem revolt and who was himself a defendant, went along with Amin, probably under duress. Aref said the Americans wanted to use the Iraqi Army in Syria to attack Communists they felt had taken power there. He said he "withstood this."

Documents were introduced at the trial purporting to show that the code word for the Americans was Rasifi, which is the Baghdad area where the United States Embassy is located. A telegram dated in 1956 from Daghistani to Aref was read into the record: "Prime Minister and Foreign Minister anxious about situation in Syria . . . Rasifi wants action. Plan A involves problems which may lead to further problems and rumors. Do not expect Communists to act in Syria because will take considerable time to consolidate their position. Disturbances may arise in Jordan. We may have opportunity to concentrate troops for the protection of Jordan using threat of Israel as an excuse. Plans should be made."

Aref testified: "The Americans wanted some action. They thought the Communists were active in Syria and wanted us to attack Syria, but we stood against it. There was no plan—just code words. I swear by the Koran there was no plan."

Another witness was Fadhil Jamali, former Premier, former Foreign Minister and former United Nations delegate. Jamali was decidedly pro-Western. He staunchly denied he knew anything about Daghistani's activities or any American-inspired plot against Syria. Specifically, he was questioned about a meeting he attended in Istanbul between Crown Prince Abdul Illah and Loy Henderson, roving United States Ambassador. "The Americans said that if we were confronted with a Communist threat, they were prepared to help us," Jamali testified. "They asked if there was any threat from Syria, and Iraq answered that there was no threat."

It is a good bet the Kassem government was giving CIA more credit than it deserved. Quite aside from whether the

United States wanted to meddle in Syria's internal affairs—which it probably did, on a much smaller scale—Kassem overlooked a major point. This was that if American intelligence had the kind of organization which could plot the overthrow of a government in the Middle East, with all the necessary connections involved, it also would have had connections to tip it off on Kassem's march to Baghdad on the night of July 13. Yet the only word CIA had on the Kassem revolt was the vaguely worded reference put out by the men captured when Jordan's King Hussein put down the rebellion against his government.

Jordan long has been linked to Iraq by close ties. The late Sherif Hussein, a Hashemite chieftain who successfully revolted against the Turks, had two sons: Faisal and Abdullah. They became the rulers of Iraq and Trans-Jordan. The King Faisal killed during the Iraqi revolt of July 14, 1958, was the great grandson of Sherif Hussein. He was the cousin of King Hussein of Jordan, son of the late King Abdullah.

Because Hussein also has had close friendships with the Western world, his regime often has been torn by internal strife. In April, 1957, Hussein's Chief of Staff, Major General Ali Abu Nuwar, led rebel troops unsuccessfully against other troops loyal to the King. He later took refuge in Egypt. Other plots were directed from outside. Working with the British, CIA put the finger on Colonel Abdel Hamid Serraj, chief of Syrian intelligence, as the chief outside plotter. It was Serraj who directed the long period of terror-bombing in Jordan after the 1957 uprising, according to CIA's information. The bombings lasted until Hussein, again with CIA and British aid, uncovered and jailed a few of the bomb throwers.

Later, in June, 1958, CIA uncovered another plot against Hussein. Agents discovered that certain Jordanian Army officers were spending money with considerable abandon in Amman night clubs. Jordanian contacts were assigned to ask some questions, and they returned with the report that the money was coming from exiled Jordanian politicians in Cairo and Damascus, who had directed that the cash be distributed through all ranks of the army to prepare for a military government which would overthrow Hussein.

King Hussein called in his top officers. He told them of a widespread Army plot and said that four or six culprits were present in the room. Everybody denied taking any Egyptian or Syrian money, but their explanations failed to mollify the King. Hussein was understandably upset because shortly before the meeting CIA men had informed him of a plot to shoot him from the ground while he was flying in one of his helicopters.

About two weeks later—a week before the Iraqi revolt—Hussein acted to put down a revolt he now was convinced was being hatched by Egyptians and Syrians to take over Jordan with the help of disloyal Jordanian Army officers. Among the more than sixty officers and noncoms arrested was the King's personal aide and bodyguard, Colonel Radi el Abdullah, who was captured in bed at three o'clock in the morning.

What particularly shocked Hussein was that so many of the persons implicated in the plot were from branches of Jordan's crack Arab Legion. This was the outfit created by the British and officered by them for nearly thirty years. In March, 1956, however, Hussein had yielded to Arab pressure and had dismissed Sir John Bagot Glubb, the famed Glubb Pasha who had developed the Legion and who had been its long-time chief of staff. This was what the anti-Hussein crowd wanted; from then on the Legion was infiltrated by pro-Nasser and pro-Communist forces.

Hussein's job, of course, was enormously complicated by the presence within Jordan's borders of 517,000 Palestinian Arab refugees, who owe no loyalty to the central government. They number roughly one third of the Jordanian population and are the target of constant attention from Arab agitators.

In addition, there are 500,000 Bedouins living east of the Jordan River, who always have been intensely loyal to Hussein but who have always lived for the day when the war against Israel will be resumed.

Faced with these pressures on all sides, King Hussein refused to rely entirely on his own 25,000-man army when Kassem overthrew King Faisal in Iraq. He appealed for, and got, a force of British paratroopers, at about the same time that American troops were landing in neighboring Lebanon. The United States troops were in Lebanon because in CIA's opinion the strangely gentle civil war which had gripped that little country for several months might become serious to the Western World as a result of Kassem's rise to power in Iraq. There was danger that forces of the United Arab Republic from Red-tinged Syria might try to take over Lebanon.

News of Kassem's coup in Iraq reached CIA Director Allen Dulles about dawn on July 14. He arranged a meeting as soon as possible with his brother. the late Secretary of State John Foster Dulles, and various military officials. It was agreed at that meeting, and later at a conference with President Eisenhower, that conditions in the Middle East were a threat to world peace. President Camille Chamoun of Lebanon, under terms of the Eisenhower Doctrine, had requested American aid on at least six different occasions since the insurrection in his country. This time it was decided to give him some. President Eisenhower dispatched the Sixth Fleet to Lebanon and ordered United States Marines and units of an Army paratroop outfit to land in the country. Somebody forgot to check with Chamoun to see if he still wanted our help because Chamoun knew nothing of the President's action until he heard of it on the radio. Fortunately, he welcomed the troops.

Trouble in Lebanon began when the United States first proposed the Eisenhower Doctrine, which would authorize our intervention in Middle Eastern affairs if Communist aggression threatened and our help was requested by a legitimate government. It was accentuated by the British-French-Israeli invasion of Egypt following Nasser's seizure of the Suez Canal. A former premier, Saeb Salam, then Minister of State in the cabinet of President Chamoun, opposed the Eisenhower Doctrine; he demanded that Lebanon remain neutral in the Cold War. Supported by the UAR, Salam asked that Lebanon break diplomatic relations with Great Britain and France, as most Arab countries did, as a result of the Suez fiasco. Chamoun, who favored the Doctrine, shrewdly told Salam to propose to the UAR a conference of Arab chiefs to discuss the matter. The meeting took place in Beirut in December, 1956, and, as Chamoun had figured, failed to reach an agreement. Chamoun then claimed Lebanon was free to act as it wished, and refused to break diplomatic relations with the Suez culprits.

Salam was furious. He and Premier Abdullah Yaffi, also a Moslem nationalist, threatened to resign unless Chamoun relented. To their surprise Chamoun immediately accepted their resignations. He also rubbed salt in their wounds by selecting Beirut University Professor Charles Malik, a decided pro-Westerner, as Foreign Minister to succeed Salam. Sami es Solh, a Sunni Moslem, was named Premier. Then the new government accepted the Eisenhower Doctrine.

In the parliamentary election campaign of June, 1957, Salam and his followers, urged on by UAR's Nasser, made foreign policy the crucial issue, hoping to defeat Chamoun because of the government's pro-Western stand. But Chamoun's candidates swept the election, taking even those seats held by Salam and Yaffi. Salam tightened the opposition into an organized "National Front" and waited for his chance to strike.

In May, 1958, the murder of a leftist newspaper editor gave Salam that chance. He accused the government of ordering the crime, called a general strike and demanded that

Chamoun resign. Salam's move came as no surprise to
Chamoun. Several hours before Salam acted, an agent of the
CIA, known in Beirut as a successful American businessman,
gave Chamoun a complete briefing on Salam's plans, including the word that the strike had been urged by Nasser agents
and would be supported financially and with hired mobs by
the United Arab Republic.

The strike, enforced with stark terrorism and given Nasser's full support, was partially successful, but Chamoun
refused to budge. It then became the kind of civil war which
probably could take place only in complex Lebanon. Salam
retired to the Moslem quarter, which he barricaded, and his
residence and Chamoun's presidential palace frequently were
under mortar fire as the opposing forces tried out their new
weapons. But it was a strange little war. Foreign correspondents passed freely between the lines, and Salam daily held
court for the press in his home. On one occasion a cease fire
was called so that Salam's daughters could make their
monthly trip to the beauty parlor. On another, Salam appeared at an old graduates' reunion at Beirut University.

Before the American landings, there was considerable fuss
raised about the United States "invasion." Adel Osserdan,
speaker of Parliament, gathered thirty of the sixty-six members to protest the United States intervention. General Fauod
Chehab, commander of the Lebanese Army, was outraged
and demanded that Chamoun withdraw his request for help
or he would resign. Chamoun refused to withdraw his request
and persuaded Chehab to stay on.

The American landings were a touchy thing. Admiral
Holloway, commanding the U. S. forces, led the column of
troops into Beirut along with General Chehab and United
States Ambassador Robert McClintock. Ordinary citizens
turned out by the thousands in their best clothes to make a
holiday of the landing and to watch the Americans disem-
bark, but nobody was quite sure what the Lebanese Army

would do—even General Chehab. Lebanese Army tanks were lined up along the road into Beirut, their guns pointed at the marching column. No one knew whether or not they would fire. But at the last moment, with their commander, General Chehab, riding along with the "invaders," the men snapped smartly to attention and saluted. The crisis was past. Later, Salam gave strict orders that the Americans were not to be molested, and his men generally obeyed this admonition, although there were a few minor scrapes in assorted saloons.

Much to American chagrin, the United Nations refused to recognize our action, and its representative had no official contact with Admiral Holloway. Moreover, Afro-Asian countries joined the Soviet bloc in demanding that American troops get out of Lebanon. Eventually, on October 31, United States forces evacuated Lebanon—and Chamoun's government promptly fell. But through the efforts of Ambassador McClintock and Robert Murphy, Under Secretary of State in charge of trouble shooting, a compromise was reached and General Chehab, a Christian, was elected President. Chamoun remained a member of Parliament, and Salam and his rebel colleague, Kamal Jumblatt, also were elected to the governing body.

On balance, then, CIA's score during that hectic period in the Middle East was a creditable one. It had prevented the spread of the Iraqi revolt to Jordan and its intelligence had helped to bring a measure of stability to the Lebanese government. But its failure to uncover the plot in Iraq returned to haunt CIA. In the summer of 1961, as we have seen, Abdul Karim el-Kassem decided that his Iraqi regime was entitled to annex the fabulous oil reservoir of Kuwait. To be sure, Kassem's grab was foiled. But the fact remains that three years earlier, while CIA was not looking, a dangerous and capricious militarist had deposed Iraq's pro-Western government to present a long-range threat to the peace of the Middle East.

7. King-Making in Iran

A FEW DAYS AFTER the suave, Sorbonne-educated Ali Amini took over as Premier of Iran in May, 1961, an agent for the Central Intelligence Agency ran into a newspaperman friend in a bar in Istanbul.

They chatted for a while over a couple of dry martinis and then the reporter put a question to the CIA man.

"What about this Amini in Iran?" he asked. "What kind of a joker is he?"

"Oh, he's all right," replied the CIA man. "He is fine. He's one of our boys."

The reporter looked aghast. "My God," he said, "Not again!"

Whether or not the newspaperman was libeling Amini, he had a right to be apprehensive. For the last time CIA had stuck its well-meaning nose into the Iranian internal situation it had fathered an administration whose corruption startled even the most hardened observers of Middle Eastern thievery and which, by the time of Amini's ascension to power in 1961, had carried oil-rich Iran to the brink of bankruptcy. This was an achievement of monumental dimensions even for Iran, because since 1953 the United States had poured nearly one billion dollars into this country of only eighteen million persons to save it for the West.

It was in 1953, of course, that the CIA stage-managed the

overthrow of Premier Mohammed Mossadegh, that celebrated compulsive weeper, who had seized Britain's monopolistic oil company and was threatening to do business with the Kremlin. At the time CIA's coup was hailed as a blow for democracy, which it was. But after disposing of Mossadegh, CIA and the State Department reverted once again to a weakness that so often has been disastrous. In the setting up of the new regime, in which CIA took a major part, no consideration was given as to whether the new men had any intention of attempting to relieve the misery of the Iranian people. It was enough for the United States that they were anti-Communist.

As in so many other areas in the world, notably Laos, it was not enough. The American-approved regime stole everything it could lay its hands on, despite the well-meaning but perfunctory efforts of the Shah. The Shah, an athletic and physically energetic young man named Mohammed Pahlevi, has felt constrained to spend most of the national budget on his 200,000-man army and 50,000-man police force, and although land reform laws have been in operation for more than a decade, by June, 1961, the Shah still was the personal proprietor of nearly half his seven hundred crown villages totaling 600,000 acres.

Iran's distress is all the more tragic because it is a country which with reasonably wise and even partially honest leadership could be the most powerful and richest in the Middle East. Its eighteen million people rattle around in a country with an area only slightly smaller than that section of the United States east of the Mississippi. From the Caspian Sea, Iran stretches a thousand miles to the Gulf of Oman and runs for a thousand miles along the border of the Soviet Union. Although one third of this area is arid, it has untapped copper and coal deposits in the mountains, and rivers where dams could provide unlimited power. And its oil fields produce more than one million barrels a day, with potential wells still to be tapped. It is a nation whose people are a proud and stubborn mixture of Arab, Mongol, Turk and Afghan, with its own Shiite branch of the Islam religion, a national ancestry that goes back to Cyrus the Great and Darius, and a culture that includes the poetry of Omar Khayyam and the magnificently sculpted architecture of Persepolis, Isfahan and Shiraz.

The Shah, who had to marry three wives before he could produce a male offspring, traces his "divine right" to the throne all the way back to his father. This hearty patriarch was Reza Pahlevi, originally an illiterate officer in the Iranian army who led his troops in a military putsch in 1921 and took over as Minister of War. Shortly, Pahlevi also was Premier, and in 1925 he proclaimed himself Shahinshah (king of kings). It was Pahlevi père who built the Trans-Iranian Railroad, with its 4100 bridges and 54 miles of tunnel, and by the time the British exiled him in 1941 for sympathizing with the Nazis, he had quelled all the rebellious tribes within reach of his iron fist and torn the purdah veils from the faces of Iran's women. His son also has had an obsession with national development. He has built more than nine hundred additional miles of railroad and instituted a Seven Year Development Plan to build irrigation dams and 1500 miles of highways.

But the Shah had barely taken his first few tentative strides toward the further rescue of his country from the Nineteenth Century when wily old Mossadegh burst on the international scene. The Shah, in 1951, had been forced to name Mossadegh his Premier during a period of fervent nationalism in Iran, and Mossadegh shoved the youthful king of kings into the background while he proceeded virtually to wrest the tail from the British lion. Specifically, Mossadegh expropriated the properties of the British-owned Anglo-Iranian Oil Company, whose royalty payments had supported the Iranian economy for nearly half a century.

Iran's resources include an estimated 13 per cent of the world's oil reserves, and as early as 1870 this mouth-watering fact had come to the attention of British interests. In that year, the Baron Reuter, founder of the news service which still bears his name, obtained a concession that gave him a monopoly over Iranian industry. Conditions in the country and throughout the world forced Reuter to put off exploiting this concession until the early 1900's. But in that period he formed a company with various European industrial and financial personages to organize the Industrial Bank of Persia, which became the financing agent for the Anglo-Iranian Oil Company.

Admittedly, there was a turning of international wheels-within-wheels during this period of exploitation, and once again Allen Dulles was lucky enough to have a front-row seat for the proceedings. For Dulles' law firm, Sullivan and Cromwell, had been legal counsel for Anglo-American Oil, and presumably Dulles was familiar with the peculiar situation long before Mossadegh decided to twist the British lion's tail. To be sure, Dulles had left Sullivan and Cromwell some time before Mossadegh appeared on the scene but, undoubtedly, the background he had acquired during his service with the firm was invaluable to the new director of CIA when that agency faced the problem, in the spring and summer of 1953, of how to save Iran from falling into Communist hands.

When Mossadegh announced the expropriation of Anglo-Iranian Oil and nationalization of Iran's oil fields, the international uproar was thunderous. Mossadegh could not do that, and the Western bankers would prove it to him. Iranian oil was virtually boycotted. Mossadegh promptly tried to swing some deals with smaller, independent companies to work the Iranian fields, but the State Department gave these companies little encouragement—which is to say it told them "hands off." Meanwhile, Iran was losing its oil revenues and going broke. Even American financial aid was not enough although the State Department, with understandable reluctance, donated $1,600,000 for a technical rural improvement program in 1951 and followed that with a foreign aid grant of $23,000,000 in 1952. Most of the latter was used to make up Iran's foreign exchange shortages, but Iran remained financially unstable.

Meanwhile, CIA learned that Mossadegh was carrying on a clandestine flirtation with Iran's furtive Communist party, the Tudeh. Soviet intelligence agents flocked into the ancient capital of Teheran and the traffic jam between them and Allen Dulles' energetic young men was almost ludicrous. Almost daily, emissaries from the Soviet danced attendance on Mossadegh as he lolled recumbent on his couch, alternately dozing and weeping. Inevitably, the old dictator put it squarely up to President Eisenhower. In a letter received by the President on May 28, 1953, Mossadegh overplayed his hand—he attempted to blackmail the United States by warning that unless Iran got more American financial aid he would be forced to seek help elsewhere. Elsewhere was the Soviet Union, with which Mossadegh suggested he would conclude both an economic agreement and a mutual defense pact.

Since Iran otherwise was broke, that meant Mossadegh would have to pledge the rich Iranian oil fields and the refinery at Abadan, the world's largest, in return for financial assistance from the Soviet. The danger to the West was clear. With Iran's oil assets in its pockets, the Russians would have little trouble eventually achieving a prime object of Russian foreign policy since the days of the Czars—access to a warm water outlet on the Persian Gulf, the free world's life line to the Far East. But even if Russia were to get just Iran's oil, the Western world would be weakened throughout the Middle East and Soviet prestige would soar. It was clear, too, of course, that Anglo-Iranian Oil had a stake of billions of dollars, and when private enterprise of that magnitude is involved State Departments and Foreign Offices are apt to react most sensitively.

The time had come for the United States to embark on an international gamble. CIA reports were that Mossadegh, although popular with the masses, had never been able to undermine the young Shah with his people. If something were to happen whereby the Shah was able to take over more firmly the reins of government, there was a good chance Mossadegh could be unseated. In any event, the Shah had a better than even chance of winning any popularity contest with Mossadegh.

So for a month the White House stalled Mossadegh, avoiding a direct reply in a welter of polite diplomatic notes seeking further discussions. Then President Eisenhower favored Mossadegh with a blunt reply: "No." Everybody agreed it was a calculated risk, a gamble that Mossadegh could be dealt with in such a fashion that he would be powerless to carry out his threat. The CIA forthwith set the wheels in motion for dealing with this tough old man.

First, on August 10, Allen Dulles flew to Europe to join his wife for a "holiday" in the Swiss Alps. Although the political situation in Teheran was becoming more ominous—Mossadegh was conferring daily with a Russian economic mission—United States Ambassador Loy Henderson decided he would like a vacation in Switzerland, too. Almost simultaneously, the Shah's sister, the pretty and tough-minded Princess Ashraf, marched into the royal palace and gave her brother the rough side of her tongue for his hesitancy in facing up to Mossadegh. Then she, too, flew off to Switzerland.

Certainly, the Russian espionage network must have surmised that something was cooking as Dulles, Henderson and Princess Ashraf turned up at the same Swiss resort. Their suspicions were strengthened when an old Middle Eastern hand named Brigadier General H. Norman Schwartzkopf suddenly was discovered in the midst of a leisurely flying vacation across the Middle East. He had been to Pakistan, Syria and Lebanon and, while the Russians fumed, he ultimately turned up in Iran.

The Reds had a right to be fearful, for Schwartzkopf had long been an anathema to the Kremlin. Americans remember him most vividly as the man who ran the Lindbergh kidnapping investigation in 1932, when he was head of the New Jersey State Police. But the world of international politics knew him better as the man who, from 1942 to 1948, had been in charge of reorganizing the Shah's national police force. In this job, Schwartzkopf spent little time tracking down ordinary criminals; he was kept busy protecting the government against its enemies, a job that required the setting up of an intelligence system to keep watch on various political cliques which might seek the Shah's overthrow.

In the course of these intriguing duties, Schwartzkopf had become a close friend and adviser to the Shah and, more important, to Major General Fazlollah Zahedi, one of his colleagues on the police force. So when Schwartzkopf turned up in Teheran in August he could explain with a straight face that he had come merely "to see old friends again." The Russians stormed and protested over his presence in Iran but Schwartzkopf went his casual way, dropping in to see the Shah one afternoon, spending the morning with General Zahedi, and renewing contacts with other old pals in the police and army.

And suddenly the Shah seemed to have located his courage and authority. On Thursday, August 13, the Shah handed down a ukase that sounded as if it had been written in collaboration by Schwartzkopf and Zahedi. Mossadegh was ousted as Premier and his successor was to be General Zahedi. The Shah ordered the colonel of the Imperial Guards to serve the notice on Mossadegh, and the wheels seemed to be turning.

But for some reason the colonel seemed seized by inaction. It was not until two days later, on midnight of August 15, that the colonel and a platoon of his troops showed up at Mossadegh's residence. There they found themselves surrounded by an array of tanks and jeeps, manned by hard-faced Army veterans Mossadegh had rounded up while the colonel vacillated.

The colonel, of course, was clapped into jail and Mossadegh announced that a revolt against the rightful government of Iran had been crushed. He also had some unkind things to say about the youthful Shah, and Iran's king of kings and his queen took the hint and hopped a plane for Rome by way of the then royally safe country of Iraq.

Schwartzkopf, however, held his ground on the Iranian stage. He took over as unofficial paymaster for the Mossadegh-Must-Go clique. Certain Iranians started to get rich, and the word later was that in a period of a few days Schwartzkopf supervised the careful spending of more than ten million of CIA's dollars. Mossadegh suddenly lost a great many supporters.

The climax came on Wednesday, August 19, four days after Mossadegh had "crushed the revolt." The tense capital was filled with troops, mounted against a new uprising, but none of them looked very happy. There seemed no reason for alarm when a long and winding procession of performers appeared on the scene for one of those impromtu parades common in Teheran. In the procession were tumblers, weight-lifters, wrestlers, boxers—all performing their specialties as they moved slowly along the streets. As usual, crowds flocked out into the streets to watch the show and to follow the parade.

Then, apparently, somebody gave a signal. The weird procession suddenly broke into an organized shouting mob

"Long Live the Shah!" they cried. "Death to Mossadegh."
The crowd joined in the shouting, some of them undoubtedly
keeping one hand tight against pockets where their American
wages were secured. Soon the entire capital was in an uproar,
and when the din was at its loudest troops who had remained
loyal to the Shah launched their attack.

For more than nine hours the battle raged, with Mossadegh's troops fighting fiercely but gradually giving ground.
Obviously, they were confused by the tactics and swift logisti-
cal maneuvers of the Shah's forces, who had been exposed to
some American who knew the ropes. Anyway, by midnight
Mossadegh's soldiers had been driven into a little ring around
the Premier's palace and they were forced to surrender.
Troops forcing their way into the palace captured Mossadegh
as he lay weeping in his bed, clad in silk striped pajamas.
Somebody telephoned Rome and the Shah and his queen
packed again, to return to Teheran and install Zahedi as
Premier.

This was a coup necessary to the security of the United
States, and probably to that of the Western World. But it
was another case of the United States not requiring tough
enough terms in return for its support. It is senseless, as some
observers have written, to say that the Iranians overthrew
Mossadegh all by themselves. It was an American operation
from beginning to end. But at the end, CIA—and the American government—stood by while a succession of pro-Western
and anti-Communist administrations, uninterested in the
smallest social reforms, brought Iran once again to the edge
of bankruptcy. And, of course, the American taxpayer has
contributed hundreds of millions of dollars to this corruption.

What seems incredible is that the United States should
have thought it necessary to pour so many millions into Iran.
Once things had settled down, an agreement was reached
whereby an international consortium was set up to adminis-

ter Iran's oil wealth, and soon the Iran treasury was being fattened to the tune of $300 million a year in oil revenues. In a country of only eighteen million persons, this would seem enough to keep the economy's head above water, but both the thieving Iranians and the naïve Americans did not see it that way.

In five years, from 1951 to 1956, the United States gave Iran a quarter of a billion dollars. In August, 1953, immediately after the overthrow of Mossadegh, the United States government began to feed mutual security funds into Iran at an average rate of five million dollars a month, and kept this up for three years to make up deficits in Iran's budget. These figures are from the 1957 report of the Committee on Government Operations of the House of Representatives. While Iran officialdom lived in palaces and rode around in Rolls Royces (Cadillacs were not chic enough), the House committee reported that American aid was administered in such "a loose, slipshod and unbusinesslike manner that it is now impossible —with any accuracy—to tell what became of these funds." One of the major projects was a multi-million-dollar dam on the Karadj River, but the committee said this project "has resulted in virtually nothing but the relocation, at a cost to the United States Government of nearly three million dollars, of a road around the proposed site."

Worse, our costly aid program administered by CIA's tame Iranian government has done practically nothing for the ordinary citizen of Iran, a fact that is serving Moscow's propagandists in good stead. The House committee in 1957 reported that literacy was so low in Iran that even in the cities it rarely was better than 7 per cent. Teachers earn less than twenty-five dollars a month and some families live on the produce of a single walnut tree. Yet the Shah and his officials have insisted on maintaining a 200,000-man army, which is larger than the armies of either Japan or Western Germany.

One general, Ahmed Ajodani, who formerly supervised

Teheran's electrical system, formed a phony consulting firm to supervise the wiring of the two-million-dollar plant. When the Shah arrived to pull the inaugural switch, the current flowed down into a nearby reservoir and electrocuted two swans.

General Haj Ali Kia, former chief of army intelligence, ran a government organization known only by the initials K.O.K. Its budget was $1,500,000 a month, and its sole chore was to compile confidential reports on the Shah's popularity. This was neither difficult for nor distasteful to General Kia, who was the *only* member of the organization and who made up his reports out of thin air.

In May, 1961, when the Shah installed Ali Amini as Premier, Amini had little comfort for the people. He reported that Iran's government debt had swelled from $10,000,000 in 1955 to $500,000,000, and said sadly, "The treasury is empty, and the nation faces a crisis—I dare not speak more openly lest I create a panic."

Even as Amini was speaking, the great masses of the Iranian people were flocking to the support of the man who supposedly had been discredited in the CIA palace coup—Mohammed Mossadegh. Eighty thousand of them packed Teheran's Jalalieh polo grounds to cheer his name at the biggest political rally in Iran in more than seven years. At seventy-nine and under house arrest, Mossadegh still was the biggest political figure in Iran and a stumbling block to Amini's program of revolution from the top. He was the undisputed boss of the National Front, a coalition of four leftist parties, and most of the experts agreed that the Front would carry away the majority of the seats in the Iranian Parliament in any free election.

The lesson of Iran apparently was one the Central Intelligence Agency learns hard. It is that in this era of Communist world conspiracy the United States cannot be content with short-term results. It is proper to seek to help pro-Western groups gain power in the strategic countries of the world, but if their only qualification is that they are pro-Western perhaps CIA should shop around a little more. For too often these Western-oriented leaders are not oriented to the needs of their own peoples and in their lush carryings-on and their indifference to social reforms they usually wind up as the finest propaganda targets Moscow can buy—with the damning label attached: Made in America.

8. Suez Snafu

IN THE TRICKY BUSINESS of king-making, it must sometimes seem to CIA that a body cannot win for losing. Allen Dulles and his operatives had shown considerable shrewdness in supervising the overthrow of Mossadegh in Iran, only to wind up with a regime notable chiefly for its sensational record of polite thievery. In Egypt, CIA assisted in the ousting of King Farouk and then found itself forced to deal with a vain, power-hungry and unpredictable ruler named Nasser.

Most international experts have continually hesitated to pass judgment on Colonel Abdel Gamal Nasser, President of the Arab Republic, whom the Central Intelligence Agency helped place in the driver's seat in the Arab world. On most occasions, even such a cautious jury has to admit bravely that Nasser is anti-West, that he is aggressively, pathologically opposed to the onetime colonial powers of Great Britain and France. But over the years Nasser also has been a hot iron for Moscow to handle. He has alternately accepted assistance from the Kremlin and turned on the Communist party in his own land. Perhaps it is safe only to put him down as a nationalist and a Nasserite who will do business with anybody who will help him strengthen Egypt, and Abdel Gamel Nasser.

Whatever history's ultimate verdict on the man, it may be difficult to pinpoint CIA's blame or credit. For, while CIA's efforts helped bring Nasser to power, there is considerable confusion as to whether CIA knew it was getting Nasser for its pains. Among those with authoritative understanding of the situation, the consensus is that while CIA was well aware of Nasser and his behind-the-scenes maneuverings, it firmly believed at one time that Major General Mohammed Naguib was CIA's contribution to Egypt as its man of destiny.

With Nasser foisted on it, CIA ultimately managed to bat a fair percentage in the turbulent years of keeping an eye on his regime. It failed to appraise correctly Nasser's affection for his $1.3 billion Aswan Dam, which caused him to nationalize the Suez Canal. But it did predict the far-flung consequences of his action—the French-British-Israeli invasion of Egypt in the fall of 1956. And at the outset, CIA had earned the gratitude of most of the world by getting rid of the fat and obscene King Farouk.

Nasser's role as the Colossus of the Arab world, a man who would stand athwart the Moslem faithful as both master and protector, had its genesis, as so many similar coups do, in the utter corruption of his country. It was a corruption personified by the porcine King Farouk, a royal personage who assumed the ancient throne as a lean, likable youth and went on to bring his nation to the brink of ruin by the absolutism of his degeneracy. The end of Farouk's regime came on July 22, 1952, with a military coup which overthrew the monarchy and sent him into luxurious Italian exile. But the seeds of dissatisfaction had been sown much earlier in an army disgraced by defeat.

Egypt had suffered a disastrous rout in her war against Israel in 1948. Officially she blamed her defeat on the West, because of the free world's close ties with the new Israeli state. But within the Army there was considerable resentment over the failures of military procurement whose corrupt practices had caused the Egyptian forces to go into battle unprepared for fighting. In a country like Egypt it was a lot easier to throw stones at the West.

Anti-Western feeling came to a head in October, 1951, when Farouk's government denounced its 1936 treaty with Great Britain and moved to drive the British from the Suez Canal zone and from Anglo-Egyptian Sudan. In January, 1952, there were violent anti-Western, anti-British riots in central Cairo in which the famed international hotel, Shepherds, was burned and much Egyptian property was destroyed. Farouk obviously had encouraged the rioters, but when they got out of hand and began pillaging property belonging to his friends he called out the Army to restore order.

It was probably at this time that the United States and Great Britain decided Farouk would have to go. That is, both CIA and British Intelligence began casting about for somebody to take over. General Walter Bedell Smith was director of CIA, but much of the planning for the Egyptian intelligence campaign was put in the hands of Allen Dulles, then Smith's No. 2 man. At first a survey was made of Egypt's Wafd Party, but the verdict was that the only potential leaders either were as corrupt as Farouk or too weak to stand up to him. With no great enthusiasm CIA turned to the Army.

The Wafd had been the ruling force in Egyptian life for nearly thirty years. At the outset a Simon-pure nationalist movement, the Wafd had gradually become corrupt and venal from feeding on absolute power. Leaders such as Nahas Pasha, who served innumerable terms as Premier, feathered their own nests and met with bland silence outcries in the Egyptian press. After the January riots, Farouk dismissed Nahas Pasha's Wafd government and appointed in his place a respected jurist named Hilaly Pasha. But the Wafd was a political machine that only the palace could contest; it derived its power from the people, from its mass appeal, and even after Nahas Pasha had been dismissed the Wafd retained its majority in Parliament.

Moreover, Wafd had the palace guard on its side in fighting any campaign against corruption. When it appeared that this campaign might become serious, the palace clique and the Wafd got together to destroy Hilaly. Farouk, too, took a hard look at the facts of life and was disturbed at their message that most of his friends would be the targets of any purity drive. Hilaly was sacked and was replaced by Hussein Sirry Pasha, a man not likely to offend anyone with his Puritanical zeal. Farouk, however, had been placed on the defensive. Younger elements in the Army let it be known that they wanted the corruption investigation continued and they made threats about what they would do if Farouk dragged his feet. CIA agents and British intelligence operators were close to these young reformers at the time and correctly gauged their strength.

That strength shortly brought about the ousting of Hussein Sirry Pasha and Hilaly Pasha was brought back to office, along with those ministers who were ready and willing to proceed with the anti-corruption campaign. With some prodding from CIA, Hilaly Pasha decided he wanted to appoint General Naguib as his Minister of War. Naguib's record recommended him to CIA, if not to Farouk. Alone among senior Army officers, Naguib had emerged from the Palestinian war, in which he had been severely wounded, with an untarnished reputation. But Farouk was determined to retain control of the Army so that he would have the force to block Hilaly if he became too inquisitive. Farouk by-passed Naguib and appointed as his War Minister one Colonel Ismail Sherine Bey, whose chief distinction was that he was married to the King's sister. Thus rebuffed, General Naguib was an easy prey for the conspirators.

By this time, the plotters had decided that Naguib was their man—their front man, that is. The real power was to be wielded by a lieutenant colonel named Abdel Gamal Nasser, who was unknown to Egypt's body politic but who was the acknowledged leader and official fire-eater of the military underground. It is not certain whether CIA was privy to the details of this plan and it may be that the Army rebels were purposely deceiving our agents. In any event, Naguib was CIA's man. And, of course, Nasser would not emerge as No. 1 for two years.

Nasser is the son of an assistant postmaster, the product of Egyptian-Arab farmer stock in the Upper Nile Valley. He went to school in Cairo and soon won his spurs as an anti-British revolutionist. In 1935, he led a group of students in a well-staged demonstration on National Struggle Day in Cairo. Police and British troops fired on the demonstrators as they crossed the Nile in boats and on rafts. Nasser was clubbed and won a lifetime scar on his forehead. The next year, Nasser was expelled from school for participating in another demonstration, but was reinstated when fellow students threatened to burn down the school building if the ban was maintained.

His revolutionary escapades in school set the pattern for Nasser's adult life. After spending six unenthusiastic months in law school, he wangled entrance to the military academy and on his first assignment, to garrison duty in the Sudan, he led a minor revolt of junior officers. Over the years, Nasser formed a hard core cell of junior officers who shared his hatred for the British. He recruited his men by dropping provocative comments into casual conversation and then sitting back to observe the reaction. He called his rebel unit the Free Officers Corps and by 1952 he had gathered around him a tough-minded little army of seven hundred. Meanwhile, he made contact with Egypt's leading Communists, always insisting that it was he who was using them. "When the Communists tried to enlist me, I refused and said I could not take orders out of the unknown," he said.

As late as a few days before the Free Officers' coup which unseated Farouk, Nasser's plan called for the assassination of thirty military and political leaders, including the King. CIA heard of this and an agent hurried to Nasser to present a horrified dissent to this blood bath. Nasser was told, in effect: "Look, it's no good killing a lot of people without any assurance that the killing will change the system. It's the system you have to kill and the only way to do that is to seize power." Nasser went before his Free Officers' Council and replayed the CIA agent's words, then talked the Council into abandoning the blood bath.

Nasser had more than the Free Officers Corps with him. Early in his revolutionary career he had formed a close friendship with Hassan el Banna, Supreme Guide of the Moslem Brotherhood, a fanatical religious group that used terrorist methods in its efforts to turn the clock back to a medieval theocratic state guided by pure Islamic principles. Although personally a religious progressive, Nasser worked with the Brotherhood because he needed the help of an influential force outside the military.

The Brotherhood, of course, was spurring Nasser on, but he made no move until he had consulted people he considered more expert on such things as military coups. This was CIA, which had sent a number of its skilled operatives to Cairo to keep a close watch on the weakening Farouk regime. Among these operatives were former Army intelligence officers who had spent most of their careers in the Middle East and with whom Nasser felt at home.

CIA gave the word late in July, 1952, and Nasser's Free Officers Corps swung into action. After securing all military establishments, the Corps placed General Naguib at the head of a force of tanks and field pieces and Naguib sent them rolling into the streets of Cairo and Alexandria. On the morning of Wednesday, July 22, Naguib proclaimed himself commander in chief of the Army and, by way of emphasizing

Farouk's untenable position, sent a jet plane to circle over the summer Royal Palace in Alexandria. Farouk took the hint and accepted Naguib as his boss; at the General's bidding he recalled Aly Maher, a rightist but a crusader against corruption, as Premier.

On Thursday a comparative calm set in. General Naguib announced that the main objective of the coup had been achieved—domestic reform. In a broadcast to the Egyptian people, he said "corruption and bribery were the main reasons for our failure in the Palestine war; they are the main reasons for troubles in Egypt's political and economic life." On Friday, the corruption cleanup began. Six members of Farouk's royal household resigned their offices. General Naguib announced the discovery of an attempted countercoup by the police and scores of police officers and officials in the Interior Ministry were arrested. It was beginning to appear that the revolution would not be safe as long as Farouk remained on the throne.

Nasser was determined to oust Farouk, but he wanted to do the job correctly. CIA suggested that Naguib present Farouk with a demand that he renounce his power to dissolve Parliament and appoint prime ministers. Naguib did so, and Farouk refused. Thereupon, on Saturday morning, Naguib's troops surrounded the summer palace and when Farouk's personal bodyguard barred the way the troops routed the bodyguard and smashed their way into the palace. Naguib ordered Farouk to abdicate in favor of his infant son and gave the King six hours to get out of Egypt. Well before the deadline, Farouk was at sea on his royal yacht, and a regency council had been named.

At least on the surface, Naguib had emerged as Egypt's "strong man." His pictures were in every street in Cairo and he rode about the city in one of Farouk's ten Rolls Royces, acknowledging the plaudits of the mobs. Nasser remained in the background, a shadowy figure the CIA suspected of biding his time for a seizure of power. At this time, a CIA appraisal reaching Washington described Nasser thus:

"His vices are vanity, obstinacy, suspicion, avidity for power. His strengths are complete self-confidence, great resilience, courage and nervous control, willingness to take great risks, great tactical skill and stubborn attachment to initial aims. He gets boyish pleasure out of conspiratorial doings. Has a real streak of self-pity. While a patient, subtle organizer, he can lose his head."

The calm, pipe-smoking Naguib ruled for two years as a kind of benevolent, paternal dictator. The Free Officers group regarded him uneasily. They had expected him to be their pawn, but Naguib soon revealed that he enjoyed the feel of power and there was a series of tug of wars in which Naguib successfully resisted the Free Officers' demands for sterner measures, a more austere economy. Some of those around Naguib compared him to the late Mahatma Gandhi in his pursuit of benevolence. Nasser and his clique believed Egypt needed a more ruthless hand.

By early 1954, Nasser had decided that Naguib had outlived his usefulness, and that a crisis would have to be created as a pretense for removing him. He was particularly disturbed by Naguib's efforts to return to the parliamentary system, which Nasser considered an obstacle to reform. A CIA report at this time said it was "obvious" Nasser would unseat Naguib.

Nasser's opportunity came without his willing it, when he was addressing an open-air meeting in Alexandria. A shot was fired and Nasser was wounded in the shoulder. The would-be assassin was a member of the Moslem Brotherhood, Nasser's religious ally, whose membership had been disillusioned by Nasser's tactics after the overthrow of Farouk. Once his wound had been bandaged, Nasser resumed his speech— an emotional exercise in which he inflamed the crowd by his references to plotters in the government. It was a simple thing to involve Naguib and, with the Army on his side, Nasser went on to depose his onetime tame general and, on April 18, 1954, to assume the premiership himself. Naguib was sent off into leisurely and luxurious imprisonment.

Foreign policy to Nasser meant annoying the British whenever the opportunity presented itself, and he addressed himself immediately to the negotiation of British withdrawal from their Suez base—a step that would lead to other and more far-reaching actions by the new Egyptian dictator. He attended the Bandung conference of neutral leaders in Indonesia, and to no one's surprise he then rejected a limited American offer of military assistance and accepted arms from the Soviet bloc.

It was the natural feeling among American policy makers that if Nasser was going to be slipping in and out of the Soviet bed he should get no subsidies from the United States to help finance his maneuvers. At the time the United States and Great Britain, in co-operation with the International Bank, were supporting loans to Nasser for construction of the monumental Aswan Dam. It was the belief, fostered in part by CIA, that if the United States acted tough Nasser would fall into line, since he could expect comparatively little economic help from the Soviet Union. In any event, Allen Dulles had succeeded to the top post in CIA with the ascension of the Eisenhower Administration in 1953, and certainly he and his brother, Secretary of State John Foster, kept no secrets from each other.

So in July, 1956, the American and British withdrew their support of the loans for the dam. Nasser was livid—"Americans, may you choke on your fury," he shouted. Still, the feeling was that he would fall into line. It must be remembered that this was in the period of John Foster Dulles' policies of toughness everywhere, massive retaliation and brinksmanship, and we had successfully handled a crisis in Egypt once before when Farouk was deposed.

Nasser almost immediately proved himself a different proposition than the corrupt Farouk. On July 26th he seized and nationalized the Suez Canal, that monument to British and French financing and imperialistic ambitions. Obviously, this was not quite the reaction the Brothers Dulles had expected; it also took the British by furious surprise. The United States could not, or would not, do anything more than engage in an exercise of tongue clucking; but the British had other ideas and quietly began to transform them into action.

That action was described initially on October 30, 1956, in a compilation of press dispatches in the *Washington Post:*

"Tank-supported Israeli troops speared to within eighteen miles of the Suez Canal early today in a lightning invasion strike almost completely across Egypt's 120-mile wide Sinai Peninsula. The attack was along a 26-mile front. The blow was described officially by Israel as an operation to wipe out Commando bases."

It was far more than that, of course. It was an attack on Egypt by three nations—Israel, Great Britain and France— and it was designed to crush the Nasser government, recover the Suez Canal and win more land for the fledgling Israeli nation. Britain and France at once ordered Egypt to cease fire and when Nasser rejected this demand, British and French bombers attacked Egypt on October 31, and landed ground troops a few days later.

President Eisenhower, who was campaigning in the South when the attack was launched, was described as having been caught by surprise. Chalmers Roberts wrote in the *Washington Post:* ". . . it began to dawn on official Washington that Britain, France and Israel had worked out, and were carrying through, a concerted military-political movement about which the United States had been almost totally unaware." In Foggy Bottom, Secretary of State Dulles would say, "We had no advance information of *any* kind . . . The British-

French participation also came as a complete surprise to us."

That was the Administration's story. The facts according to CIA's Allen Welsh Dulles were startlingly different. "My brother said the State Department was taken by surprise," he told this author a few years later. "That was only technically correct. What he meant was that the British, French and Israeli governments had not informed our ambassadors. But we had the Suez operation perfectly taped. We reported there would be no attack by Israel on Jordan but that there would be a three-nation attack on Suez. And on the day before the invasion CIA reported it was *imminent*."

CIA was specific in its defense. It insisted and continues to insist to this day that American intelligence agents in Israel reported the mobilization of the Israeli Army, and that other CIA operatives reported on British and French activity on Cyprus, where combat craft were being loaded and bombers and fighter planes were being marshaled. They reported also that French newspaper correspondents had been briefed by commanders of the invading units.

Yet, White House Press Secretary James C. Hagerty was telling reporters that President Eisenhower got his first information on the invasion "through press reports," and Secretary Dulles was reported by the *Washington Post* as being "angry—or worse—at America's chief allies." State Department officials were saying that the British-French military move, "certain to be widely condemned around the world, unhappily would serve to offset similar condemnations of the Soviet Union for its use of force in Hungary."

The only explanation seemed to be that although the United States had been informed of the attack in advance, it had been decided there was nothing we could do to dissuade the attackers. Therefore we took the position that we should, in John Foster Dulles' words, "shut our eyes and see nothing."

Once the attack was launched, however, and international

public opinion was aroused, the United States acted with considerable vigor. It urged the British, French and Israelis to agree to a cease fire and when that plea failed, the United States took the matter to the United Nations Security Council, thereby putting a strain of enormous proportions on the Atlantic Alliance.

What happened next can only be guessed at. The invaders had victory in their grasp and were prepared to present the UN with a *fait accompli*. But at this point a mysterious letter from Russian Premier Bulganin was delivered to the White House. It is generally accepted that Bulganin threatened to unleash his intercontinental rockets on Britain and France in support of Egypt. Whether this is true or not, the fighting ended as suddenly as it had begun. Britain, Israel and France withdrew their troops and Nasser emerged stronger than ever.

As for CIA, there has never been an official denial that Allen Dulles' agents did, indeed, keep the Administration informed up-to-the-minute on the invasion plans of the three nations. Some critics have suggested that Brother Allen's information became snagged in the transmission belt to the White House once it had reached Brother Foster's desk. That remains speculation, but the fact remains that President Eisenhower informed the world that the first word he had of the invasion was from press dispatches.

9. *The Black Lady*

PONDERING THE COMPLEXITIES and mutual frustrations of the Cold War, historians of the Twenty-First Century may well conclude that the intelligence coup of that tense period was scored by a little band of American airmen sequestered on a bleak plain near the Turkish town of Adana. The group were members of the top secret 10-10 Reconnaissance Detachment which for nearly four years staged secret flights over the Soviet Union and brought back plane loads of intelligence—in photographs and in the millions of radio words and radar signals etched on the tapes of recording machines.

Among other things, these flights located missile stations, military airfields, troop concentrations, the nature of industrial establishments and the design of railroad bridges. From fifteen miles above the earth, the planes could take pictures of such clarity that our intelligence could distinguish between a man on a motorcycle and a man on a bicycle. Their radios located radar stations and the recorded signals laid bare the Soviet antiaircraft defense system in given areas. It is almost certain that no other espionage operation ever provided any nation with such a wealth of vital detail.

Unfortunately for American prestige throughout the world, the Eisenhower Administration reacted with all the naïvete of a child caught raiding the cookie jar when one of these airmen was captured by the Russians. First a cover story

112

was put out that was patently and amateurishly false. Then, after a few days of confusion, President Eisenhower decided to admit to the world that we were spying on the Russians. To the surprise and disgust of our allies, he not only broke the first rule of espionage, which is to admit nothing, but he insisted the United States had a right to do such things and implied that the flights would continue.

To be sure, the argument is most valid that a nation has a right to protect itself by gathering intelligence in any way it can. But this is not to be said publicly by anyone in an official position. When it is said, it wrecks the polite little accommodation by which enemies in peacetime manage to do diplomatic business with each other while seeking the soft spots in one another's defenses. In the famous case of the U-2, it wrecked the 1960 summit conference in Paris, caused Nikita Khrushchev to revoke an invitation to President Eisenhower to visit the Soviet Union, and generally spread alarm throughout the world.

Nevertheless, the U-2 flights remain as perhaps the greatest triumph achieved by the Central Intelligence Agency since its founding. The operation's success at avoiding detection over so long a period earned high praise from such cynical intelligence experts as the French and the British. One Britisher told CIA Director Allen Dulles: "We'll never be able to match that one. Those flights were intelligence work on a mass production basis."

The story of the 10-10 Reconnaissance Detachment began back in 1953, when the Lockheed Aircraft Corporation of Burbank, California, instructed its engineers to design an airplane that would go higher and farther than the F104 went at that time. It shortly became apparent that it would take an entirely new kind of aircraft to do the job.

A designer named Kelly Johnson went to work—and came up with the U-2. It was a plane that was like a glider with a jet engine. The wing span was more than eighty feet, and although the wing was extremely light it was designed to carry the whole weight of the aircraft, including a large amount of fuel. In addition, it was necessary for stability's sake on takeoffs to make the wing tip a part of the landing gear. This was done by attaching what Johnson called a "pogo"—a wheel on a stick—to each wing tip.

Finished, the U-2 was an amazing plane even in an era of extraordinary aeronautical achievements. It ranged as high as ninety thousand feet—seventeen miles above the earth—and during the eight hours it could stay aloft it could half fly and half glide for nearly four thousand miles. Before takeoff, the pilot had to spend an hour and a half relaxing and breathing pure oxygen in order to prepare himself for high-altitude conditions. His helmet was airtight and sealed to his body by a cork ring, which meant he could neither eat nor drink before or during a flight. Often, when a pilot was in the air for as long as eight hours, he landed in a state of physical exhaustion, his body chafed and raw from the tight fitting suit and helmet and burning with thirst.

The Air Force and other agencies, which later included the National Aeronautics and Space Administration, eagerly seized upon the U-2 for use in high-altitude scientific research, to observe missiles in flight and to track missile nose cones on the way down. It was used, too, to check on radiation fallout and to measure atmospheric turbulence at high altitudes as a guide to aircraft designers and pilots.

Shortly, too, CIA became interested in the U-2. It was the best plane ever designed—for spying. It could fly higher and farther than any interceptor aircraft, and it could carry the kind of equipment necessary for the mechanical and electronic collection of intelligence. And so, by 1956, a group of American airmen had arrived at Incirlik Air Base in Turkey. There were eight civilian pilots in all, including a personable young man named Francis Gary Powers. The pilots and their wives and families moved into a trailer camp at the western end of the base, where they lived in mystery and seclusion for nearly four years, having little or no contact with the rest of the base.

For the record, Powers and his colleagues were employed in a program of upper atmosphere research being conducted by the National Advisory Committee for Aeronautics, which was the predecessor of the National Aeronautics and Space Administration (NASA). Also for the record, they were listed as employees, not of NASA, but of the Lockheed Aircraft Corporation. The explanation was that when the research program was started NASA did not have enough pilots, and so it signed a contract with Lockheed to provide the men to fly the U-2. Actually, the pilots had a contract with CIA, whereby they were paid the handsome salary of $2500 a month.

Soon, however, the Russians began protesting the flights of this dark blue plane, which they called the Black Lady of Espionage, and which they claimed was systematically probing deep into Soviet territory. A leak in security was caused by a crash landing by a U-2 on a glider strip near Tokyo in 1959, but no information was released about the plane. Meanwhile, a British flight magazine carried an article about the mysterious aircraft, and there were reports of a "mystery plane" in which a Lockheed test pilot named Robert Seiker crashed to his death. In 1958 and 1959, the newspaper *Soviet Aviation* periodically attacked the espionage flights. Officially, the United States kept its mouth shut.

On a fine Wednesday morning, April 27, 1960, a transport plane flew Powers and other members of the 10-10 Detachment from Incirlik to the United States Air Force Base at Peshawar, Pakistan. Several U-2's were ferried to Peshawar by other pilots. The group waited at Peshawar for four days, waiting for the right flying conditions. Then, early on Sunday morning, May 1, Francis Gary Powers was awakened as he had been many times before to prepare for another U-2 flight.

That morning, Powers was ordered to make a flight of thirty-three hundred miles from Peshawar across the Soviet Union to Bodo airport in Norway. He was to fly at approximately 68,000 feet and his course was to take him over the Aral Sea, Sverdlovsk, Kirov, Archangel and Murmansk. Powers was familiar with the Bodo airport, having flown there in 1958 during one of his reconnaissance missions.

At his espionage trial in Moscow, Powers told of how his commanding officer "brought the maps and showed them to me. He told me that this was the route I was to fly. It was the route on the maps found in my plane. He told me that he had some information about some airfields and if I wanted to I could put the places on my map. I wanted to do so and did mark some of them. There was also a place where he said I might see a missile launching site. I also put it down. There was one place that he said he thought there was something but he did not know what. I also put this down. I was to follow the course of the route which was plotted on the map with red and blue pencils and to turn on and off the controls of the equipment over the points indicated on the map."

The equipment, of course, was the cameras, radio receivers and tape recorders by which CIA gathered its intelligence wholesale. But Powers also carried other instructions and equipment. He testified that "the colonel said that just in case anything should happen, he was giving me some packages with Soviet money and gold coins. He also had a silver dollar coin which he showed me which had a pin installed in it. He said that there was no danger because no USSR aircraft or rocket could get to my altitude, but in case something should happen and I was captured, the pin contained poison and if I were tortured and could not stand it I could use the pin to kill myself."

Powers' plane also was equipped with a special device by

means of which the pilot could blow it up in the event of a forced landing in the Soviet Union; CIA did not want the Russians to get the secret of the U-2. There was, too, a blasting mechanism fitted to the tape recorder, so that Powers could destroy evidence that CIA was monitoring the Reds' radio messages and radar signals.

It is a fact that Powers was armed—with a revolver equipped with a silencer and with two hundred rounds of ammunition. His personal and survival equipment also included a dagger, fishing gear, a pneumatic boat, topographical maps of the Soviet Union, chemical aids for the making of campfires, signal flares, an electric flashlight, a couple of compasses, a small saw, food concentrates, 7500 rubles in Soviet currency and, in addition to the gold coins, several rings and wrist watches with which he presumably could buy the favor of Soviet citizens should he be forced down.

Dawn was breaking in Moscow as Powers' U-2 crossed into Soviet territory, but already street sweepers were at work cleaning the city for the annual May Day parade dedicated to the glorification of the Communist regime. In the United States it was still the night of April 30. Guards kept watch over an empty White House, because President Eisenhower was spending the week end at his farm in Gettysburg. Scattered lights were burning in the State Department, where aides were working on papers in preparation for the first summit conference in five years, due to open in Paris in two weeks.

After taking off from Peshawar, Powers took the plane to about 60,000 feet and flew over Afghanistan's peaks before soaring across the Soviet border. As he crossed the border, he became preoccupied with the special controls that operated his intelligence-gathering equipment. There were five such controls, and as Powers reached certain points he switched them on—to take photographs and to record the operation of Soviet antiaircraft defenses. As his plane soared over the Soviet Union, his cameras automatically recorded on film the sites of Russian ammunition depots, oil-storage installations, the number and type of aircraft at military airports, electric transmission lines.

The circumstances which surround the downing of the U-2 are still a mystery. That is, the public has its choice between the Soviet version, which says Powers' plane was shot down by a rocket, and the American version, which claims that the U-2 was disabled by a flameout in its jet engine. In any event, it seems fairly certain that from the time Powers took off American communications networks kept fairly good contact both with him and with Soviet planes attempting to track him down.

Through the network which monitored Soviet communications, American eavesdroppers have always gained a great deal of information. Two years before the U-2 incident, they listened in on the conversations between a group of Soviet fighter pilots moving in to attack a real or dummy invader. This is what they heard at that time:

"The target is a four-engine transport . . . Roger. 201—I am attacking the target . . . the target is burning . . . there is the target . . . the target is banking . . . it is going toward the fence. Open fire. 218, are you attacking? Yes, yes. The tail assembly is falling off the target. I will finish him off, boys. I will finish him off on the run. The target is falling . . . yes. Form up . . . go home."

As Francis Gary Powers aimed his U-2 across the Soviet land, the United States monitoring system was operating efficiently. It brought the information that Russian radar crews apparently expected Powers' flight and had located him almost from the moment he crossed the Afghan border. It was evident from conversations of fighter pilots that the Reds had set up relays of supersonic fighters in an attempt to shoot Powers down.

Suddenly, as Powers neared Sverdlovsk, he radioed there had been a flameout in his jet engine and that he had begun to descend to an altitude where he could start the engine again. This was at about 40,000 feet. Not hearing from Powers again our monitors presumed that he had gone down in the area of Sverdlovsk, and that the plane had suffered a mechanical failure. They did not know if Powers was still alive or what the condition of the aircraft was when it hit the ground.

Later the Russians claimed that, "in view of the fact that this was a case of the deliberate invasion of Soviet airspace with hostile aggressive intent, the Soviet Government gave orders to shoot down the plane." They said that Powers' plane was shot down at 8:53 A.M. by a rocket that blasted the U-2 at 68,000 feet.

Powers eventually testified that at 68,000 feet, while flying in the Sverdlovsk area, he saw "an orange flash," and that after that his plane began to lose altitude. During the plane's swift descent, Powers was pressed against the controls and was unable to use the catapulting device to bail out. But after a struggle he managed to raise the canopy, to unfasten the straps securing him in the cockpit and to lift himself out of the plane through the top. As he emerged, the parachute opened automatically.

Powers landed by parachute, and his plane crashed in a field near the city of Sverdlovsk, some nine hundred miles east of Moscow. His landing, according to Soviet authorities, was witnessed by four residents of Sverdlovsk—V. P. Surin, A. F. Cheremisin, L. A. Chuzhakin and P. E. Asabin. According to testimony at Powers' trial, these four "apprehended and disarmed" the American pilot. They gave him a drink of water and a cigaret and then drove him to the local Rural Soviet, where he was turned over to security police.

Powers' plane had penetrated 1200 miles into the Soviet Union. By the time he fell into the field, crowds already had almost filled Moscow's Red Square, where the May Day parade would begin at 10 A.M. Shortly thereafter, the high command of the Soviet government, headed by Nikita Khrushchev, filed into their places on the reviewing stand. Joe Michaels, NBC correspondent in Moscow, has described the scene:

"Exactly at 10 A.M., as always, the May Day ceremony officially began. The first part of the parade was the military section. I watched the mobile units going by to see if there was anything new. There wasn't. Most of the time, I kept my eye on the reviewing stand. From a reporter's point of view this is the most likely place to pick up anything of interest.

"And at about 10:45 A.M.—three-quarters of an hour after the parade began—I did notice something most unusual. An excited Marshal Vershinin, the head of the Soviet Air Force, arrived late. He entered at the rear of the reviewing stand, went up to Khrushchev, and whispered something in his ear. Of course it's only a guess, but I am inclined to believe that this was the moment Khrushchev found out that the U-2 was down."

It is probable the news came to CIA and other government agencies involved a short time later, about noon. The U-2 was due at the NATO base at Bodo, Norway, at seven o'clock in the morning, Washington time. When it failed to arrive, and after allowing for a reasonable delay, the information about the missing plane was communicated to Washington, to the headquarters of CIA in that drab complex of buildings on E Street. At about the same time that CIA Director Allen Dulles was being advised, the word also came to Defense Secretary Thomas Gates. Secretary of State Christian Herter was abroad, but Under Secretary Douglas Dillon was informed. So were Director Keith Glennan of NASA and his Deputy Director, Lawrence Dryden.

But, unfortunately for what was to follow, nobody but the Russians knew that Francis Gary Powers was alive and about to arrive by plane in Moscow for incarceration in the dark fastnesses of Lubyanka Prison.

On the night of May 1, a meeting of various Intelligence, Defense and State Department representatives was held to discuss what to do "just in case." It was decided to put out a cover story which would cover for the record the fact that the plane was missing without revealing anything of its true mission. The cover story had been in the files for a long time in preparation for just such an occurrence. The decision was flashed to all lower levels concerned, including officers at the Incirlik base in Turkey.

Nothing happened immediately; that is, neither side made any announcements about the plane. The Russians apparently were busy interrogating Powers and, of course, there was no reason for the Americans to do anything at that stage except try to locate the plane, especially since it was assumed that Powers probably was dead.

Then, on May 3, reporters were covering a meeting of NATO countries at the Municipal Palace in Istanbul, Turkey. Among those at the conference was Secretary of State Herter.

Zeyyat Goren, bureau manager in Istanbul for United Press International, was in his office writing a story on the NATO Council meeting when a stringer—a part-time correspondent—telephoned him. The stringer said he had heard a story about an American plane being missing somewhere in eastern Turkey. The plane, he said, was based at Incirlik. Goren called Incirlik and talked to the information sergeant at the base. The sergeant confirmed the story. He said the plane had been missing two days and that the last they had heard from the pilot he was having trouble with his oxygen supply somewhere over the Van Lake area. The sergeant described the area as being near the Iranian border, but Goren also knew that it was close to the Russian border, which was a better angle for his story.

Goren's dispatch about the missing plane was received in the New York offices of United Press International at eight o'clock on the morning of May 3. It was always noteworthy when an American plane was reported missing anywhere near the Soviet border, so the day cable editor, Bill Fox, rewrote the story, adding the information that another American plane had been downed in the same general area about a year previously.

As the story went out on the transcontinental A wire for simultaneous transmission to all UPI subscribers throughout North America, it read something like this:

A single-engine U. S. Air Force plane with one man aboard was missing today near the Soviet border in the rugged mountains of Southeastern Turkey. The plane was one of two that took off Sunday morning from Incirlik Air Base near Adana on a weather reconnaissance mission. One plane returned but the pilot of the missing craft reported that his oxygen equipment was out of order. Three C-54 planes from Wheelus Air Force Base in Libya under the command of Major Harry E. Hayes of Clarksville, Texas, were combing the area in search of the missing plane, but thus far without success.

Journalistically, nobody seemed to think the cover story very important. Only a handful of newspapers across the country carried it, and only one, the *Washington Post and Times-Herald,* ran it on Page One. But it was a small story that was eliminated in later editions to make room for a headline on a Washington Senators ball game. Yet there was not much else in the newspapers, either. That morning President Eisenhower had breakfast with a group of Republican Congressmen, and later he signed a wheat agreement with India. In the afternoon he played a round of golf at the Burning Tree Club. In Paris, workmen were busy getting the Elysée Palace ready for the coming summit conference.

Having bided his time until the United States committed itself, the wily Khrushchev made his first move, on the morning of May 5. He made it in the Hall of the Kremlin Palace at the opening of a three-day meeting of the Supreme Soviet.

As usual, the Premier gave the opening speech and he obliged with the customary tedious harangue about such matters as currency regulations, tax reform, wages and prices. But after nearly three hours of this recital, Khrushchev had a shock for his audience.

In a voice that started almost casually and rose to a shout, Khrushchev announced that an American U-2 spy plane had been shot down in the Soviet Union. He did not say where it had been shot down and he gave no indication that the pilot had been captured alive. But he went on to warn those countries where there were United States bases that they were "playing with fire," and he declared that he would make a stern protest to both the United States and the United Nations. Rather curiously, then, he added: "I do not doubt President Eisenhower's sincere desire for peace. Reason must guide us."

In Washington the response was immediate, but not very intelligent. Due to the time difference between Moscow and Washington, Khrushchev's announcement was transmitted to the White House in time for discussion during the regular meeting of the National Security Council that same morning. After the NSC had adjourned, President Eisenhower called together a small group to discuss how to handle the situation. It was agreed to continue with the cover story that had already been planted. Nobody raised the question of how this story might be affected if it was discovered that the U-2 pilot was alive.

Yet the cover story potentially was full of holes, as cited by the *St. Louis Post-Dispatch*'s military affairs analyst, Brigadier General Thomas R. Phillips, U. S. Army, retired. "From an intelligence point of view," Phillips said, "the original cover story seemed to be particularly inept . . . A cover story has certain requirements. It must be credible. It must be a story that can be maintained [no live pilots knocking about] and it should not have too much detail. Anything that's missing in a cover story can be taken care of by saying the matter is being investigated."

But the United States insisted on fooling itself. At 12:45 P.M. on May 5 at the State Department, Press Officer Lincoln White held his regular daily briefing at which he read the following statement:

"The Department has been informed by NASA that, as announced May 3, an unarmed plane—a U-2 weather research plane based at Adana, Turkey, piloted by a civilian, has been missing since May 1. During the flight of this plane, the pilot reported difficulty with his oxygen equipment. Mr. Khrushchev has announced that a United States plane has been shot down over the U.S.S.R. on that date. It may be that this was the missing plane. It is entirely possible that having a failure in the oxygen equipment, which could result in the pilot losing consciousness, the plane continued on automatic pilot for a considerable distance and accidentally violated Soviet airspace. The United States is taking this matter up with the Soviet Government, with particular reference to the fate of the pilot."

White volunteered the information that "infinitely more detail" was being given out at the National Aeronautics and Space Administration. But at NASA, the press section at first did not seem to know what White was talking about. There was a lot of conferring and bustling back and forth and finally, at 1:30 P.M., Information Officer Walt Bonney did release a statement.

Bonney's statement went into considerably more detail than White's had done. It gave details of the flight plan and insisted, with White, that it was on a weather reconnaissance mission and that the U-2's course had called for it to make a left turn at Lake Van and return to Adana. Bonney reported that the pilot was a civilian employed by Lockheed and under contract to NASA, that NASA had ten U-2's and that they were stationed in various countries from England to Okinawa.

There was a great deal about how the U-2 was obtaining more precise information about clear air turbulence, convective clouds and the jet stream.

Under questioning, Bonney admitted the U-2 had cameras aboard, but said they were not reconnaissance cameras but cameras "to take cloud cover." He said the plane had NASA markings and was painted an indigo "Russian" blue, like Navy planes. He was asked if he could give reporters the identity of the pilot, but said he could not. He added he believed this would be given out later in the day, probably by Lockheed—"after all, it is a Lockheed pilot."

CIA—or somebody—seemed to be operating with a certain amount of efficiency in Moscow, because, on the afternoon of May 5, a coded cable was received by the State Department from United States Ambassador Llewellyn Thompson in Moscow. Its purport was that there was a good possibility Powers might still be alive. This should have caused consternation, or at least concern, but apparently it did not. For on the next day, at his daily press conference, the State Department's Lincoln White was still stuck with the cover story his superiors had foisted on him.

In response to questioning, White said "It is ridiculous to say we are trying to kid the world about this." He added later, "There was absolutely no—N-O—no deliberate attempt to violate Soviet airspace and there has never been."

Meanwhile, President Eisenhower's manner was most casual, even when he said something that sounded significant. The same day on which White was sticking to the cover story, the President attended a Union Industry Show in the Washington Armory. Chatting with George Meany, president of the AFL-CIO, Eisenhower remarked that he was going to give a hydrojet boat to Khrushchev on his forthcoming trip to Russia. Then he added, "If I go." It was the first sign that the Administration was concerned that the U-2 incident might disturb our relations with the Soviet Union.

After the show, Eisenhower climbed into his helicopter outside the Armory and flew to Gettysburg where he played a round of golf that afternoon. At about the time Eisenhower was holing out on the ninth green, Secretary of State Herter returned from abroad. But despite the gravity of the situation, it would be another two days before Herter would see the President.

Next day Khrushchev played his hidden ace. Standing before the Supreme Soviet in the Kremlin palace, Khrushchev let his colleagues and the world in on a secret. He displayed photographs which he said had been taken from the captured U-2 and which, he said, proved that it was a spy plane. And he announced that Francis Gary Powers was alive and had confessed to being a spy. Of the Americans, Khrushchev remarked, "When they learn that the pilot is alive, they will have to think of something else . . . and they will."

On that morning President Eisenhower was playing golf again on the Gettysburg course, but White House Press Secretary James C. Hagerty had promised reporters a story. Everybody, of course, was sure it would have to do with the U-2. But to the surprise of the press, Hagerty's statement was to the effect that the United States was prepared to resume nuclear testing, for the purpose of improving means of detecting underground blasts—a step toward policing a nuclear test ban.

Hagerty said he had informed the President of Khrushchev's speech, but that he would have no comment. He added that any reaction would have to come from the State Department.

Eisenhower finished his round of golf at about 11:30 A.M. He then returned to his farmhouse where he spent the remainder of the day. Meanwhile, high officials of the State Department were holding a stern-faced meeting to work out an answer to Khrushchev's speech. Hagerty informed reporters that the President was in contact by telephone with Secretary Herter during the day. Late in the afternoon a statement was read to the President by Herter and the President approved it without change.

That statement was read by Lincoln White at the State Department at six o'clock Saturday evening. It was an admission that the government had been lying. It said: "As a result of the inquiry ordered by the President it has been established that insofar as the authorities in Washington are concerned, there was no authorization for any such flight as described by Mr. Khrushchev. Nevertheless it appears that in endeavoring to obtain information now concealed behind the Iron Curtain, a flight over Soviet territory was probably undertaken by an unarmed civilian U-2 plane." It was the first time a nation had ever admitted it was involved in espionage.

Moreover, more backtracking was to come. For on Wednesday, May 11, President Eisenhower retreated from that part of the statement which said there was no authorization for any such flight as Powers'. At his regular press conference, he assumed full responsibility for authorizing the program of intelligence flights, including Powers'. He said: "Our deterrent must never be placed in jeopardy. The safety of the whole free world demands this. As the Secretary of State pointed out in his recent statement, ever since the beginning of my Administration I have issued directives to gather, *in every feasible way,* the information required to protect the United States and the free world against surprise attack and to enable them to make effective preparations for defense."

Informed in advance of this statement, Allen Dulles was furious, and so was his aide, Colonel Stanley Grogan, who handles relations with the press. Dulles offered to make himself the scapegoat and resign, in order to avoid the spectacle of the President of the United States admitting that, in effect, he sent a spy plane over the Soviet Union. But Eisenhower had been sold on his course of action by a high official of the

State Department, who got to him by phone and told him it was the only thing to do. Later, at another press conference, he told a questioner he had done so to protect Pilot Powers, to let the Soviet Union know that Powers was only acting under orders.

Hagerty, an astute and pragmatic practitioner of public relations, also had opposed the President taking the responsibility. But Hagerty was a good team man who accepted decisions once they were made and did his best to implement them on a public-relations basis. He told reporters, in effect, it would have been impossible to disown Powers: "If you gentlemen are spies, and I am the government, and you get caught, I can say I never heard of you, or saw you before. But if you strap a U-2 to your back, it is a little difficult, to say the least, not to admit and assume responsibility."

Others were just as furious as Allen Dulles. The Russians took great glee in quoting an editorial in the *Des Moines Register and Tribune* which declared: "Let us assume that the man in charge of the Russian air detection system had interpreted pilot Powers' flight as an attack and had pushed the button for a retaliatory blow . . . in a few hours those who survived would have found themselves in hell. When will we at last realize that espionage, counterespionage and all such idiotism belong to the dead past?"

Senator William Fulbright, the Arkansas Democrat who was chairman of the Senate committee that investigated the U-2 affair, took the viewpoint that had been conventional among all nations almost since the beginning of time. "The President need never have *avowed* or *disavowed*," Fulbright said. "He should have taken the position of silence in this matter and if anyone had to take responsibility it should have been the head of the intelligence. It shouldn't have been the President, who embodies the whole sovereignty and dignity of the whole American people."

There also were differences concerning our attempt to justify our right to engage in such flights. Hagerty told reporters that "when a closed society makes threats against our very welfare, it is up to us to find out everything we can about such a closed society, whether they are preparing for war, whether they are building up . . ." Fulbright saw this as illogical, as something we could not expect the Russians to swallow. "To say you need something such as intelligence in international relations certainly is no justification for it," Fulbright said. "The President was in fact asserting the right to do this and not the need. They (the Russians) could understand the need. They understand that espionage goes on within certain areas all the time. But they never take full responsibility for it. The head of state does not. I think that it's responsible to believe that this avowal put Mr. Khrushchev in the position where he could not proceed to treat with a man who at the same time is asserting the right to violate the sovereignty of his country."

Still one more significant question was raised following our avowal of the U-2 flights. It was whether the flights would be continued. During the week before the summit conference, there was considerable confusion on this point. The *New York Times* carried a story saying it had been learned that the President had ordered a cessation of all flights over or near the borders of the Soviet Union. But at his news conference that day, Hagerty said the President had not canceled the flights, and that he knew of no orders from anyone else to stop the flights. The impression, of course, was that the flights were still going on, although the Administration later denied it had intended to imply such a thing.

At any rate, there was enough confusion so that international tension increased as the summit conference approached. Nikita Khrushchev furnished a startling example of that increased tension in an explosion that rocked the confused world. He was touring an exhibit in Gorki Park of the remnants of the U-2 plane the Russians had salvaged from the Sverdlovsk field, plus its various equipment and Francis Powers' personal effects. He seemed happy enough, but when newspapermen trailing him caused him to stage an impromptu press conference he boiled over at what he termed the American threat to continue the flights. As though on the spur of the moment, he canceled his invitation to President Eisenhower to visit the Soviet Union the following month. He explained that he could not expect his countrymen to give the President a cordial welcome after the U-2 affair.

After that, it must have been apparent that there was little hope for the summit conference in Paris, but there was nothing for the United States to do but carry on. As the President prepared to leave for Paris, the *New York Times'* James Reston summed up his predicament: "The tragedy of President Eisenhower in the spy plane case is that he and his colleagues have created almost all the things he feared the most. He wanted to reduce international tension and he has increased it. He wanted to strengthen the alliance and he has weakened it. He glorified teamwork and morality, and got lies and administrative chaos. Everything he was noted for—caution, patience, leadership, military skill, and even good luck—suddenly eluded him precisely at the moment he needed them most."

The President was warned in a CIA briefing before he departed for the summit meeting that Khrushchev almost surely would turn the conference into a propaganda stage for the Soviet Union. Still, nothing could be done about it but go through the motions. At the first preliminary meeting, Premier Khrushchev verified CIA's prediction. After bitterly attacking Eisenhower, he stalked out of the session. Before returning to Moscow, leaving the summit wreckage behind, he gave the world more of the same in a shouting, table-pounding press conference.

Nobody, of course, could have looked into Nikita Khrushchev's mind and learned what his plans were for Paris. From what CIA was able to learn, it was entirely possible that he decided on his outburst at the last minute, perhaps en route to the conference. At any event, he had shown no outward signs, while still in Moscow, that he was bent on torpedoing the conference but only, from CIA's information, on putting on a good propaganda show. But the fact remains that it was the United States that opened the door for him. By justifying the U-2 flights and by the implication that they would be continued, we made it easy for Khrushchev. If he had intended to wreck the conference, we now gave him an excuse. If he intended sincerely and seriously to negotiate, we put him in a position where it was awkward if not impossible for him to do so.

Nevertheless, the fault lay with the Administration's handling of the situation, not with the flight itself, which was CIA's only responsibility. Numerous critics, of course, have bitterly questioned CIA's judgment in sending Powers on such a ticklish assignment just before the summit conference was to convene; no chances should have been taken, these critics say, on jeopardizing the conference. CIA's answer, unofficially, was that it had weather conditions to contend with. Cloud formations prevalent in the area most of the time made it impossible or extremely difficult to get the kind of intelligence results that were desired. The weather was favorable at the time Powers took off, so he took off. Moreover, Khrushchev claimed he had known about the U-2 flights for a long time, and both the Pentagon and CIA had evidence that Soviet pilots regularly plotted and tracked the flights.

As for the accomplishment of this Black Lady of Espionage, the nation did not have to depend on leaks by CIA to favored newsmen because the facts were made public. Testifying before the Senate Foreign Relations Committee on June 2, 1960, the then Secretary of Defense Thomas S. Gates, Jr., reported that U-2 missions in previous years had supplied "vital information" on Soviet "airfields, aircraft, missiles, missile testing and training, special weapons storage, submarine production, atomic production and aircraft deployment." This just about runs the gamut of what the United States needed to know.

It is also certain that such information was of considerable value to the Joint Chiefs of Staff in their strategic planning. General Lyman Lemnitzer, chairman of the Joint Chiefs, said later that the void in our intelligence occasioned by suspension of the U-2 flights would be seriously felt until it could be filled from some other source. President Eisenhower, in an address to the nation following the summit fiasco, apparently referred to this need when he said that "new techniques, *other than aircraft,* are being developed." He was referring to Midas II, the missile warning satellite the United States had just put into orbit, and Samos, the photo-reconnaissance satellite. Meanwhile, the Pentagon hinted that U-2 photographs furnished the bulk of the data on which we based our estimates of the Soviet Union's war-making capabilities.

It was Secretary Gates, of course, who approved all U-2 flights, and he told the Senate Foreign Relations Committee he did so because he "remembered Pearl Harbor."

Senator Alexander Wiley, Republican of Wisconsin, asked: "You had in mind, did you, what the condition of this country was at the time of Pearl Harbor, how we were asleep?"

"I certainly did."

"During negotiations?"

"I did indeed."

President Eisenhower made the same reference. He said there was "no time when vigilance can be relaxed," and added that the United States at Pearl Harbor learned that "even negotiation itself can be used to conceal preparations for a surprise attack."

Khrushchev, of course, has tried to downgrade the intelligence importance of the U-2 flights. In a speech at the third

Congress of the Romanian Communist Party in Bucharest June 21, 1960, he said the U-2's missed photographing the Soviet Union's strategic rocket bases, discovered nothing of importance to United States defenses and failed to uncover "powerful military means" the Soviet Union had developed. "We knew two or three years ago they photographed the areas of the proving grounds where we conduct experimental rocket launchings," Khrushchev said. "But it was a rocket testing grounds that they photographed, and not strategic rocket bases."

Other Soviet officials whose statements went into the record during the August, 1960, espionage trial of Pilot Powers must have neglected to read Khrushchev's speech to the Romanians. The prosecuting officer, for instance, declared that the five intelligence-gathering controls in Powers' plane "functioned normally and faultlessly," during Powers' flight "over big industrial centers and important Soviet defense installations." Later he said that it had been established that "the pilot photographed the territory of the Soviet Union for the purpose of espionage." He also pointed out that when the tape-recording machine was examined and the tape decoded it was found that "the signals recorded belonged to ground radar stations of the radar antiaircraft defense system of the Soviet Union."

In summing up the case before announcing their verdict, the judges also gave Central Intelligence Agency a grudging pat on the back. Powers, they said, "photographed important defense objectives and recorded signals of the country's antiaircraft defense radar installations. The developed . . . films established that Defendant Powers photographed from the U-2 plane industrial and military objectives of the Soviet Union—plants, depots, oil storages, communication routes, railway bridges and stations, electric transmission lines, airfields, the dislocation of troops and military technique." The photos were excellent, too, the judges concluded. They said the films "make it possible to determine the nature of industrial establishments, the design of railway bridges, the number and type of aircraft on the airfields, the nature and purpose of military materiel."

Since the Sverdlovsk flight was referred to among U-2 pilots as "the milk run" because it was so frequently flown, the CIA would seem to have had a right to gloat over the results. The only trouble, of course, was that after four years the Russians managed to get their hands on one of the U-2 pilots and some pieces of the plane. This eventuality certainly was anticipated by CIA, and yet the philosophy of espionage was well summed up in terse comments made by two government officials as the hurly-burly was dying down.

In Washington, Press Secretary Hagerty was asked by NBC Correspondent Ray Scherer what lessons had emerged from the U-2 incident for the future.

"Don't get caught," Hagerty replied.

Similarly, Secretary of State Herter was asked what he had learned from the U-2 affair.

"Not to have accidents," he replied.

In Moscow, the man who had had an accident and who had got caught kept his final rendezvous with Soviet justice. Francis Gary Powers, the boy from Burdine, Kentucky, was sentenced to ten years of "confinement," with the first three years to be served in prison. That scratched one American operative, but fortunately there were others at work in the shadow of the Kremlin.

10. *Spy in the Kremlin*

IN THE WASHINGTON HEADQUARTERS of the Central Intelligence Agency, a woman researcher named Alice routinely scanned press dispatches concerning the shifting of various officials—mostly middle-level operatives—in the Soviet Union. With the list of new appointees on her desk, she checked a fat folder from a filing cabinet containing dossiers on Soviet politicians believed to be marked for future promotion by the Politburo.

The appointments seemed to have gone according to expectations except in one case. CIA's folder pinpointed a functionary named Andrei as the logical successor to an aging hack who had been replaced, but the post had not gone to Andrei but to a relatively obscure party handyman from Kiev.

Whether this information had any significance for America's top spy outfit, it was not Alice's job to pursue it further. A memo from her desk to another cubicle down the hall merely noted that Andrei had been passed over for promotion. In the second cubicle, a male analyst named Roger opened the complete folder on Andrei, a folder which contained every bit of information about him that CIA had been able to gather. Almost immediately Roger found what he wanted: This was the second time Andrei had been passed over for promotion. Moreover, in the last month or so there had been added to his dossier the report that he had been close to Soviet officials who had been in the camp of the deposed Georgi Malenkov. Andrei was an intense intellectual, who might be expected to look with a certain amount of disdain on the blunt tactics of Nikita Khrushchev. At any rate, he sounded interesting enough so that his dossier and a memo on both the findings and the significance of those findings went to still a third office.

It was in that third office that the decision was made. That decision was that CIA should attempt to recruit Andrei as a "defector in place"—a man who deserts the Communists without telling his bosses and remains in his official job in order to be able to feed secrets to CIA. Such a man, obviously, is of far more value to CIA than the announced defector, who tells all but subsequently is unable to operate behind the Iron Curtain. Quite aside from Andrei's natural resentment at being passed over for promotion, as an intellectual he was apt to have ideological differences with the party on which CIA perhaps could capitalize.

In reaching this decision, CIA had to accept one obvious risk: Andrei might be a plant; that is, the Russians might have arranged the snub, with Andrei's knowledge, in an attempt to draw CIA into trying to do business with him. If this were so, CIA's network in the Soviet Union could be damaged seriously, but the risk was worth taking for two reasons. First, Andrei would be quite a catch. Second, even if he were a plant it was doubtful if he could involve more than one or two of our agents because of CIA's classic doctrine of so compartmentalizing operations that one agent seldom knew anyone else in the apparatus but his own contact.

The approach to Andrei would be a cautious one. There was no thought of having the CIA case officer in Moscow contact him because we could not afford to have this agent exposed and expelled from the country—perhaps even imprisoned or executed. Another check was made of another folder, and the man was found for the job. His name was Georgi and he was a clerk in the division where Andrei was one of the high executives. In his job, Georgi would not be close to Andrei either professionally or socially, but he could make it his business to see enough of Andrei so that he probably could report on Andrei's moods and problems. The democratic operation of middle-level Soviet operatives is such that there would be no suspicion if Georgi were to strike up an acquaintance or even a fairly close friendship with Andrei. Georgi was an intellectual too, and young enough and competent enough to have a Soviet future.

Georgi was contacted in Moscow—in the lobby of the Bolshoi Ballet Theater—and given his assignment verbally. He was also given several typewritten sheets of paper which contained an analysis of an article in an American scientific magazine. The conclusion of the analysis "exposed" a "secret" American device for the testing of jet engines. It was a device which was certain to become international public knowledge in a month or two and so there was no great need to protect it. Georgi was to seek an appointment with Andrei and give him this analysis which he would pass off as his own. This would bring Georgi favorably to Andrei's attention and pave the way for further friendly contacts.

There was no word from Georgi for seven months. Then one day his contact made a routine check of a "dead drop"— the underside of a wooden slat on a bench in Gorki Park. There he found a report from Georgi which stated that Andrei indeed was dissatisfied and moody, that he was disillusioned with the cold and calculating materialism of the Khrushchev regime. He was resentful about having been passed over for promotion and was beginning to wonder whether he had a future in Soviet politics.

In West Berlin there was an important conference on the Andrei matter. Other information on his activities was sifted and analyzed. His family life was studied; it was apparent that he was a devoted husband and a loving father to his two young boys—the kind of father who would seek security for his family. There was every evidence that he had been upset by the fall of Malenkov. It was decided that Andrei was ready for the approach, that he was ripe for recruitment.

The big decision now was the choice of the man to put the proposition to Andrei. He was important enough so that he would be more impressed by a bona fide American agent, but the conclusion was that it was too early in the game to risk such an operative. Georgi apparently had won Andrei's confidence; it seemed safe to let Georgi make the approach. If the approach failed, it might mean the death of Georgi, but that was one of the risks a spy took. Georgi would represent himself as an innocent go-between who was used as little more than a messenger. Georgi was willing, and anxious, to do a job that would net him a great deal of money and also bring him closer to the day when, with CIA help, he could flee the Communist dictatorship.

In case something went wrong, Georgi's rendezvous with Andrei was set for a CIA "safe house," that is, an apartment occupied either by Soviet citizens friendly to the West or by an American with a "cover" occupation. From there, Georgi could be whisked to safety if Andrei refused to go along and denounced Georgi for treachery. Chances would have to be taken all along the line, but the prize was worth the risks. If Georgi failed, CIA would lose a valued operative, but fortunately it had others in Andrei's department.

Andrei and Georgi met in the "safe house" on a dark and rain-filled night in the fall of 1955. After some small talk, Georgi bluntly put the proposition to Andrei. He waited nervously, while Andrei stared at him for nearly a minute without speaking. Then Andrei replied. He was interested because of his dissatisfaction with the regime and his resentment at the snubs he had received. But he would not do business with Georgi. He wanted evidence that this was not a Soviet plot, that there were Americans at the other end of the line. What he was being asked to do was of the utmost danger and he wanted assurances that he would be protected by the American government. Georgi told him he would contact his superior and report back.

The decision had to be made quickly, and it was. Several nights later the American case officer met with Andrei in the "safe house" and again made the proposition. Additionally, however, he provided Andrei with details on how he would be spirited out of the country if anything went wrong and assured him that CIA would support him in the United States until he could get decent employment. In the meantime he would be paid well for his pains—in funds deposited to a dummy account in a Swiss bank. Andrei agreed to the proposition. He was especially impressed by the agent's outline of the plan for getting him out of the country some day, and by the documented arrangements for depositing his salary in the Swiss bank.

With considerable relief, the CIA agent went on to make the specific arrangements for Andrei's secret job. Andrei was told the type of information he was to gather and pass on. He was given the location of a "dead drop"—in this case an address in Moscow—and also a "live drop" in an office building where he could leave his reports disguised as merchandise. He was told that his personal contacts with the apparatus would be with a "cut-out," another agent whose occupation and activities made it safer for him to meet Andrei. The original agent was too valuable a man to see Andrei more than occasionally, and then only in times of emergency. Andrei would meet the "cut-out" on the street or in a "safe house," and signals were devised and memorized for use by both Andrei and his contact in case either believed he was being followed, or if either was unable to keep an appointment.

Andrei worked for CIA for several years; it is not known

whether he still toils at the chore of betraying his government. But in a coincidental course of events, CIA was able to get its hands on a document that spread uncertainty, confusion and resentment throughout communism's conspiratorial empire.

That document was the secret speech delivered by Nikita Khrushchev at the 20th Party Congress of the Soviet Communist Party in 1956 in which he denounced the crimes of Josef Stalin and called for an end to the "Cult of the Personality." Khrushchev purposely had tried to keep the speech a secret because, although it was necessary to brief his own Soviet colleagues on the change in the party line, he felt it would be unwise to let the full impact of the speech be felt throughout the world. His plan was to give the new policy to the world's Communist faithful a little at a time to avoid both confusion and resentment among those who had been indoctrinated with the theory of Stalin's divinity. By carefully issued statements and policy switches, he had hoped to accomplish Stalin's downfall by degrees.

But CIA got its hands on the speech, turned it over to the State Department and it was released to a startled world. As a result, thousands of disillusioned Communists deserted the party and the masses remaining became locked in bitter factional disputes which in countries like Poland, Hungary and East Germany eventually were climaxed by bloody physical violence. On the one hand, supporters of Stalin launched vigorous attacks on Khrushchev; on the other, Khrushchev's disciples were kept busy explaining to those under them how Khrushchev could have mustered a stomach strong enough to do business with a Stalin whose bestiality Khrushchev himself had catalogued. Additionally, of course, the United States was put on notice that in Khrushchev it was faced with a man who had abandoned the straightforward diplomatic brutality of Josef Stalin to embark on a program of underhanded cajolery.

Since CIA will not talk, there is no way of knowing—except for that coincidental course of events—whether Andrei delivered the Khrushchev speech into American hands. But he was in a position where he had the opportunity to do so. It is possible it was not a one-man job; the theft of the speech may have required the co-ordination of various other CIA operations.

In the period preceding the theft of the speech, for instance, certain Communist couriers certainly had their pouches rifled and the contents photographed and replaced, all without their knowledge. Especially in Eastern Europe, CIA has some really spectacular experts in this kind of thing. Other experts undoubtedly picked up some information by breaking Communist codes. But the best guess would seem to be Andrei, who as a "defector in place" was a man who had broken with his party without his party's knowledge and who therefore was admirably placed to get his hands on all kinds of documents.

Much the same probably happened in Communist China, where CIA brought similar consternation to Mao Tse-tung. Mao had addressed a "secret" meeting of a Communist delegation from several Latin American countries and had given them instructions on new infiltration methods. CIA had a detailed report on the session before the delegation arrived back home.

CIA succeeds in such instances because of its happy faculty for leaving no stone unturned, as in the case of the campaign the Soviets launched in 1950 to persuade White Russians in France to return to their homeland. CIA agents immediately tackled the job of contacting and interviewing all those who expressed a willingness to return. One of them was a boy who was going back with his parents but who was violently anti-Communist. CIA had several chats with the boy and gave him certain material as well as ideological assurances. Nine years later, the boy made contact with a CIA man in the Soviet

Union where he was working in a sensitive technical establishment, and since then he has turned over reams of important intelligence.

All over the Communist world, too, CIA has the services
of hundreds of émigrés—Germans who fled Hitler, Eastern
Europeans trapped by the Communist takeover of their countries, anti-Communist Chinese who, when Mao and his henchmen arrived, stayed behind for the express purpose of
espionage. CIA regularly obtains funds through Mutual Security legislation for "financing the activities of selected persons who are residing in, or are escapees from, the Eastern
European countries either to form such persons into elements of the military force supporting the North Atlantic
Treaty, or for other purposes." Among such are the National
Committee for a Free Albania and the Polish underground
organization known as W. I. N.

In this connection, one of CIA's vital roles is the counterintelligence chore necessary to the combating of Communist
attempts to discredit the United States with both its friends
and the millions of people in the world's uncommitted areas.
Much of this Communist plotting revolves around the forged
document, which the Kremlin circulates through the press in
its satellites or in Communist or fellow-traveling newspapers
in neutral or free-world countries. This is a Cold War trick
lifted from Russian tradition, for the Russians have a long
history of the use of the art of forgery in intelligence operations. Just before the turn of the century, the Czarist intelligence service concocted and peddled a fable called the Proto-
cols of the Elders of Zion, and as late as 1958 this confection
was still being pushed by psychological warfare organizations
specializing in anti-Semitism. Hitler's propagandists, of
course, borrowed it in the 1930's and 1940's and added re-
finements.

CIA has discovered, in its labors with microscope and double agents, that these Soviet forgeries are manufactured and

spread according to plan and that they have three main purposes. The first is to discredit the West generally and the United States specifically in the eyes of the rest of the world. The second is to sow suspicion and discord among the Western allies, especially between the United States and its friends. The third is to drive a wedge between the peoples of non-bloc countries and their governments by fostering the line that these governments do not represent their citizens because they are the puppets of the United States.

In the four-year period ending in the spring of 1961, CIA discovered and exposed thirty-two forged documents designed to look as if they had been written by or to officials of the American government. Almost all of them were planted in the satellite press, in such newspapers as the East German *Neues Deutschland* and the Bombay scandal sheet, *Blitz.*

One of the first of these forgeries appeared in *Neues Deutschland* in February, 1957, when the newspaper published several pages of what was alleged to be the facsimile of a letter in the "original English" from Governor Nelson Rockefeller of New York to President Eisenhower. Headlined, "Rockefeller Gives Directive for Supercolonialism of the United States," it spelled out a cynical plan for American manipulation of military and economic aid in order to gain domination of the world.

This was a fairly stupid job. In the first place, there were several misspellings and even fellow-traveling readers would be loath to believe they could have been committed by an educated man such as Governor Rockefeller. As Richard Helms, assistant director of CIA, testified before the Senate Subcommittee on Internal Security: "This is not the kind of letter that Nelson Rockefeller would have written. He wouldn't have cast them in this way and wouldn't have used certain terminology."

Moreover, the letter stated that Rockefeller was reluctant to refer to "a tiresome discussion [with the President] that took place at Camp David." This prompted Senator Kenneth B. Keating, the puckish Republican from New York, to comment: "That strikes me as not exactly the way you address the President of the United States."

During the next three weeks other Communist newspapers reprinted the letter to reinforce the campaign. In early March of 1957, *Neues Deutschland* proudly announced that it had linked the Rockefeller forgery with another incriminating document, a purported memorandum from the late Secretary of State John Foster Dulles to President Eisenhower.

The falsity of the memorandum was exposed when CIA got its hands on a *secret* manual issued for the use of Soviet propagandists which carried a translation of the *Neues Deutschland* article. It said:

"Dulles reasoned that England and France could never again become masters of the situation in the Near and Middle East . . . that Egypt and other Arab countries were beginning to understand that they could decide their own affairs . . . Proceeding from this, Dulles planned the course of American policy. The main problem, he declared, was the overcoming of Arab nationalism (that is, the movement for freedom from the colonizers), and the filling up of the 'vacuum' which formed. Dulles proposed to accomplish the overcoming of 'Arab nationalism' by the formation in this region of aggressive military blocs. He wanted to fill up the vacuum with American military bases and by sending into this region American military units designated for 'special purposes' on 'the Formosa pattern' . . .

"To seize these positions [the former imperialistic positions of England and France]," the memorandum said, "it is necessary to strengthen the military positions of the U. S. in the Near East. To expand the program of the creation of air bases, to place in certain places American military forces equipped with atomic weapons, to achieve the consciousness of 'an African military pact.' "

Eleven of the forgeries discovered by CIA charged United States intervention in the private business of Asian nations, according to Helms. He ticked them off:

One was a faked secret agreement between our Secretary of State and Japanese Premier Kishi "to permit use of Japanese troops anywhere in Asia." Another alleged that American policy in Southeast Asia called for U. S. control of the armed forces of all SEATO nations. Four more were supposed to make the Indonesian Government view us as a dangerous enemy. Of these, two offered forged proof that the Americans were plotting to overthrow President Sukarno, and the other two purported to demonstrate that the United States Government, despite official disclaimers, was secretly supplying the anti-Sukarno rebels with military aid. Of the remaining five, two announced that the Americans were plotting to assassinate Chiang Kai-shek. Another had the American Embassy in Phnom Penh deeply involved in a conspiracy with a Cambodian dissident, Sam Sary, to overthrow the government of Prince Sihanouk. The fourth fable told the world about a State Department order that American intelligence agencies were to "screen the loyalty" of the King of Thailand and the members of his government. The fifth recited that the United States Information Service was directing the press of one Asian country in attacks upon another.

There was, also, the letter supposedly written by the Secretary of State to Ambassador Chapin in Iran, which was filled with insults to the Shah. This letter was not published but was transmitted to the Iranian Government through official Soviet channels. There were two phony orders which directed American diplomatic missions to help in overthrowing the United Arab Republic. A forgery keyed to the landing of American troops in Lebanon in 1958 purported to prove that American troops would occupy Lebanon for fifteen months and said their purpose was the installation of atomic and other military bases and the "wiping out of millions of Arabs."

Sometimes the Communists combine forgeries telling of American ambitions in former colonial areas with implications of racism designed to inflame Africans. Such a forgery was the alleged letter from the State Department to Ambassador Clare Timberlake in the Congo. The letter represented Premier Tshombe of Katanga Province as a paid and probably reliable agent of the United States Government, then added "but God knows what these blacks will do."

Eventually, of course, these Communist lies catch up with them, but the exposure of the forgery is never as sensational as the original charge and, as Helms said, "People's memories are somewhat short. What you read one day, a week later you tend to forget. The people take the forgeries at face value, even if the line shifts later." Moreover, the Soviets do not care whether they are exposed or not, so long as they have been able to get their story across. They rely on the Hitler Big Lie technique: If you say something often enough people will believe it.

It probably is for this reason that the Communists are careless about mistakes and overlook usage and phraseology that rob their forgeries of authenticity. Once they put out a forged "letter" from Frank Berry, Assistant Secretary of Defense for Health and Medical Affairs, to the then Defense Secretary Neil McElroy. The letter asserted that 67.3 per cent of all flight personnel in the United States Air Force were psychoneurotics, and charged flyers with excessive drinking, use of drugs and sexual excesses. The forgery, however, had no written signature and made such errors as referring to "the Internal Zone" instead of "Zone of Interior" and to "Air Force Command," which is not an Air Force term.

Still, it is a fact that however sloppy these forgeries and planted newspaper stories may be they too often fall on receptive ears, even in friendly countries. This is especially true in countries where certain segments are distrustful of American ambitions in newly liberated colonial areas. The Soviet seeks to feed this distrust in England and France, and it managed some degree of success with its planted story, in an Italian newspaper, of CIA's alleged complicity in the revolt of the French generals in Algeria. It was a telling illustration of the effectiveness of this line of Communist attack that it took the French Government so long to back away from the allegation. And, of course, the Reds here were operating in an area where CIA's activities throughout the rest of the world made it a likely suspect.

11. CIA's Ex-Nazi

ON A GLOOMY NIGHT in March, 1953, Josef Stalin finally was discovered to have something in common with humanity. He died. This startling intelligence was flashed immediately over the air waves from Moscow to sputter its message on a teletype in the Washington headquarters of the Central Intelligence Agency late in the evening of March 5.

Allen Dulles, director of CIA, had long since departed his office and was having a last pipe in the living room of his home, "Highlands," a tall, vine-covered mansion on busy Wisconsin Avenue in Washington's Georgetown section. He learned the news when he picked up the telephone which linked his residence to CIA by a direct wire. After issuing a few instructions, Dulles got into his coat, put on his hat and went back to the office.

There were scores of questions raised by Josef Stalin's death, and it was CIA's job to provide the answers to them as quickly as possible and then to transmit those answers to President Eisenhower. It was probable that the squat Georgi Malenkov would succeed to Stalin's premiership, if not his power. As soon as possible, CIA had to be able to tell the President what kind of a ruler Malenkov would be. It had to collect and analyze information that would tell it whether the Soviet Union would be torn by revolution or internal power struggles, whether her posture would be more warlike, or whether her new ruler would adopt a soft line. At the White House, at the Pentagon, at the State Department, at the Atomic Energy Commission and on Capitol Hill the answers to all these questions were needed to guide the formulation of American foreign policy in the period to follow.

The news of Stalin's death had been received by CIA's watch officers, who are on duty twenty-four hours a day, and by comparable officers in the Pentagon. Since the news showed up a critical situation, Dulles immediately called a meeting of the Intelligence Advisory Council, a kind of board of directors made up of all the nation's intelligence-gathering organizations—CIA, State Department, armed services, Atomic Energy Commission and the FBI.

Given raw intelligence by his CIA subordinates, Dulles immediately submitted it to key government leaders. Then he set in motion the machinery needed to obtain a "crash" estimate of the changed world situation. Orders went out to CIA agents and secret operatives all over the world and to other government agencies with listening posts abroad. He wanted to know as soon as possible what diplomatic or military moves to expect, information on troop movements, purges and arms shipments, the condition of morale behind the Iron Curtain.

Reports poured into CIA headquarters all night—from Moscow, from Sofia, from Peiping—via friendly countries. Embassy personnel all over the world were called back to work. Coded telephone and teletype conversations were conducted with intelligence units in London, Paris, Madrid, Helsinki. All through the night Dulles and his CIA experts, flanked by experts from other intelligence agencies, pored over the reports and studied the bulging files on Malenkov and the other men in and out of the Politburo who were likely to help him wield his power.

Next morning, Allen Dulles hustled over to the White House for a long conference with President Eisenhower and other Administration officials. In a nutshell, he was able to report that the Soviet Union did not appear to be prepared for war, no immediate foreign policy changes were expected, although Malenkov was inclined toward increasing the production of consumer goods and thus might soften the aggressive tone of Moscow's propaganda machine, and there was little likelihood of an internal revolution.

As it turned out, this was to prove a good estimate to deliver virtually on the spur of the moment. After all, in a single night's work CIA could hardly be expected to predict the forthcoming liquidation of Stalin's sinister boss of the secret police, Lavrenti P. Beria. A year later, however, shortly after the overthrow in Guatemala of the Communist regime of Jacobo Arbenz Guzman, CIA offered the National Security Council a long-range estimate of the situation in the Soviet Union that seemed tinged with wishful thinking.

CIA acknowledged the menace of Russia's military might, with its 4,000,000-man army, 20,000-plane air force and nuclear weapons estimated in four figures. But it claimed that all was not splendid in the Soviet Union. Communist industry was progressing only reasonably well, although it was being spurred by an intensive program to train young scientists and engineers. CIA here warned, correctly as it turned out, that this drive threatened to overtake the United States in the vital field of technology. It noted that food was a problem to the Russians due to a breakdown in the Communist collective farming system and that the Soviets recently had had to divert 100,000 workers from industry to agriculture. Finally, CIA said it was unlikely that Russia would go to war before 1957 or 1958, because the committee in the Kremlin headed by Malenkov could not be sure their regime could survive the death, damage and suffering which would be inflicted on the Soviet population by a retaliating United States.

Partially as a result of this appraisal, the Eisenhower Administration in 1954 sponsored a $7,400,000,000 reduction in

Federal taxes, and Secretary of the Treasury George M. Humphrey was talking about the possibility of another $2,000,-000,000 cut in national defense spending. For the first time the United States gave proper attention to a strategy of countering the Communists underground, where the real Soviet conquests were being scored. That year, of course, CIA had staged its first publicly spectacular coup in Guatemala, and success gave the government ideas.

CIA has always insisted that its principal chore is not so much to pinpoint a future happening but to flag those critical situations which the government should watch and try to turn to its advantage. In this era of supercharged public relations, however, even CIA has been guilty of announcing its opinions and then having them come back to haunt the agency. Dulles, who was an indefatigable speechmaker, stuck his neck out in the summer of 1957 when he suggested in a speech that a military dictatorship under Marshal Georgi Zhukov might be "one of the possible lines of evolution" in the Soviet Union. A month later Zhukov was unceremoniously demoted and sentenced to obscurity.

Critics jumped on Dulles for failing to predict a major shift in the Kremlin's power struggle, but Dulles was unperturbed. He admitted he had pulled a boner, but pointed out that Zhukov's demotion also surprised a lot of people in the Kremlin and noted that Zhukov himself did not know it was coming or he would not have been in Albania when the ax fell.

The average citizen, who joins in the catcalls when CIA falls on its face, nevertheless would be surprised and delighted to know that the nation's intelligence agency does not have to depend entirely on its own home-grown spies for information on what is going on in the Kremlin. The fact is CIA gets considerable help from the Communists themselves. CIA is mum about this kind of thing, for obvious reasons, but it can be said that some of its lines of communication lead to high officials of the Communist regimes in such places as Moscow, Peiping, Budapest and Warsaw. These are men who have managed to indicate in the most clandestine fashion that they would be willing to defect to the United States— for a price, or for a taste of Western freedom.

In most cases they have been persuaded not to desert. Their defection, of course, would be a great propaganda coup for the United States, but CIA is interested in something more important than propaganda: a continuing stream of information. Therefore it has managed to keep a number of these Communist officials on the job, usually by depositing sums to "cover" accounts in Swiss banks which will enable the officials to finance their experience in democracy on the day they are permitted to defect. Elaborate plans are stowed away in a CIA vault by which, on the appointed day, these VIP spies will be sprung from their homelands. Meanwhile, they furnish more than a trickle of information which CIA could get nowhere else.

This is risky business, because the Communists are most adept at planting false intelligence. But the information is checked and triple-checked against what CIA already has learned from other espionage agents, and in any appraisal of a situation CIA analysts keep the source well in mind.

In addition, CIA uses many currently active Communists as well as former Communists. They are not employed directly—that is, they are on no continuing official payroll— and they have no contact with CIA except through go-betweens. CIA preserves their isolation by having these go-betweens pose as fellow travelers who get information from Reds or Pinks who are not aware they are being used. In the normal course of international espionage Communists are always trying to infiltrate CIA and sometimes Red sympathizers have been detected in minor jobs. Usually these individuals are not discharged immediately but are put under twenty-four-hour surveillance by CIA counterintelligence agents who frequently are able to locate and identify the double agent's contact in the Soviet spy apparatus. Meanwhile, the double agent is fed a pile of false information to keep his bosses happy—and unknowingly confused.

CIA, of course, also does its best to infiltrate the Soviet's KGB, or international spy organization, and the indications are that its record in this respect is satisfactory. The American people can accept as a good bet that the United States has at least some representatives in Communist spy units in most of the leading countries of the world. This bet is bolstered by the cautious suggestion that despite the Communist announcements that they are daily rounding up infiltrators into their spy apparatus Moscow apprehends only about one American operative out of three. For the record, however, CIA notes that it is ten times more hazardous for an American spy behind the Iron Curtain as it was behind the Nazi lines during World War II.

On a continuing basis, a great deal of intelligence is obtained from Iron Curtain defectors, especially those of high rank in Soviet intelligence. Such a defector was Josef Swiatlo, the high-ranking internal security officer in Poland, who fled to West Berlin and gave the West its first information on the arrest of the three notorious Fields—Noel and his wife, Herta, and Noel's brother, Hermann. Swiatlo was kept under cover in the United States for nine months before he appeared at a Washington news conference in September, 1954.

There was, too, Yuri Rastvorov, who deserted the Russians in Tokyo and who poured out to CIA all kinds of secrets on the operation of KGB. There were the Vladimir Petrovs, man and wife, who defected in Australia after Mrs. Petrov had thrown her dessert in the face of Mrs. Nikolai Generalov, wife of the Soviet Ambassador. Petrov revealed operation of a Red spy apparatus based in London and covering Britain, Canada, the United States, Australia, South Africa and New Zealand.

CIA prizes these defectors even more, perhaps, than the KGB gloats over Western turncoats because they tip the scales in CIA's battle with Soviet intelligence a little more in our favor. Yet CIA will never be on an equal footing with its Communist counterpart; circumstances stand in the way. That is to say, the KGB has built-in advantages accruing from the Communist system and from our own easy-going democratic institutions.

In the first place, the Communist countries are sealed in with a military curtain which makes operations in the Soviet Union and its satellites highly difficult as well as dangerous. Neither the United States nor any of its allies has the barbed-wire barriers, the frontier guards and the dictatorial grasp on its subjects that the Reds boast. Furthermore, every traveling Communist citizen is a potential spy. These include, as a matter of course, all Communist diplomats and newspapermen; the Soviet news agency, Tass, is an arm of the KGB. Businessmen and athletes, theatrical performers, chess players—all are subject to espionage assignments when they travel beyond the Iron Curtain. All over the world the Communist conspiracy can expect assistance from members of the Communist Party in democratic countries—25,000 of them in the United States. The World Peace Council was established by the Soviets as an espionage front; a session in Vienna was financed to the tune of $500,000 by the Soviet Military Bank in Vienna.

CIA gets what it can from Communist publications, but it is a trickle compared to the mass of information Red spies can pick up in our technical and scientific journals—and in our daily newspapers. Even the day-by-day working of the United States government provides the Reds with valuable intelligence and is often damaging to CIA's efforts to preserve secrecy and protect its operatives.

There was, for instance, the Senate Subcommittee on Internal Security hearings which went into allegations brought against a career Foreign Service officer named John Paton Davies. Davies purportedly had suggested that CIA employ Communists and party-liners as a means of getting closer to the Communist conspiracy apparatus. When the transcript of the hearings was published it destroyed the cover of two valuable CIA secret agents, since the text carried their unwilling testimony before the subcommittee. And certainly the Communist espionage operation found much gold in the hearing record of the special investigation into the loyalty of the nuclear physicist, Dr. J. Robert Oppenheimer.

The romanticists will be pleased to know that CIA still employs women as spies, some of them with the traditional blonde tresses and pretty faces. Most women are in the "white" category, working in research jobs in Washington or doing analysis of espionage reports. In these latter jobs women have always had CIA's official respect because of their skepticism and thoroughness.

But out in the field there are women who do such dangerous jobs as blowing up bridges and fomenting discontent among labor unions. They live in foreign countries as stenographers or housewives and do courier work or act as contacts with local individuals working for CIA. Notable among these feminine operatives is a woman with a wooden leg who has parachuted into enemy territory twice and once was forced to shoot her way out of a trap in West Berlin. CIA has no worries about female courage. During World War II, the OSS conducted a parachute school where 3800 men and 38 women were trained. The officers supervised 20,000 jumps in all and had only 50 refusals—none by women.

In the turnabout atmosphere of the post-World War II era, CIA has been forced by circumstances to do business— usually profitable—with a strange assortment of characters. Suddenly, even in the midst of the Potsdam negotiations, there were indications that Germany and Japan would become our new allies and that the Soviet Union, our wartime friend, would become our new enemy. By the time CIA's predecessor, the Central Intelligence Group, was organized in 1946, the first steps had been taken to make use of our new allies in the intelligence field against our new antagonist. Among the new helpmates we acquired at the time, none brought to CIA more firsthand knowledge and caused more controversy among the more delicate observers of the espionage scene than a Germany Army intelligence chief named Lieutenant General Reinhold Gehlen.

Some critics have called Gehlen a Nazi, but he was long vouched for by Konrad Adenauer and other usually impeccable high officials of the West German regime. He served Adolf Hitler, but not without disagreeing with the dictator, and when the Third Reich went down to defeat Gehlen hastened to mend fences with the victors. Nazi or not, opportunist or not, he brought to the Allies truckloads of intelligence on the Russians and a reputation as a master spy.

Reinhold Gehlen is a life-long professional soldier, despite his early background as the son of a German publisher and a youthful frequenter of literary salons. From that early background he acquired a quiet and scholarly manner; from his service in the Reichswehr he developed the terse and precise tones of the commanding officer. He had joined the Army in the decrepit days of 1920 but stayed with it to fight in the invasions of Poland and France when the misery of the Twenties seemed worthwhile. When the Russian war broke out he was transferred to the Eastern Front, where in April, 1942, he was named head of the German Army's Intelligence Section and eventually ended his World War II career as a lieutenant general.

One of the items in Gehlen's past which some of his supporters use as a recommendation is that he opposed Hitler's policy of exterminating the Russians or using them as slaves. He maintained throughout the war with Russia that the Germans should try to win over the Russian people by generosity and fair dealing, while liquidating the Communist system. When Hitler persisted in treating the Russians like animals, Gehlen took a pessimistic view of the war and at one time was in danger of arrest as a defeatist, but the Army somehow managed to protect him.

When the war ended and the Hitler regime collapsed, Gehlen conveniently—for both sides—was captured by the Americans. Back in Washington, the government was well aware that it had laid its hands on an extremely important prisoner of war, and Gehlen immediately was put to work. For eighteen months he toiled at the chore of organizing his files of secret material on the Soviet Union and arranging indexes and cross indexes in English for use by the American intelligence units. Then he was assigned to organize a small army of secret agents, given several million dollars and told to take charge of espionage in the Soviet Zone for the United States. His job was to identify and locate at all times the forward Soviet and satellite armed forces for the protection of the 400,000 American, British and French troops in West Germany.

In other words, over the years, we have trusted a former enemy to tell us pretty much everything we wanted to know about the Soviet Union's activities in Europe. This has caused eyebrow-raising, not only by critics in the United States, but by the British, who are more cynical about such things. CIA's attitude, though never publicly expressed— since it has never acknowledged Gehlen—undoubtedly is that he was the best man for the job and that we were lucky to get him. Presumably, there were safeguards installed lest Gehlen prove undependable.

Most authorities—if such exist in intelligence matters— have estimated that Gehlen and his thousands of agents have cost the United States $6,000,000 a year. It is a reasonable guess because Gehlen's secret force always included the elite of the old German Army's counterintelligence corps, plus a weird but knowledgeable assortment of cloak-and-dagger operatives scattered throughout Eastern Europe and the Balkans. And the fingers of Gehlen's organization have extended as far east as Siberia.

Up to 1955, Gehlen's army was supported by the West German government as well as the United States, but it had no official German status and its money came almost exclusively from Washington. The West German security responsibility was in the hands of Dr. Otto John's security section, and there appears to have been no love lost between the handsome, suave Dr. John and the small, thin-faced Gehlen. The results showed by Gehlen's army were impressive, and they impressed Chancellor Adenauer, who was in the habit of inviting Gehlen to his hilltop house in Bonn for night-long discussions. CIA, of course, was officially neutral, since it did business with Dr. John as well as with its personal spy, Reinhold Gehlen.

For example in July, 1954, Dr. John visited the United States and had dinner with Allen Dulles. It seemed a logical meeting between two prominent spies. But then Dr. John returned to Bonn, and on July 20 he suddenly deserted to the Communists in East Berlin. The knowledge that the chief of West Germany's Office of Internal Security—a kind of German J. Edgar Hoover—had defected so soon after a private conversation with America's top spy reddened necks in every capital of the free world. Presumably Dr. John had taken with him a goodly supply of secret papers because shortly after his defection the East German Communists announced a round-up of alleged Western agents.

Dr. John's defection left Reinhold Gehlen as the top intelligence authority in West Germany, and Adenauer promptly gave him official status. He took over Gehlen's organization and named Gehlen to Dr. John's old job. Friedrich Wilhelm Heinz, boss of the intelligence section of the Defense Ministry, was sidetracked. Commenting on the Gehlen appointment, The *New York Times* noted that Gehlen "has been credited by some with great intelligence and denounced by others as a sinister figure."

In a pamphlet written in 1961, *A Study of the Master Spy* (Allen Dulles), a leftist member of the British Parliament was a lot tougher on Gehlen. The author was Bob Edwards, who had been elected to Parliament with Labor and Co-operative support since 1955. He fought with Loyalist forces in Spain during the civil war and has been general secretary of the Chemical Workers Union since 1947. He has been vociferous in pointing out the danger of permitting the Germans to establish bases in Spain.

Edwards wrote: "It is particularly worrying that Mr. Dulles and his agency should be maintaining close contacts with General Reinhold Gehlen's West German secret service. Though it can be counted as a NATO intelligence organization, we think there is great need for caution in our dealings with it. It is extremely unlikely that General Gehlen has any very warm feelings for us. As for Mr. Dulles, he actually advertises his friendship with the General and after a recent visit to London went straight off to Bonn. But we have reason to believe that General Gehlen does not confine his interests to the East. The German secret service never has done so. So much the worse for us . . . Beware the Germans, when they come bearing gifts!"

Other critics have been worried about United States dependence on Germany. They fear that the Germans, under the guise of friendship, are merely intent on recovering their military might and that once they do so they will proceed unilaterally to annex East Germany—a step that can only lead to World War III. Specifically, these critics point out that in using Gehlen we may discover we have been used by him; that he may have been deliberately withholding information and issuing misleading reports of Russian activity. Notably, this view is held by many official observers in Great Britain and France.

There have been indications that Gehlen has wielded considerable influence within the CIA, in addition to being our main German source of intelligence. Of particular note was the brouhaha in August and September, 1955, involving a celebrated American Army officer.

On September 1, the Army announced in Washington that Major General Arthur Gilbert Trudeau, head of Army's G-2 (Intelligence) was being transferred to the Far East. This routine announcement was not quite the complete story, according to certain officers in the Pentagon who got the attention of John O'Donnell of the New York *Daily News*. They told O'Donnell that Allen Dulles personally had demanded that General Trudeau be transferred and that his demand had been carried all the way up through the Defense Secretary to President Eisenhower for action.

O'Donnell wrote that Dulles told the Defense Secretary that "the Army's top intelligence officer, 'without consulting the Central Intelligence Agency,' had talked with West Germany's Chancellor Adenauer here last June in 'an effort' to 'undermine' the confidence of Adenauer in a hush-hush CIA-bankrolled setup in Germany, headed by the mysterious Reinhart [sic] von Gehlen. Furthermore, said Dulles, the General had expressed doubts about the reliability of Gehlen as an individual and the security safeguards of the mystery organization."

General Trudeau was popular with the Army brass as the commander who had spearheaded General MacArthur's drive to take Manila, and the brass came to his defense. All General Trudeau had done, said the Pentagon, was to express doubts about Gehlen's security safeguards. But the transfer stuck, and General Trudeau was shunted to the Far East; later he was named the Army's Assistant Chief of Staff for research and development.

Allen Dulles has always refused to discuss the case. "Trudeau and I are very good friends," he said. "I don't want to talk about it." In the meantime, Gehlen was kept on as America's principal eyes and ears in Europe as CIA continued on its difficult path of trying to mastermind the events of the Cold War.

12. *Trouble In Paradise*

Nikita Khrushchev's angry outcries that West Berlin is a bone in his throat is splendid Soviet propaganda, of course, but it is one of the few Russian complaints that has some basis in fact. West Berlin, by the very nature of its free population, is a menace to the regimented masses of East Germany, and when Khrushchev contemplates this menace he must have thoughts about certain events in June, 1953, when the bone threatened to choke him.

On June 17, for one day, 2,000,000 bare-fisted East German workers defied the dictatorship of the Communist party and Russian occupation troops. These workers and students fought Russian tanks and guns, ripped open jails to free political prisoners, beat Communist officials to death and roared their demands for free elections.

The revolt began with a "spontaneous" strike of construction workers in East Berlin over a 10 per cent increase in work norms without any corresponding increase in pay or other benefits. It spread to Magdeburg, Halle, Leipzig and Rostock-on-the-Sea and more than two hundred other smaller cities and towns in all corners of the Eastern Zone. At least a third of the demonstrators were proven later to be skilled workers and most were settled persons over thirty years of age. In Berlin alone, in two days, 569 people were killed and 1744 wounded. Fifty thousand more were arrested. Police

Chief Wilhelm Zaisser was fired and so was Justice Minister
Max Fechner, who had admitted publicly the constitution
gave the workers the right to strike. Among the official heads
that rolled was that of the gruesome "Red Hilde," Judge
Hildegarde Benjamin, a fanatic Communist who had sentenced hundreds to death or prison. And Russian martial
law was in force for two grim weeks.

The Central Intelligence Agency naturally has always
denied any connection with this revolt. But from evidence at
hand from unofficial sources it is obvious that American intelligence operatives, if they had no part in planning the
"spontaneous" gesture, gave considerable aid and comfort to
the rebels. It was, after all, built to order for CIA's program
of spreading anarchy and confusion in the Communist camp,
as Allen Dulles outlined it—rather fuzzily—for *U. S. News
and World Report* in 1954.

Q: It is often reported in the papers that you send in provocateurs to stir up revolution in the satellite countries. What
truth is there in that?

DULLES: I only wish we had accomplished all that the Soviets attribute to us . . .

Q: Is that part of your function—to stir up revolution in
these countries?

DULLES: We would be foolish if we did not co-operate with
our friends abroad to help them do everything they can to
expose and counter this Communist subversive movement.

There were plenty of signs that CIA co-operated with its
friends in the East German revolt, including the reaction of
the Kremlin. Allowing for the Soviet's congenital inability to
tell the whole truth about anything, Radio Moscow's revela-
tions about American complicity were at least interesting. It
reported that the riots were part of a plot by a mysterious
United States two-star general named Sievert who allegedly
had called a meeting of ninety West Germans on the morn-

ing the riots began and ordered them to go into action. They were told, Radio Moscow said, "to infiltrate East Germany and East Berlin, set buildings afire, loot shops, attack the People's police and generally upset order, not excluding the use of weapons." The Soviet said its source for this story was a confession by a jobless West Berliner named Werner Kalkovsky.

The United States Army promptly retorted that it had no general named Sievert. We did not seem to know anything about Werner Kalkovsky, but on June 19 Major Gen. P. T. Dibrowa, military commandant of the Soviet sector, announced the execution before a firing squad of an unidentified West Berliner accused of having helped start the riots "on the orders of a foreign intelligence agency." West Berlin authorities shortly identified the man as Willi Goettling, an unemployed painter who had been living in the French sector with his wife and two children. The Western powers denounced Goettling's execution as "an act of brutality which will shock the conscience of the world."

It is feckless to believe that CIA would use a general in uniform to direct any of its plots, but sources with considerable access to the story of what went on behind the scenes indicate that CIA nevertheless had at least a sly finger in the pie. The reasoning, supported by background knowledge, is that some of the provocateurs captured by the Communist authorities were too well equipped with blueprints for sabotage to have managed the business alone.

These rioters had in their pockets plans for blowing up railroad bridges and railway terminals and detailed floor plans of various governmental buildings. They had forged food stamps and fake bank drafts to be used to spread confusion in the food-rationing system and to disrupt East German bank credits. It seemed indisputable that they were getting their espionage pay checks from CIA's top German spy, the aforementioned unprepossessing Reinhold Gehlen.

At the East German trials of some of these agents, the Communists made themselves look ridiculous by claiming they had found on the agents lists of names of prominent West German anti-Nazis marked for liquidation. The Reds did not explain why these provocateurs had been impelled to carry these incriminating lists around with them while engaged in the dangerous work of violent revolt.

It was sheer and heart-rending tragedy that the revolt failed after such valiant efforts by those ordinary East German citizens. But at a time of stern repression, the revolt threw a monumental scare into the Soviet. Even during the period of martial law, no policeman or Communist official dared walk alone on the streets of East Berlin, and more than 12,000 East Germans succeeded in the frightful risk of fleeing to West Germany. The frightened Reds resorted to bribery—they unlocked the doors of their food supplies and loaded shops with fruit, vegetables and meat, offered at a 10 per cent reduction in prices. Work quotas were rolled back to get production going again, but the workers switched to passive resistance and in some big plants slowdowns lowered production by as much as 50 per cent.

Moreover, the East German rebels showed that, with help and organization, they could make things at least temporarily miserable for their masters. By midafternoon on the 17th, they had spread so much terror in East Berlin that an estimated 50,000 workers were threatening to seize the East German government and calling for a general strike via commandeered loud-speaker trucks that toured the streets. Soviet troops were moved into the city at 6:30 the next morning and on the Unter den Linden they fired over the heads of the threatening crowds. East German youths tore down the Red flag from over the Brandenburg Gate, which separates East from West Berlin. Otto Nuschke, an East German deputy prime minister, was dragged from his car, beaten up and then driven into the American sector, where he was held for three days and questioned by intelligence officials. Rioters attacked headquarters of the East German "Peoples Police," set fire to the plant of the newspaper *Neues Deutschland*, and cut power cables for the elevated railway connecting East and West Berlin.

In Washington, the Voice of America broadcast statements in support of the demonstrators by President Eisenhower, Senator Alexander Wiley, Republican of Wisconsin, chairman of the Senate Foreign Relations Committee, West Berlin Mayor Ernst Reuter, and West German Chancellor Konrad Adenauer. Unfortunately, this official cognizance of the revolt was limited to giving moral assistance.

Despite the arrival of an entire Russian armored division, the mobs continued to do well. They held command of the streets all night, and prompted the hyperbole-shy *New York Times* to describe the scenes as "a time of high emotion," and to report that at times "a single deep-throated shout" arose from the mob and could be heard for miles. When, the next morning, government and party workers gathered under the protection of Soviet troops and pleaded with the rioters to go back to work, they were met with jeers.

"You are smashing everything the workers have created," shouted one of the government functionaries.

"What do you know about the workers?" retorted a youth.

Meanwhile, Dr. James Conant, former president of Harvard University and then U. S. High Commissioner in Germany, described the disturbances as "a spontaneous manifestation of the spirit of freedom," and gave tribute to "the courage of desperation." As he spoke, young East Germans were attacking Soviet tanks with their bare hands in East Berlin, and in Magdeburg one Albert Dartsch was executed for having seized a pistol from an East German policeman and slain him with it. In Jena, workers stormed the offices of the Socialist Unity (Communist) Party, and the Free German Youth headquarters were wrecked and typewriters were thrown into the streets.

It seems beyond doubt that these bloody but stirring events were the violent results, at least in part, of what Enno Hobbing in *Esquire* later described as CIA's role in moving "swiftly through foreign political backrooms, to rescue and revive a friendly government and a friendly people who were on the verge of being choked by Communist pressure." Yet as the Kremlin completed its crushing of the revolt, there was little the United States could do but order its armed forces in Germany to observe a period of five minutes' silence and the lowering of flags to half mast when West Berlin buried its victims of the uprising. The result has been criticism of CIA for moving too soon in East Berlin, or at least for not dissuading the East Germans and those recruits from West Germany to postpone action until there was more promise of a general uprising. American intervention was out of the question unless we were prepared to risk World War III, and so it was even more important that intelligence be assured that the East Germans could handle a revolt successfully without official outside help.

The situation was virtually identical in Hungary during those tragic months of October and November, 1956. The important difference was that the Hungarian insurgents actually succeeded in ousting the puppet government and installing a regime headed by the ill-fated Imre Nagy which at the very least leaned toward an accommodation with the West. The Hungarians proved they could handle a revolution without the help of foreign intervention—until the Russians moved in.

CIA claims that it accurately predicted the Hungarian outbreak, and there is evidence from other sources which supports this claim. It is also a virtual certainty that CIA managed to smuggle arms to the rebels and generally gave them assistance before the uprising. CIA was correct in reporting that Hungary was ripe for revolt and in predicting that the Hungarian Army was honeycombed with dissidents who would defect to the rebel cause. But in the international atmosphere of our time, it seems incredible that CIA should not have given more emphasis to the possibility of Soviet intervention. Looking back at the events it seems clear that the Kremlin could not have permitted this "most docile" satellite to slip over to the side of the West.

Some critics have attacked CIA for whipping up the Hungarian rebels to sacrifice themselves in a hopeless cause. This might have been true once the revolt got underway if one agrees with those critics that Radio Free Europe is a kind of arm of CIA, for RFE's broadcasts were filled with hints of United States intervention. But CIA had nothing to do with the scheduling of the revolution except for supplying the arms and counsel which helped the Hungarian people to prepare themselves for the big day. When that day came it caught CIA as well as the rest of the world unawares because, as a United Nations commission later reported, "events took (even) participants by surprise." CIA knew of the boiling opposition to the Communist regime of Erno Gero but, because no date for the uprising was fixed in advance by the rebels, it had no way of knowing when it would come.

It had not been difficult for CIA to come to the conclusion that things were getting hot in Hungary. Quite aside from its lines to underground plotters, it had benefited from the publicly announced fact that the Hungarian people already had won one concession from their Soviet masters. The hated Matyas Rakosi, First Secretary of the Hungarian Communist Party and a Stalinist who had ruled the country with cruel repression since World War II, had been deposed and succeeded by the more moderate Gero, who seemed to promise better things.

Naturally, too, CIA was watching carefully for the Hungarian reaction to events in Poland where in September and

October the Polish government had successfully resisted Russian pressures and won a great degree of independence from the Soviet Union. Some CIA experts felt Gero would do something about the Hungarian people's grievances; others appraised him as a man too subservient to Moscow to do anything constructive for his country. The pessimists were proved right.

Gero had recognized the grievances, but his public utterances indicated he felt they were unreasonable, and in a speech on October 23 he declined to meet any of these demands and adopted a truculent tone toward the petitioners. Hungarian students had anticipated his attitude. Encouraged by the news, received on October 19, that the Poles had successfully defied the Kremlin, the students gathered at a number of rallies on October 22, and adopted sixteen demands expressing their views on national unity.

The students asked the immediate withdrawal of Soviet troops, reconstruction of the government under Nagy, the former Communist Premier who had been imprisoned by Rakosi, freedom of expression, re-establishment of political parties, and sweeping changes in the condition of the workers and peasants. The Hungarian Writers Union said it would express its solidarity with Poland by laying a wreath on the statue to General Bem, a hero of the Hungarian War of Independence of 1848-49, who was of Polish extraction. Meanwhile, according to the UN report, "Soviet authorities had taken steps as early as October 20 to make armed intervention in Hungary possible. Evidence exists of troop movements or projected troop movements from that date on. It would appear that plans for action therefore had been laid sometime before the students met to discuss their demands."

What the UN was referring to may have been the movements described by General MacArthur's former intelligence chief, Major General C. A. Willoughby (retired). Willoughby, a man who keeps his finger on the intelligence pulse, wrote in

1961 that "Budapest was engulfed frontally by four divisions." Moving four divisions about in secrecy is a difficult accomplishment, but it would seem these movements did not come to the attention of American intelligence.

By the morning of October 23, the students' demands of the night before were well known throughout Budapest. There was an atmosphere of elation and hopefulness. At first, the Ministry of the Interior banned the planned demonstration, but later the prohibition was lifted when the demonstrations already were underway. The thousands of young people in the crowd included factory workers and soldiers in uniform as well as students. By six o'clock in the evening, a crowd of from 200,000 to 300,000 was massed outside the Parliament building across the Danube where they shouted for Nagy to come out and address them. A shy Nagy eventually did so.

The next day, some of the students went to Radio Budapest to force authorities to broadcast their demands. State Security Police guarded the building against the surging crowd, and tear-gas bombs were thrown from the windows. Suddenly, the police opened fire on the crowd, killing and wounding hundreds. At this moment the peaceable demonstration became a violent uprising. It vented its initial fury when white ambulances with Red Cross markings drove up and disgorged not doctors or nurses but security police wearing white doctors' coats. The crowd hurled itself at these reinforcements and wrested their weapons away from them. Then, when Hungarian Army troops were rushed to the scene, the crowd persuaded the soldiers to join the revolt.

The job of bringing the Hungarian government to its knees was done in five days of hard and brutal fighting. Its spearhead was the gallant Hungarian civilians, but their fellow countrymen in the police and Army gave them unexpected reinforcement. Police gave the rebels their weapons or fought by their side. Certain units of the Army fought as such on the side of the insurgents, hundreds of soldiers handed over their weapons to the Freedom Fighters and deserted individually or in squads. The UN reported that "There was no single instance recorded of Hungarian troops fighting on the Soviet side against their fellow countrymen."

As a last resort, Imre Nagy assumed the office of Premier in an attempt to quell the revolt. He formed a government which included such pro-Westerners as Anna Kethley, who later escaped to the United States, and he retained the pro-Westerner General Pal Meleter as commander of the armed forces. But his Minister of Interior was a rat-faced man named Janos Kadar who later would succeed and execute the mild-mannered Nagy.

Moscow had no intention of permitting Nagy to bestow any crumbs of freedom on his countrymen. The first Soviet tanks appeared on the streets of Budapest about two o'clock on the morning of October 24, by invitation, said Moscow, "of the Hungarian Premier, Nagy." Nagy denied he had asked for Soviet troops or even had been aware the invitation was extended; besides, he held no government post at the time the tanks had received their orders. The UN report suggests that the invitation may have been extended privately by Gero, who then was still boss of the country, or by Andras Hegedus, his puppet Premier.

In any case, Nagy's first step after taking over the Prime Minister's portfolio was to begin negotiations with the Russians for the withdrawal of Soviet troops. Nagy was a Communist, but a soft-liner and an advocate of more independence from the USSR. He lacked the courage to defy the Soviet leaders openly, but he believed he could persuade the Russians to leave by argument, and at first he seemed to have succeeded. Late in October Soviet armored and other vehicles began to evacuate Budapest with the exception of certain key positions such as the neighborhood of the Soviet Embassy and the main approaches to the Danube. They also surrounded the Budapest Airport. Promptly, the Hungarian Air Force adopted a resolution stating that unless the Russians withdrew in twelve hours they would make an armed stand.

Nagy, Meleter and other Hungarian leaders were in conference with the Soviets when Mikhail A. Suslov, head of the Soviet secret police and a member of the Soviet Presidium, who had come to Budapest with First Deputy Premier Anastas I. Mikoyan, burst into the room. He placed all the Hungarian leaders under arrest. Meanwhile, the Soviet armed forces had turned at the border and raced back into Hungary so that by the evening of November 2 Hungary again was invaded by Soviet troops whose numbers were variously estimated at from 75,000 to 200,000 men.

By this time most Hungarians were happily at work tidying up and repairing their capital city. Rubble and glass were being removed and holes in the streets were being patched. Then it was learned that Russian troops had surrounded the capital and that hundreds of tanks were advancing on the city. Nagy pleaded with the Hungarians not to open fire on the Soviets lest they be massacred, but his countrymen paid him no heed. Almost the entire population of Budapest fell upon the invaders. Molotov cocktails were hurled from apartment windows by women and children while the men battled tanks with weapons as ineffective as rifles and machine guns. The Soviet troops, unable to identify their attackers in the buildings, staged a series of punitive sorties in the side streets, killing noncombatants indiscriminately. For example, they shot up a breadline of women and children outside a bakery and killed and wounded several doctors and nurses in a Red Cross ambulance.

It has been charged that all this time the Central Intelligence Agency was urging the Hungarians to continue their hopeless resistance. The basis for this charge would seem to be the broadcasts of Radio Free Europe, a powerful propaganda weapon about which the most that can be said publicly is that it is on the same side as CIA. RFE kept droning the message, "America will not fail you . . . America will not fail you," but to suggest that this was done at the instigation or with the encouragement of CIA is pure speculation because officially RFE is an independent organization purportedly financed by private funds.

The UN found that RFE indeed had offered encouragement to the rebels, and that under the emotional stress of the moment this was often misinterpreted as an offer of physical assistance against the Russians. This was unfortunate, said the UN, but at no time was such hope actually held out. Nor did the UN hold with the thesis later advanced by Khrushchev's puppets in the reconstituted Hungarian government that the uprising "was fomented by reactionary circles in Hungary and drew its strength from such circles and Western imperialists." From start to finish, said the UN, the uprising was led by students, workers, soldiers and intellectuals, many of whom were Communists or former Communists.

By that time it mattered little anyway. Kadar had replaced Nagy as Premier; Nagy had been executed as a traitor after being offered safe conduct from the Yugoslav Embassy by the appalling Kadar. To punctuate its claims that the United States was involved, the Kadar regime ordered the U. S. legation to reduce the size of its Budapest staff by half, and expelled the American air attache, Colonel Welwyn F. Dallam, Jr., on the grounds he had photographed military installations.

Whatever the claims about CIA's role in the Hungarian uprising, neither blame nor credit can be assigned to the agency for the events in Poland in that fall of 1956 which helped spark the Hungarian revolt. To be sure, CIA had done its best to propagandize both the Polish people and, through its undercover connections, certain members of Poland's Communist government. But the agency's principal contribution in the Polish revolt was as an excellent report which kept President Eisenhower and the National Security Council au courant with what was happening in Poland's highest councils. Much of the material is in the public domain now, but CIA had it and passed it on swiftly to the White House during the same hours when these events were taking place.

Poland's start toward a greater measure of independence from the USSR can be measured from the death of Josef Stalin, and Nikita Khrushchev's subsequent denunciation of the "Cult of Leadership." The Poles, a vigorously irrascible people, were among the first in the satellites to cry for more freedom. A small part of the Polish leadership, centering around the Polish-born Soviet Marshal Konstantin Rokossovsky, wanted to dig in and resist the popular pressures. Rokossovsky's sentiments were logical; he had been installed by the Kremlin as Polish Defense Minister and commander in chief of the armed forces.

But the majority, including Communist Party First Secretary Eouard Ochab, favored going with the tide, and emphasized its sentiments by releasing the onetime Communist Party boss Wladislaw Gomulka, who had been imprisoned for Titoism after the Yugoslav break with Stalin in 1948. Once back in the club, Gomulka prodded the Polish Communist leadership to take steps which would lessen the Soviet Union's hold on the country. Soon Moscow's No. 1 man in the Polish party, Jacob Berman, was dropped as Deputy Premier, and shortly thereafter the head of the secret police was sacked. There were serious riots in Poznan in June, 1955, and Ochab blamed "serious troubles inside the party." In July, 1955, Gomulka was readmitted to the party and helped arrange for the public trial of the Poznan rioters—and probably for the light sentences they received. As CIA reported promptly, the Politburo was deeply disturbed and kept a succession of top Communist leaders shuffling back and forth between Moscow and Warsaw. Marshal Bulganian showed up in the Polish capital to demand a harsh crackdown. Khrushchev tried in vain to persuade Tito to preach a go-slow attitude to the Polish leaders.

At about this stage of developments, CIA was able to suggest that a showdown seemed imminent between Warsaw and Moscow. It came a little sooner than the agency had expected —on September 19, 1956—and it was an extraordinary episode in the relations between the Soviet Union and its satellites. Through espionage communications lines which extended into at least the secondary levels of Polish Communist leadership, CIA reported what happened:

Polish Party leaders, including Gomulka, had met to plan steps for further "liberalization" of the regime when Nikita Khrushchev suddenly showed up with a corps of Soviet party chieftains. These included Deputy Premiers V. M. Molotov, Anastas A. Mikoyan and Lazar Kaganovich, Defense Minister Marshal Georgi Zhukov, and a group of high-ranking Soviet Army officers headed by Marshal Ivan Konev.

Khrushchev demanded an end to the "liberalization." Ochab and Gomulka stood up to defy him. Poles and Russians then went into a loud-talking conference that lasted for six hours, with the Russians demanding that at least the Polish Stalinists be retained in leadership of the Communist Party. Ochab and Gomulka, and others, said that was impossible.

"Go carefully," Khrushchev warned the Poles. "Rokossovsky's troops are near Warsaw and a Soviet division in Silesia is on the move toward Warsaw at this very moment."

Ochab's face turned pale and he replied to Khrushchev through thin lips: "If you do not stop them immediately, we will walk out of here and break off all contact. Any attempt at a putsch in Warsaw will mean war."

Khrushchev was livid. "I will show you what the way to

socialism looks like," he shouted. "If you don't obey, we will crush you. We are going to use force to kill all sorts of risings in this country. Russian soldiers were slain liberating Poland in World War II. We will never permit this country to be sold to the American imperialists."

But Khrushchev strangely failed to get down to specifics. He talked tough, but seemed unwilling to go beyond the point of no return. As he bellowed, there were two incidents that seemed to point up his threat. Polish frontier troops barred with gunfire an attempt by a Soviet regiment to move into Stettin from East Germany. A Soviet armored division was reported to have smashed through a crossing and rammed a train during a movement toward Warsaw.

When the meeting broke up, the Poles went back to the Council of Minister's building to debate Khrushchev's ultimatum. The Stalinist faction argued for its acceptance. The Gomulka faction flatly refused. Meanwhile, word of the ultimatum spread through Warsaw and throughout the night Polish workers, armed, stayed at their posts in the factories. A mass rally of students and workers at the Polytechnic Institute cheered the mention of Gomulka's name.

The rest of the story eventually wound up in the newspapers around the world. Sidney Gruson of the *New York Times* wrote that "the victory of Poland's Communist leaders in their momentous struggle with the Soviet Union seems complete." The Soviet military threat collapsed. The Polish Communist Party's Central Committee elected a new Politburo on its own terms and ousted Marshal Rokossovsky. Gomulka was named the party's First Secretary, with Ochab stepping down to a post as one of the secretaries. The Soviet troops Rokossovsky had started toward Warsaw were back in their barracks in Lodz and Posnan, and the next day it was revealed that Rokossovsky had returned to the Soviet Union on leave.

Rokossovsky had departed just in time, because a special

commission of inquiry had assembled "proof" that he had prepared a military coup against Gomulka. Also implicated was Lieutenant General Kazimierz Witaszewski, former chief of the Polish Army's Political Education Division, who was dismissed and replaced by General Marian Spychalski, a close friend of Gomulka's. At the same time, the government announced the release of Stefan Cardinal Wyszynski, Roman Catholic Primate of Poland, who had spent three years in prison.

Since then, anti-Soviet feeling has continued among the common people of Poland. Periodically, both Moscow and Warsaw, the latter probably with tongue well tucked in cheek, have charged CIA with provoking and encouraging such attitudes. While CIA maintains its usual discreet silence on such matters, those diligent enough to look into such matters and add the customary two and two cannot help being impressed by the stubbornness with which Poland's workers, students and peasants have managed to sustain and strengthen their national antipathy toward anything Russian.

13. *Deaf Ears in Korea*

ONE OF THE CANARDS which is fast becoming a legend of modern American history is that in the Korean War the United States was twice caught by surprise—first by the invasion of South Korea by the North Koreans and then by the mass intervention of troops from Communist China. Neither is true so far as the Central Intelligence Agency is concerned, for in both instances CIA gave adequate warning.

What happened in the first instance is that Korea was only one of many places where the Communists "possessed the capability" to attack—the list also included Berlin, Trieste, Greece, Turkey, Iran and the small countries of Southeast Asia. Therefore, whether rightly or wrongly, the top-level command could give Korea no more attention than the other countries where the hammer and sickle hung over the heads of free men.

What happened in the second instance is that, until the Chinese Reds fell on him like a load of coal, General Douglas MacArthur stubbornly refused to believe those CIA reports which said the Reds might intervene in force.

Curiously, the tragedy of Korea dated from the first free election in Korean history. It was held on May 10, 1948, in that part of Korea south of the 38th Parallel now known as South Korea, and it was limited to that area because the Soviet occupying forces of the northern section refused to permit the United Nations Commission even to enter the area north of the 38th Parallel. Shortly, the National Assembly of this new southern Korea republic elected Synghman Rhee as its first President, and on August 15, 1948, the government was transferred from American military forces to the Rhee Administration. Except for an advisory group of five hundred engaged in training the South Korean Army of 65,000 men, the last United States troops left Korea on June 29, 1949.

On September 9, 1948, the Soviet occupation authorities in the area north of the 38th Parallel set up their own puppet North Korean "republic," but without benefit of a free election. It was called the "Democratic People's Republic of Korea," a euphemism that was a Soviet trademark, and its capital was placed in Pyongyang. Ten days later, the Soviet Foreign Office advised the United States Embassy in Moscow that all Soviet forces would be withdrawn from Korea by the end of December, 1948. Later, the U.S. was informed that this had been done on schedule.

The United States, and especially President Harry S. Truman, were in favor of the troop withdrawals, despite the fact the Russians had built up one of their "People's" armies in North Korea and intelligence showed that Communist infiltration in South Korea was considerable. Truman wanted to avoid the creation of antagonisms that always accrue with the presence of unwanted foreign soldiers in a country. General MacArthur had concurred in the withdrawal; he reported that the training and combat readiness of the new South Korean security forces made such a withdrawal practical. Meanwhile, for fiscal 1949 and 1950 the United States appropriated $210,000,000 to bolster Korea's economy.

But the Soviets had their eye on South Korea. Throughout the spring of 1949, Admiral Roscoe H. Hillenkoetter's CIA poured a stream of reports into the White House, Pentagon and State Department concerning military build-ups in

North Korea and guerrilla incursions into South Korea. By the spring of 1950, CIA reported an increase in incidents along the 38th Parallel, where armed units of the two Korean republics faced each other. CIA warned that at any time the North Koreans might decide to change from isolated raids to a full-scale attack. But, like CIA reports on other danger spots throughout the world, there was no information on when such an attack would take place. Admiral Hillenkoetter, the first director of CIA, noted a year later in an interview that any intelligence agency would need a "crystal ball" to offer an accurate report on an enemy's intentions.

The North Koreans invaded South Korea on June 24, 1950, with more than 60,000 troops spearheaded by one hundred Russian-built tanks. President Truman was spending the week end in Independence, Missouri, when Secretary of State Dean G. Acheson called him to tell him the bad news. They agreed that the United States should ask the United Nations Security Council to meet at once and declare that an act of aggression had been committed against South Korea. Meanwhile, Truman ordered that the armed service secretaries and the Joint Chiefs of Staff start working on recommendations as to possible American military aid to the Rhee regime.

Unfortunately, the United States had no plans for protecting South Korea against satellite aggression or limited war. Unfortunately, too, Secretary Acheson in a National Press Club speech had ruled Korea outside the American defensive perimeter in the Far East and this undoubtedly had had an effect on North Korea's calculated action. We knew from CIA's reports that the North Koreans were building up their military muscle and that their patrols were picking up intelligence on their sorties into South Korea, but we just did not do anything about it. As Harry Howe Ransom of Harvard reported in his book, *Central Intelligence and National Security,* "Intelligence, in a sense, was thus falling on deaf ears."

Within twenty-four hours, the UN Security Council had

voted 9 to 0 for a resolution declaring that the North Koreans
had committed a breach of the peace and ordering the Communist forces to cease fire and withdraw. On June 27, the UN
asked members to help carry out the demand by sending
troops to South Korea. Harry Truman had anticipated the
UN. Several hours before the UN's call, he had ordered General MacArthur to use air and naval forces to support the
South Korean forces and he had directed General J. Lawton
Collins, Army Chief of Staff, to prepare for the dispatch of
two or three divisions of American troops from Japan to
Korea. Additionally, he dispatched the Seventh Fleet to Formosa, both to prevent Communist attacks on that Nationalist
Chinese stronghold and to prevent Chiang Kai-shek from
raiding the Chinese mainland in a move that might result in
reprisal actions by the Chinese Reds and an enlargement of
the conflict.

On July 8, President Truman, at the request of the UN,
named General MacArthur commander in chief of United
Nations troops in Korea. American ground troops had entered the conflict June 30, but other UN members were slow
to send forces to take part in what Truman called a "police
action." It was some police action, inasmuch as the North
Koreans by that time had occupied the South Korean capital
of Seoul.

For more than two months UN troops did little more than
fight holding actions while MacArthur directed an organization of his forces and regrouped the battered South Korean
troops. But the North Korean drive had been checked, and
on September 15 MacArthur staged a brilliant landing at
Inchon by the 1st Marine Division and the Army's 7th Infantry Division which left the enemy confused and badly shaken.
Seoul was freed and the Rhee government moved back into
its capital.

Under directions from the National Security Council, Mac-
Arthur now prepared to pursue the North Koreans north of

the 38th Parallel—into Communist territory—in order to destroy their forces. However, he was placed under a limitation. If there was no indication or threat of entry of Soviet or Chinese Communist elements into the struggle he could go as far as he liked. But no ground operations were to take place north of the 38th Parallel in the event of Soviet or Chinese Communist intervention. Once again, intelligence was about to fall on deaf ears.

CIA had reported that the Chinese Communists would view with considerable seriousness any UN move across the line dividing North and South Korea. Its appraisal was supported by a free-lance operative, Supreme Court Justice William O. Douglas, the peripatetic world traveler. Douglas returned from a rambling trip through Southeast Asia during the late summer of 1950 and told Truman in the course of a White House visit that if UN troops crossed the 38th Parallel the Chinese Reds would enter the war on a massive scale.

Although CIA reported movements of Chinese Communist troops along the Manchurian-Korean border and noted the official irritability of the Chinese Red regime over the possibility of UN action north of the 38th Parallel, the agency declined to warn bluntly that the Chinese *would* intervene; it merely cited their *capacity* and *inclination* to do so. Obviously, what was needed was a man with the courage to throw cold water on the military's ambitious plans for conquering all of North Korean by telling them: "Gentlemen, if you invade North Korea the Chinese Reds are going to enter the war." But everybody seems to have been so enthusiastic about winning a complete victory that they discouraged any argument that was colored with pessimism.

At hearings before the Senate Armed Services Committee in May, 1951, General MacArthur said flatly CIA had reported the Chinese Communists would not intervene. This led President Truman to observe tartly that if such a report had come in from CIA he had not seen it. But even if CIA had not forecast intervention, it would seem that MacArthur was given plenty of warning. General Omar Bradley, then Chairman of the Joint Chiefs, was asked about it in a general way by Senator Alexander Wiley, Republican of Wisconsin.

WILEY: Is it true that the government had intelligence that the Chinese Reds stationed opposite Formosa were moving north some time before they entered the war; and that you had that intelligence?

BRADLEY: Yes, sir.

WILEY: Did you inform MacArthur?

BRADLEY: I am told that all of that information was sent to General MacArthur.

On October 2, South Korean Army units were operating north of the 38th Parallel and there was little enemy resistance. On October 3, the State Department received messages from Moscow, Stockholm and New Delhi reporting that Red China's Chou En-lai had called in the Indian Ambassador to Peiping, K. M. Panikkar, and had told him that if United Nations forces crossed the 38th Parallel China would send troops to help the North Koreans. But Panikkar was suspect. As Truman wrote in his *Memoirs,* "Mr. Panikkar had in the past played the game of the Chinese Communists fairly regularly, so that his statement could not be taken as that of an impartial observer." Still, MacArthur was directed to exercise caution. He was told that if major Chinese Communist units entered the war he was to "continue the action as long as, in your judgment, action by forces now under your control offers a reasonable chance of success." He was also warned not to take any military action against objectives in Chinese territory without authorization from Washington.

United Nations troops continued to attack north of the 38th, along the western coastal corridor and in an amphibious landing by the X Corps at Wonsan on the east coast. About this time, Truman decided he wanted to have a chat with MacArthur. Truman was disturbed by the Peiping reports of intervention and, as he wrote, "I wanted to get the benefit of (MacArthur's) firsthand information and judgment." The meeting took place on Wake Island on October 15.

Truman and MacArthur first had a private session that lasted about an hour. "The general assured me that victory was won in Korea," Truman wrote. "He also informed me that the Chinese Communists would not attack and that Japan was ready for a peace treaty . . . I told him something of our plans for the strengthening of Europe, and he said he understood and that he was sure it would be possible to send one division from Korea to Europe in January, 1951. He repeated that the Korean conflict was won and that there was little possibility of the Chinese Communists coming in."

The second session was attended by MacArthur, Truman, Admiral Arthur W. Radford, Commander of the Pacific Fleet, Ambassador to Korea John Muccio, Secretary of the Army Frank Pace, General Bradley, Philip Jessup and Dean Rusk from the State Department and Averell Harriman, head of the Mutual Security Agency. There was a considerable fuss made later when it was discovered that Jessup's secretary, Miss Vernice Anderson, had made stenographic notes of the conference while sitting in the next room. Truman said neither he nor Jessup had told her to do so.

Miss Anderson's notes confirmed Truman's own report of the conference. He wrote: "General MacArthur stated his firm belief that all resistance would end, in both North and South Korea, by Thanksgiving. This, he said, would enable him to withdraw the Eighth Army to Japan by Christmas . . .

"Then I gave MacArthur an opportunity to repeat to the larger group some of the things he had said to me in our private meeting.

" 'What are the chances,' I asked, 'for Chinese or Soviet interference?'

"The general's answer was really in two parts. First he talked about the Chinese. He thought, he said, that there was very little chance that they would come in. At the most they might be able to get fifty or sixty thousand men into Korea, but, since they had no air force, 'if the Chinese tried to get down to Pyongyang, there would be the greatest slaughter.'

"Then he referred to the possibilities of Russian intervention. He referred to the Russian air strength, but he was certain that their planes and pilots were inferior to ours. He saw no way for the Russians to bring in any sizable number of ground troops before the onset of winter. This would leave the possibility of combined Chinese-Russian intervention, he observed, with Russian planes supporting Chinese ground units. This, he thought, would be no danger. 'It just wouldn't work,' he added, 'with Chinese Communist ground and Russian air.' "

Meanwhile, CIA was having its troubles with MacArthur. Most of the public statements on the matter are contradictory, but it seems clear that there was considerable friction between CIA agents and MacArthur's intelligence chief, the strong-willed Major General C. A. Willoughby. CIA claims that Willoughby not only declined to give CIA agents any assistance but complained to them that they were not doing any good and should get out of the theater.

By this time Admiral Hillenkoetter had been succeeded as CIA director by General Walter Bedell Smith, and much has been made about a trip by Smith to Tokyo to confer with General MacArthur. CIA sources insist that Smith made the trip to try to get MacArthur to co-operate with Smith's agents. The word is that after that conference CIA operatives were able to work much more efficiently. But MacArthur pooh-poohed all this.

Asked about it by Senator William F. Knowland, Republican of California, MacArthur told the Senate hearing: "That statement is all tommyrot. Every possible assistance has been given by me to the Central Intelligence Agency. The only thing I insisted upon was that the Central Intelligence Agency, when they came into the theater, would not act surreptitiously so they would co-ordinate with my own intelligence. I have given them every possible assistance."

But the Senators kept after the subject. Senator Wayne Morse of Oregon, then a Republican, asked the general: "Now, General, I ask a question with no implications on my part at all, but in answer to what I have read. The question is this: Is it true that two CIA men had been sent to Tokyo and were in Tokyo prior to the trip to Tokyo General Bedell Smith made to confer with you, but that those CIA men were not given access to your intelligence files and they were confronted with an order that they could not have access to the battlefield?"

MacArthur: Pure bunkum, Senator . . . The Central Intelligence Agency—I think any theater commander would be glad to have any assistance he could get in intelligence. The only question that ever could have arisen between a theater commander and the Central Intelligence Agency was that there should be proper co-ordination between his own intelligence services and the Central Intelligence Agency. The Central Intelligence Agency out in my command had worked in complete unity with my own Chief of Intelligence, General Willoughby, G-2 . . . General Smith went to Tokyo two or three months ago and at that time the purpose of his visit was to perfect and expand the Central Intelligence Agency; it was not to iron out any friction, it was not because of any difficulties. It was largely due to expanding and increasing the effort that was being made to gather intelligence.

Morse: General, you know of no friction between the Chief of your Intelligence Service, General Willoughby, and the officers of the CIA under the jurisdiction of General Smith?

MacArthur: Nothing that would not be normal and minor, nothing that ever reached me.

MORSE: You know of no instance in which the CIA was denied access to whatever intelligence your intelligence system could supply?

MACARTHUR: That would be ridiculous.

The late Senator Brian McMahon, Democrat of Connecticut, then took over.

McMAHON: When did the CIA leave Korea?

MACARTHUR: I couldn't tell you. The CIA doesn't operate under me.

McMAHON: Were they directed to leave Korea after the Inchon landing by your command?

MACARTHUR: I don't know what you are talking about, Senator.

McMAHON: I understood the CIA agents disappeared from Korea after the Inchon operation . . .

MACARTHUR: The CIA agents, Senator, are not under me. As far as I know, they were never in Korea. They may have been, but it is not an agency that functions under me.

Senator Richard B. Russell, the Georgia Democrat, and chairman of the committee, did not have much better luck with the late General George C. Marshall, then Secretary of Defense.

RUSSELL: The next question I am going to ask you is as to your knowledge as to whether or not there was co-ordination between Central Intelligence and General MacArthur's staff.

MARSHALL: I don't know in regard to that, sir, just what happened.

RUSSELL: Was it ever brought to your attention by CIA that there was any failure of co-operation between Central Intelligence and General MacArthur's staff?

MARSHALL: I have not a very distinct recollection of that. I do, I think, recall some discussion, informal entirely, with General Smith regarding, I will say, the attitude of General Willoughby.

RUSSELL: I don't understand you. You say you had no formal complaint?

MARSHALL: I do recall in a hazy sort of way a conversation with General Smith of the CIA referring to some difficulty in relation to General Willoughby, General MacArthur's G-2.

RUSSELL: Well, General Smith paid a visit to Japan. Did you know the purpose of his mission? Were you instructed on that or did you request him to go to Japan?

MARSHALL: Yes, I knew he was going out there, director of all relationships, and he reported to, I think, the National Security Council on his return.

RUSSELL: Did he go on his own initiative, or under your orders?

MARSHALL: He is not under my orders, sir.

RUSSELL: Did he go on the orders of the National Security Council, of which you are a member?

MARSHALL: No, I don't think he did, sir.

In the summer of 1961, General Willoughby was much more blunt in offering his own, and, presumably MacArthur's, version of the contretemps. Willoughby gave the impression he regarded the Central Intelligence operation in China and Formosa as a joke.

"Chiang had to leave the mainland," Willoughby recalled. "CIA left with him. This was ridiculous, an outrageous thing. By its very nature, an intelligence organization should plan to stay behind when our lines are overrun. Chiang Kai-shek's men still operate on the mainland. But, of course, Chinese can disappear among Chinese. CIA was all Western, so it had to leave.

"Chiang didn't want them; wouldn't take them. Oh, he was polite enough about it, but firm. So CIA had to find a home, a haven, had to go into exile. They applied to us for asylum, so to speak. Wanted to come to Japan. It was an absurd request, to plan to go back into a country after you've left it.

"So Bedell Smith came out to arrange it. I've known him for years. He's a friend of mine. There's a rapport between us. We said, 'All right, what do you want?' They wanted housing, logistic support, facilities, the whole works. And we gave it to them. Glad to. And then what did they do? They moved in with the Navy at Yokusuka. We didn't consider this a very friendly thing after all we'd done. CIA was where we couldn't reach them, and that was bad because one thing General MacArthur insisted on was that anyone in his theater of operations had to be under his direct control. It's the old idea of command responsibility.

"CIA had its own radio down at Yokusuka. That's why we never let OSS operate in our theater; no telling what they're sending back. Of course, we knew what CIA was sending. My cryptography boys merely broke their code."

At those Senate hearings, however, General Marshall let it be known publicly for the first time not only that CIA had warned of trouble in Korea but that its information had gone to MacArthur's headquarters. He did so in response to a long question from Senator Leverett Saltonstall, Republican of Massachusetts, who noted that Admiral Hillenkoetter had testified that CIA repeatedly warned the Pentagon and the State Department of a North Korean build-up, "with a final warning given on June 17."

"Is there anything in the records to show that these warnings went to General MacArthur to give him or his staff information concerning this build-up?"

Marshall said he had checked and had been assured that the information had been transmitted to MacArthur. Saltonstall prodded him further: "So far as you know, the information that General Bedell Smith and his CIA was getting and evaluating was going to General MacArthur's headquarters?"

Replied Marshall, "It was going to General MacArthur's headquarters."

Throughout October, MacArthur's drive to the Manchurian border proceeded almost unhindered. The North Korean capital of Pyongyang was taken on October 19. Meanwhile, in order to preserve international amenities, the Joint Chiefs of Staff instructed MacArthur that in his advance north he should not place non-Korean elements near the Manchurian and Soviet borders. But MacArthur ordered that the drive be spearheaded by American units. After the border was reached, South Koreans were to take their places "where feasible." Concerned, the Joint Chiefs asked MacArthur why he had disobeyed orders.

First, MacArthur said he had not disobeyed orders; that the Joint Chiefs' directive had told him: "We want you to feel unhampered tactically and strategically . . ." Then he explained that the Republic of Korea forces were green and inexperienced and he considered it essential to use more seasoned troops to lead the drive.

Troop movements continued on the Red Chinese side of the border, and Chinese "volunteers" began to show up in the North Korean Army. On October 20, CIA handed President Truman a memorandum which said it had reports the Chinese Communists would move in far enough to safeguard the Suiho electric plant and other installations along the Yalu River which provided them with power. From the State Department came a suggestion that General MacArthur issue a statement to the United Nations that he did not intend to interfere with the operation of the Suiho and other power plants. But both the Joint Chiefs and MacArthur opposed such a move from the military point of view, and it was dropped. By that time it would not have made much difference, anyway; the Red Chinese had begun crossing the Yalu four days earlier.

Headquarters of MacArthur's X Corps provided the first

DEAF EARS IN KOREA

official report of Chinese intervention. Prisoners captured on October 26 had been identified as Chinese and had told interrogating officers they were members of organized Chinese units. They said they had crossed the Yalu on October 16— the day after MacArthur had assured Truman the Chinese would not enter the war. The Joint Chiefs asked MacArthur for an up-to-date estimate. His reply was to recommend "against hasty conclusions which might be premature," and to say that "a final appraisement should await a more complete accumulation of military facts." He specifically discounted the possibility that the intervention of the Chinese Communists was a "new war."

Yet two days later, on November 6, MacArthur pleaded for, and received, permission to bomb the bridges over the Yalu River. "Men and materiel in large force are pouring across all bridges over the Yalu from Manchuria," he reported. "This movement not only jeopardizes but threatens the ultimate destruction of the forces under my command." Having got permission to bomb the bridges, however, MacArthur on November 7 told Washington that although things were tough, he had been confirmed in his belief that this was not a full-scale intervention by the Chinese Communists. But in a second message that day he was demanding that his planes be authorized to pursue enemy aircraft . . . which were "appearing in increasing numbers . . ." across the Yalu into Chinese territory.

CIA was ready with its own estimate, which was a grave one. General Smith reported that there might be as many as 200,000 Chinese Communist troops in Manchuria and that their entry into Korea might stop the UN advance and perhaps force the UN troops to withdraw to defensive positions. Smith called one fact inescapable. It was that with their entry into the Korean War, the Chinese Communist had staked not only their armed forces but also their prestige in Asia. Presumably they knew the risks they were taking, that is, the danger of a general war. Truman and his associates refused to give MacArthur permission for the "hot pursuit" of Chinese planes because they feared a general war, although CIA estimated that the Russians were not themselves willing to go to war but that they wanted to involve the United States as heavily as possible in Asia so that they could have a free hand in Europe.

MacArthur launched his Eighth Army on a major attack on November 24. He called it a "general offensive . . . to end the war." Although he has since denied it, he also was reported to have told one of his commanders to tell the troops they would be home by Christmas. He launched this attack despite a national intelligence summary from CIA, which Truman has said was "made available to General MacArthur." The summary stated that the Chinese Communists would "at a minimum" increase their operations in Korea, seek to immobilize the UN forces, subject them to prolonged attrition, and maintain the semblance of a North Korean state in being. CIA also warned that the Chinese possessed sufficient strength to force the UN troops to withdraw to defensive positions.

CIA was as right as it could be. By November 28 the Eighth Army found itself facing a vastly larger force, and X Corps on the east coast seemed to be beset on all sides. The communique called X Corps' situation "fluid," which as Truman later remarked "is a public relations man's way of saying that he can't figure out what's going on."

The world learned in brutal fashion what was going on. Hordes of Chinese Communist troops smashed at the UN forces, sending them into wild retreat. By Christmas Eve these 200,000 "volunteers" had forced evacuation of 105,000 UN troops and 91,000 Koreans at Hungnam. The Chinese pushed across the 38th Parallel and drove seventy miles into South Korea before UN reinforcements stopped their drive and eventually, on April 3, 1951, nudged the Chinese back into North Korea. Meanwhile, MacArthur was removed from his command for publicly threatening, on March 25, to attack Communist China with air and naval units.

Subsequently, at the Senate hearings in May, 1951, MacArthur was most casual about his references to CIA, but did say that, "In November, our Central Intelligence Agency here had said that they felt there was little chance of any major intervention on the part of the Chinese forces." Either he had forgotten about the national intelligence summary "available" at his headquarters before the Eighth Army's November 24 attack or he had not bothered to read it.

The Senators were given the impression by General Bradley that if anybody erred on the Chinese entry into the war, it probably was MacArthur's own intelligence officer, General Willoughby. Bradley was asked by Senator Margaret Chase Smith, Republican of Maine: "If we fell down, was it MacArthur's intelligence staff or was it the CIA? Could you say as a military man whether MacArthur was to blame for the apparently wrong intelligence on the Chinese coming into North Korea?"

Bradley replied that the intelligence on which MacArthur had to base his decision had to be "primarily field intelligence," that is, information gathered by his own military intelligence personnel. He noted that MacArthur had reported on November 6 that the Chinese were pouring across the bridges over the Yalu in great numbers, then added: "Now, what happened between November 6 and the time he was hit by the Chinese attack of about November 26 or 28, it was hard for us here to know, because a lot of that intelligence should have come from his own field command. That concentration on the right flank of the Eighth Army should have been picked up by air reconnaissance and ground reconnaissance; in other words by patrol and aviation put in there . . . Certainly there was enough coming in to indicate that there was a considerable Chinese build-up in North Korea."

SMITH: Was General MacArthur prevented from sending reconnaissance planes across the border in Manchuria to see whether there were any accumulations of troops?

BRADLEY: We knew all the time there were concentrations *in Manchuria.* It was a question of how many of them had been moved over *into Korea,* and that, as I say, could have been obtained or *should have been obtained* by air reconnaissance and ground reconnaissance . . . He may have had certain information and may have evaluated it wrong.

Aside from CIA's unwillingness to go out on a limb on Chinese intervention, despite its accurate information on troop build-up and movements, MacArthur has claimed that his error was in misreading the intentions of the United States. He has said that he did not think the Chinese would intervene because he believed the United States would meet such intervention with massive retaliation, and he felt the Chinese would not risk such a showdown battle with American might. But, of course, the United States had no intention of any such showdown with Red China, and there is plenty of evidence to show that this was made plain to MacArthur.

MacArthur, who presumably had no reason to get romantic with CIA, nevertheless pinpointed the fact which is CIA's strongest defense against complaints that it should have flatly predicted the North Korean attack on South Korea. The general told the committee: "I don't see how it would have been humanly possible for any men or group of men to predict such an attack as that, any more than you could predict such an attack as took place at Pearl Harbor. There is nothing, no means or methods, except the accidental spy methods—if you can get somebody to betray the enemy's higher circles—that can get such information as that. It is guarded with a secrecy that you cannot overestimate. Not even, probably, the commanding officers of the units, military units, concerned knew what was going on until they got the order to march."

Allen Dulles put it another way during a chat with a journalistic visitor who had asked what was CIA's current crying need. Dulles grinned. "That's easy," he said. "Mind readers."

14. *Foggy Bottom's Chiang*

IN THE TENSE YEAR OF 1952, when the world was preoccupied with the Korean War, other events were taking place far to the southeast of the official battlefront in the struggle between communism and the free world. But the events in Burma, though fascinating to historians intrigued by the bland machinations of Oriental confidence men, were more than a little confusing to the young American.

This youth was a comparative newcomer to the Central Intelligence Agency, which was itself still wet behind the ears. He had come to Northern Burma fresh from Chiang Kai-shek's Formosa bastion, and he was convinced by Chinese Nationalist assurances that shortly the Burmese branch of Chiang's Far Eastern Benevolent Association would be giving the Chinese Communists an extremely hard time. Thus the young man, trim in well-tailored tropical elegance, could be excused for his puzzled air as he sat across the table from a Nationalist colonel presumed to command one of the exiled regiments pledged to the harassment of the Reds. The colonel was equally fresh in white mufti, and when the CIA agent entered the tidy bungalow the officer was busy with some long forms which looked like bookkeeping sheets.

"But where are your men?" asked the CIA man. "I don't see any guerrillas. This looks like a—well, like a plantation."

The Chinese Nationalist colonel smiled warmly. "Oh, they

196

are at work in the fields," he replied. "You see, it takes money to run an operation like this and so temporarily we have gone into agriculture. We're growing opium."

Old Burma Hands would have smiled right back at the colonel, because they knew the score; this young man from CIA was shocked. He had been told that Chiang's gallant exiles were smiting the Chinese Reds hip and thigh, and he found something unwholesome in American taxpayers' money being used to help finance the production of a dangerous drug. Unfortunately, however, this was one of the cases where a CIA operation fell flat because the men we chose to help could not have cared less about fighting communism.

At the time there were several thousand of Chiang's old followers in Northern Burma. When Chiang's regime collapsed, he had not been able to take everybody with him to Formosa, and these opium growers had fled across the Yunnan border into Burma. They took with them on their flight considerable quantities of American arms and ammunition, and CIA saw in this exiled little army a military thorn in the side of the Chinese Reds across the way. Under the direction of top-level agents, more arms were dispatched to these exiles and American dollars were entrusted to their leadership to finance the project.

By that time, however, the exiles had had enough fighting; they wanted to get rich, like so many of the top officials of Nationalist China. So they settled down as planters on requisitioned acreage acquired by the simple process of chasing away those Burmese who occupied it. They grew opium and supplemented their income on the side by selling their arms to the Chinese Communist guerrillas who operated in the area. A scattered few gathered in small bands and staged an occasional hit-and-run raid on the Chinese Reds. CIA men worked feverishly to pressure and persuade the others to get on with the fight, but somebody had neglected to take a long, hard look at the character of the exiles in advance of committing American aid. Before long they became an international embarrassment to the United States.

Notably, these so-called freedom fighters displayed a colonial spirit that would have been applauded in Fifteenth Century Spain. They not only took over the best land in Northern Burma, but they annexed all but a few acres of the state of Kengtung and organized their own squatter government. This flouting of Burmese sovereignty understandably aroused the ire of the Burmese government and a strong protest was filed with the United States.

This confused the American Ambassador, William J. Sebald, who had not the slightest idea of what CIA was doing in Burma. He issued an unequivocal denial that Chiang's opium growers were being financed with American dollars and advised by American agents. Burmese Premier U Nu was flabbergasted by this denial, since the CIA operation was well known in Burmese government circles. He broke off all American Point Four activities and threatened to sever diplomatic relations. Sebald resigned because he had been hoodwinked.

It took a four-power conference finally to settle this problem. With American financing, slightly less than 6000 of the Nationalist soldiers were shipped off to Formosa where they rather unwillingly joined the regular Nationalist Army. But a thousand or so managed to elude capture and continued to prowl the Northern Burmese countryside, fighting small battles with regular Burmese troops. By 1961, indeed, there was evidence that some of these Nationalist irregulars were accepting arms from Mao Tse-tung to fight the Burmese. Meanwhile, the Burmese government in the spring of 1961 claimed it had discovered and confiscated American arms airlifted into Burma and intended for Chiang's exiles.

The tragic snafu in Burma was only one of many that have accrued to the United States and CIA during the nation's

often unrewarding relations with the Chiang Kai-shek regime. CIA has worked with Chiang and his cohorts ever
since the agency was established shortly after World War II,
and the result has been a continuing situation of utmost pre-
cariousness that often has seemed about to drag the United
States into war with Communist China. One reason for this
has been that in Formosa CIA has detoured from pure intelligence work into what President Kennedy calls paramilitary
operations.

Since well before World War II Chiang Kai-shek has benefited from the affectionate attentions of probably the world's
most powerful international agency of apologia—the China
Lobby. To the China Lobby, with its influential sprinkling of
members of Congress, Chiang Kai-shek is a genius. On the
other side are the critics, both sincere and professional, to
whom Chiang is a corrupt leader who slept with the Communists when it was to his advantage, who lost China to the Reds
because of his wanton cruelty and corruption and who is always trying to get the United States embroiled in a war with
Communist China so he can have the country back. To United
States policy makers, beginning with Franklin D. Roosevelt
and continuing through Harry S. Truman, Dwight D. Eisenhower and John F. Kennedy, Chiang has been—like Franco
in Spain—merely the lesser evil with whom it is convenient,
if not hugely profitable, to do business. CIA has been one of
the instruments of this often hazy and sometimes downright
confused policy.

The Chiang who shakes his fist across the Formosa Strait at
Communist China today began his political career in the
1920's as a fellow traveler. He studied revolution and Marxist
philosophy in Moscow and was friendly with Lenin and
Trotzky. The Reds helped subsidize him as a Chinese warlord, and Chiang went along with them until China's frightened bankers made him a better proposition. Then he turned
conservative and by shrewd maneuvering managed to take

over China. In the process, Chiang and his cronies grew rich, but unfortunately they neglected to permit any of this wealth to filter down to the peasant masses. Worse, his aides pocketed money intended for their soldiers' salaries, pillaged food supplies sent by other nations to feed the starving peasants and ran a flourishing black market. Mao Tse-tung's Communists moved into this vacuum and chased Chiang and his elegant footpads out of China.

Entrenched in Formosa with American aid—some three billion dollars' worth—Chiang went to work to build up a military machine capable of recapturing the Chinese mainland. In the process, Chiang's critics say that some of his henchmen looted and intimidated the Formosans who were no match for the police state Chiang established. Still, his regime represented a harassing anti-Communist force of 500,-000 troops under Mao's nose, and the United States sided with him; moreover, he did initiate needed land reforms. Roosevelt and Truman distrusted him, but used him, and Eisenhower had his troubles with him, but Chiang remained an important fact of life in the Far East.

CIA, of course, has always maintained a large organization in Formosa under various covers. Its most spectacular involvement in Chiang's fortunes was the direct result of a switch in America's China policy put into effect by the then Secretary of State John Foster Dulles in early 1953. This switch had two facets. First, President Eisenhower announced that the American Seventh Fleet no longer would be used to shield Communist China from attack by Chiang's Formosa forces. Second, Dulles' State Department let Chiang know that the United States would not oppose any moves Chiang made to strengthen his forces on the offshore islands, a figurative stone's throw from the Communist Chinese coastline. Foster Dulles later said that State did not encourage this build-up, but merely "acquiesced." It was a remarkably vigorous acquiescence.

Thus, in the early 1950's, CIA set up an elaborate cover operation on the offshore islands to direct and assist the Chinese Nationalists in their harassment of the Chinese mainland. The operation was known as Western Enterprises, Incorporated, and purported to be a trading company. Nobody ever found out what the company traded in or what profit there could be in dealing with the natives of these specks of land utilized as military outposts by the Chiang regime. But the Western Enterprisers managed to keep busy

Specifically, they kept busy organizing and equipping and training the Nationalist guerrillas who used the offshore islands as bases for hit-and-run raids on the mainland. They had their own planes, and there were daily flights between Formosa and Quemoy and Matsu. The Western Enterprisers themselves were a mysterious lot, soldier-of-fortune types who kept to themselves and lived well if not handsomely in large barracks with all modern conveniences, including a well-stocked PX. Presumably they did not lead any of the raids on the mainland, but they organized them so efficiently that often whole battalions of Nationalist guerrillas took part in the sorties. Planes were used for reconnaissance, leaflet dropping and for blockading the Chinese port of Amoy, just opposite Quemoy.

American correspondents and other foreigners in Formosa were amused by these Western Enterprise "spooks" because of their mysterious maneuverings reminiscent of those wonderfully ridiculous Grade B movies of the Twenties. For practical purposes, an occasional attempt was made to penetrate their cover. Stewart Alsop in the *Saturday Evening Post* told about a female journalist who visited one of the Tachen Islands early in 1954 and was chagrined to discover that while she was billeted in a bug-ridden shack, the spooks were living it up in their private complex. "She tried to exercise her charms on the spooks . . . but, faithful to their nonexistent cover, they refused to speak to her. So she sent the head spook a note: 'If you won't speak to me, you might at least let me sleep with you.' She was assigned a comfortable billet."

Although the presence of the Western Enterprisers in effect committed the United States to an interest in the defense of Quemoy and Matsu by Chiang, since everybody knew for whom the spooks worked, the commitment remained unofficial. That is, there was no admission that the Enterprisers represented the American government. But early in 1954 American foreign policy put the official stamp on our presence on the islands. At that time, CIA's Western Enterprises, Incorporated, was gradually liquidated except for a small group of top-level agents, and their mission of aiding and abetting the Chiang commandos was taken over by officers of the American Military Advisory Group, which had been stationed on Formosa since 1951.

Both State's Dulles and President Eisenhower later would complain that the build-up of Chiang's guerrillas on Quemoy and Matsu was foolish and even General MacArthur, a fast friend of Chiang, agreed that the islands were militarily worthless pieces of real estate. But in 1953 and 1954 there is no doubt that both CIA, through Western Enterprises, and the Pentagon, through the Military Advisory Group (MAG), not only encouraged but assisted in the build-up that was to cause the United States considerable uneasiness. Part of this was due to the fact that Admiral Arthur Radford, a veteran China-Firster and advocate of a showdown with Red China, became chairman of the Joint Chiefs of Staff in 1953, and the evidence is clear that the Pentagon went its Chiang-oriented way without waiting or asking for a directive from either the State Department or the White House.

At any rate, America's stake in Quemoy and Matsu was symbolized by the American flag flying over MAG headquarters and the presence of uniformed United States military officers. Chiang's forces were being strengthened and American uniforms were on the premises; obviously these two items added up to a significant sum for Mao Tse-tung and he felt something had to be done about it. What was done was the Reds' first heavy artillery attack on Quemoy in September, 1954. To the great elation of the Chinese Communists, the shelling killed two American officers of MAG—Lieutenant Colonel Alfred Menendorp and Lieutenant Colonel Frank W. Lynn.

Reaction in the United States was one of outrage, although there were those possessed of a few facts who pointed out that if we were going to station military personnel on an island used by Chiang for sorties against the mainland we should not expect Mao's gunners to show discrimination in their aim. Unfortunately, however, the outrage was shared by Admiral Radford and by two other members of the Joint Chiefs, General Nathan Twining and Admiral Robert Carney. They immediately recommended that Chiang's Air Force be permitted to bomb both military objectives opposite Quemoy and targets far inland. Moreover, they urged that American Air be committed if the Reds attacked either Quemoy or Formosa.

General Matthew Ridgway dissented vigorously. He rejected the theory of his colleagues on the Joint Chiefs that a conflict could be limited to the sea and air and, as an old ground soldier, he predicted that the action would spread to all-out war with Red China and, probably, World War III. Foster Dulles may have leaned toward the Radford-Carney-Twining recommendation, but he changed his mind when he asked them two questions, to which he received negative replies. They were whether Quemoy could be defended against an all-out assault, and whether Quemoy and the other offshore islands were essential to the defense of Formosa.

Foster Dulles therefore proposed a compromise. It was that American forces would intervene only if an attack on the offshore islands was clearly the prelude to an attack on Formosa. A full-scale discussion was waged at a meeting of the

National Security Council in Denver, where Eisenhower was vacationing, and Eisenhower went along with Dulles' plan. Furthermore, Eisenhower tried without success, several months later, to persuade Chiang to evacuate the offshore islands to eliminate a situation which might drag the United States into war. His message was entrusted to Radford and Assistant Secretary of State Walter Robertson, good friends of Chiang, but even their arguments failed. Furious, Chiang refused to abandon the islands. In 1958 the Communists shelled Quemoy and Matsu again, and once again Washington went into the frantic, scrambling exercises required to avert war.

The curious facet of this situation was that Chiang continued to retain and strengthen his forces on Quemoy and Matsu despite eventual and outspoken American opposition to it. In 1958, President Eisenhower told a press conference that "I believe, as a soldier, that was not a good thing to do, to have all those troops there." Assistant Secretary Robertson said only a "military moron" would consider the islands as bases from which to attack the mainland. Apparently, however, the feeling has been that since certain segments of the American government encouraged Chiang to build up his forces on the islands we could not insist that he evacuate them.

There has been the suggestion that the United States hesitated to interfere in the military organization of a sovereign power, such as the Formosa regime. "We can't *order* Chiang to evacuate Quemoy and Matsu," one official has said. But we *did* order him not to bomb the Chinese mainland and our Seventh Fleet *did* prevent him from attacking the mainland, and thus perhaps spreading the conflict during the Korean War. Moreover, since the United States is Chiang's sole financial support, he would seem to be in a poor position to defy us. But CIA did some of its homework on the matter, and in 1958 there were intelligence reports that the Chinese had made peace overtures to Formosa—and that Chiang had let it be bruited about in subtle whispers that he would have to consider these overtures if the United States insisted on the demilitarization of Quemoy and Matsu.

As a realistic, opportunistic warlord, Chiang is fully capable of this kind of tactic because his one aim in life is to preserve his regime, by any means. Even in relatively minor matters, Chiang and his hand-picked officials plot and maneuver against American interests which conflict with their own, and on at least one occasion such conniving led to open violence against Americans. This was the sacking of the United States Embassy in Taipei on May 24, 1957—an outrage which caught CIA with its cloak and dagger in the closet.

The mob violence was an example of how the Chiang regime creates pressures and incidents to serve its own means, in this case renegotiation of a status-of-forces agreement with its emphasis on legal jurisdictions. The instrument in this case was a dead man—a Chinese named Liu who had been shot to death by an American soldier when the latter allegedly caught Liu watching the soldier's wife in her bath.

During the court-martial, the GI testified that he killed Liu in self-defense after a struggle. Officials from the Chinese Department of Justice attending the trial filled the Chiang-subsidized newspapers with their charges that the trial was unfair, that there was no justice for a Chinese in an American military court. When the soldier was acquitted, the howls became louder. It became common knowledge—but apparently only among the Nationalists—that something was going to be done about it.

Several days later, Liu's widow showed up at the American Embassy carrying a sign protesting the injustice of the trial. The sign was printed in English, although Mrs. Liu neither wrote nor spoke the language. As Mrs. Liu marched up and down the street, Chinese began to drift into the neighborhood. Before long there were more than a thousand persons in the streets about the Embassy. When a representative of the official Chinese Broadcasting Service appeared, Mrs. Liu read a prepared speech into the microphone. Her recorded complaints, played back by the newscaster, infuriated the mob and, as if by signal, they broke into the Embassy and went to work. In less than an hour the Embassy was wrecked; staff members were threatened and several American flags were torn, spat upon and trampled.

Despite the organized nature of the demonstration, CIA had dug up not so much as a hint that it was scheduled. American officialdom was caught so flat-footed that the Ambassador had taken off for a vacation in Hong Kong. Yet the United Press International reported later that several Catholic priests had received mysterious telephone calls the day before the riot warning them to stay off the streets the next day and, if they had to go out, to shun the neighborhood of the American Embassy. Newsmen also reported that children in Taipei schools had been instructed on how they should march to the Embassy and what they should do there.

Moreover, there was the mystery of what had happened to Chiang's police and his soldiers. Formosa is a tight police state, and yet no attempt was made to disperse the mob. One answer probably was in the pictures taken of the mob by Chinese photographers—and later confiscated by the Chiang regime. These pictures showed that some of the leaders of the mob were plainclothesmen in the secret police bossed by Chiang's oldest son, Chiang Ching-kuo. It is perhaps notable that Chiang Ching-kuo lived in Moscow for a time and is married to a Russian wife; what is indisputably notable is that the mob obviously not only had official approval but official leadership.

In any case, CIA did a little better after the event. A Chinese operative who had been out of town returned to Taipei a few days after the riot and was put to work to find out the whys of the demonstration. His report was based on conversations with several officials of the Chinese Department of Justice. They told him that they had evidence before the trial that might have resulted in a different verdict, but they had withheld this evidence from American military authorities because Nationalist China was seeking concessions from the United States in the new status-of-forces agreement and it suited the Chiang regime's purpose to brand American courts as unfair. The riot had been staged to give the Americans a few second thoughts about those concessions.

Confronted with this example of Chiang's deviousness, the ordinary citizen cannot be blamed if he suffers the cold shivers whenever he considers the Nationalist leader's fetish for reconquering the Chinese mainland with its 700,000,000 regimented souls. Chiang certainly could not do that job alone; he would have to drag the United States in with him and he realizes this would take a bit of doing despite the help of the China Lobby. In maintaining a surveillance of his maneuverings in the international back alleys, it could only be hoped that CIA would be more successful than it was in finding out about the well-planned and well-rehearsed sacking of the American Embassy.

In the meantime, however, the conclusion was inescapable that for CIA things were tough all over in the Far East, complicated as they were by the loss of half of Indochina to Ho Chi-minh's Communists and by the incredible muddle that was Laos. In the field of selecting and supervising strong men, however, CIA's harrowing experiences in Formosa and in Laos fortunately were balanced by its competence, good judgment—and good luck—in the Congo.

15. *Weak Man, Strong Man*

ANTHONY EDEN is said to have remarked once that the United States was too young to play politics in the Far East. Most neutral diplomats are inclined to agree with the onetime glamour boy of British diplomacy, and they point to the little country of Laos as a good example of the sometime ineptness of American operations in this area of the world.

CIA, and the State Department, failed in Laos because they overwhelmed this tiny country by their expensive dealings with the wrong people. This is made all the more tragic by the fact that CIA had made a good start in what used to be a part of French Indochina.

In 1952, following negotiation of a truce in Korea, the Intelligence Advisory Committee predicted that Mao Tsetung's next move would be large-scale support of the Red Vietminh in Indochina. On a schedule almost precisely calculated by the Central Intelligence Agency, Chinese Communist troops, by infiltration and direct military action, started their drive to impose a Red regime on French Indochina. Eventually, when the Reds had all but overrun Vietnam, diplomatic talks in Berlin moved toward a meeting in Geneva for the negotiation of a peace settlement in Indochina. At the time, a valorous but foolhardy French general named Henri-Eugene Navarre grouped eighteen French Union battalions in the city of Dienbienphu without bothering to secure a route of withdrawal should the Communists attempt an encircling attack.

French intelligence insisted that the Communists would infiltrate the country surrounding the jungle fortress, rather than attempt to attack the stronghold in force. But CIA frantically warned that the Vietminh would launch a head-on assault on Dienbienphu. CIA's reasoning was logical, for it followed a pattern previously established by the Reds. In Korea, our experience had been that whenever the truce parley with the Communists reached a critical stage, the Communists would mount an offensive in an attempt to confront the Allies with a fresh Communist military victory that would strengthen the Reds' hand at the bargaining table. CIA predicted the same strategy in Indochina. It estimated that the attack on Dienbienphu would be timed with the fixing of the date in Berlin for the Indochinese peace talks in Geneva.

Unfortunately CIA's estimates were disregarded. The Communists took Dienbienphu and General Navarre lost his entire defense force—and the Reds showed up at Geneva's "poker game" with a full house.

Again, these operations in Indochina showed CIA at its best—in the pure intelligence field of gathering information. It is unfortunate that CIA did not similarly limit itself in the matter of Laos, whose pathetic plight became a black eye to American prestige all over the world. As usual, CIA's intentions were of the best; it was determined to freeze both Communists and Communist-leaning leftists out of the Laotian government. But this kind of operation is, in essence, diplomacy. And, since diplomacy is merely politics on an international scale, it remains the art of the possible. CIA and the State Department tried to do the impossible in Laos and the result was that the United States suffered another defeat in a country on which it had lavished military and economic aid at the rate of $300,000,000 a year.

Although the Laotians as a people and as a kingdom go back into the mists of antiquity, Laos did not become a nation in the modern world until 1955, when the Geneva conference split French Indochina into its so-called nationalist components. This agreement created a Communist North Vietnam and a democratic South Vietnam and decreed that landlocked Laos, with its one thousand miles of border along Red China, become a neutralist nation. Neither Communists nor the West wanted any such thing, but Laos' national personality recommended such a decision to the wishful thinkers.

Laos is a country of about two million people, about twice the size of Pennsylvania. It is more a collection of tribes than it is a nation, and the country is 99 per cent agricultural, with a primitive economy largely based on the barter system. It is a country without railroads and with few highways. Cambodia and Siam (now Thailand) ruled Laos from the Eleventh to almost the end of the Nineteenth Century, when the French took over. The French influence is still strong and Frenchmen continue to hold strong places in what passes for the economic community, but the educated Laotian has considerable bitterness toward his former rulers. Laos' ties with Thailand remain firm however. The American "strong man," Major General Phoumi Nosavan, is a first cousin of Marshal Sarit Thanarat, the Premier of Thailand, many of the people of Laos are Thais, and Thai is the country's principal language.

During the Indochina war, Laos got little mention in the world's headlines, but it was the target of periodic invasions by the Vietminh troops of Communist leader Ho Chi Minh. They made three military expeditions into the kingdom and once approached within a few miles of the royal capital of Luang Prabang, to the north of the official capital of Vientiane. During these so-called "raids," they buried depots of arms and recruited partisans, some of them Laos-born Vietnamese, some mountain tribesmen and some lowlanders. For the most part these recruits were unhappy about the graft and corruption in government.

For a time, in 1953, it appeared that the Vietminh planned an all-out drive against Laos. Then, with startling suddenness, the Vietminh turned back and retired into Red territory in North Vietnam, despite the fact they had marched through a third of Laos. The Communists had achieved their purpose. They had buried caches of arms for later use, and they had recruited cadres of loyal Reds on which to build their organization for a later drive on Laos. The organizational base the Reds took over was the Pathet Lao (Land of Laos), with a political arm, or party, named the Neo Hak Xat. Pathet Lao's leader, Prince Souphanou Vong, usually is referred to as the Red Prince, and there is little doubt he is a dedicated Communist although he is fond of denying it. Souphanou Vong was born into a collateral branch of the royal family, and his early inclination toward radicalism probably stemmed from the fact that his mother was a commoner, as was the mother of his half-brother, Prince Souvanna Phouma, the "neutralist" who has often played ball with the Kremlin, but who also has given the back of his hand to Souphanou Vong and the Pathet Lao.

By the time of the Geneva conference the Laotian insurgents under Souphanou Vong had become strong enough to obtain terms permitting them to "regroup" in the two northern provinces of Samneua and Phongsaly. The Pathet Lao was supposed to use this "regrouping" period to prepare for integration into the national community, but as in neighboring Vietnam and in Korea, Souphanou Vong's forces used it to consolidate their dominance of the provinces. From Red China they received supplies and technical aid, developed an administration and trained guerrillas and political cadres. They also continued to plant agents and bury caches of arms all over the rest of Laos.

Souvanna Phouma had become prime minister again when

the French returned briefly after World War II, and by 1957 he was trying to convert Laos into the image conceived by the Geneva conference. At this time, the Pathet Lao shifted from military to parliamentary maneuver. Souphanou Vong made a great show of returning the two nothern provinces to the royal government, and pretended to disband the Pathet Lao's six-thousand-man army. As a result, Souphanou Vong and another Communist were taken into Souvanna Phouma's new cabinet.

Ideologically Souvanna Phouma was a hard man to figure. By early 1958, he was saying that the Pathet Lao had never been and never would be a Communist organization. The Pathet Lao, he said, was simply "ultra nationalistic." Yet there was considerable friction between Souvanna Phouma and his brother, the Red Prince. Joining the cabinet, Souphanou Vong insisted that Laos accept Red Chinese as well as American aid, but Souvanna Phouma refused. He could do so because, whether his stand as a neutral was real or posed, Souvanna Phouma had enormous popular support in the country.

Nevertheless, the country and the royal government were in serious trouble, due largely to the sloppy and corrupt handling of American financial aid. Curiously, although the CIA distrusted Souvanna Phouma, it either did not hear or did not listen to reports that a ground swell of disgust was rising over the corruption of royal government officials. The trouble was that both CIA and State Department had little contact with anyone but the ultrareactionary ruling class, whose thievery and crooked politics were driving moderates into the Communist camp. They refused to do business with anyone, including Souvanna Phouma, except those they considered to be militantly anti-Communist. Souvanna Phouma presumably was no better than he should have been, but he was at least a Nehru-type fence walker and his relations with the Pathet Lao were cool and watchfully correct. Yet, because he had leftist tendencies—which he insisted on describing as a desire to institute social reforms—he was snubbed repeatedly by United States Ambassador J. Graham Parsons during Souvanna Phouma's in-and-out career in the Laotian government.

Practically none of the American aid went to help the Laotian people; on the contrary, the influx of these huge amounts of money all but wrecked the Laotian economy and the cost of living doubled between 1953 and 1958. The Laotian kip was selling on the black market for 100 to the dollar, but the legal rate was 35 to one, a fact that substantially increased the cost of American aid. In October, the kip was devalued from 35 to one to 80 to one, which eliminated some of the graft but embittered those who had waxed rich and fat without winning any appreciable number of friends among the less affluent.

Yet nobody on our side seemed to sense that anything was wrong. During the Laos elections in May, 1958, Ambassador Parsons told the House Committee on Government Operations he had reliable information that the elections would be virtually a landslide for our side. The information, of course, came from CIA, which had been listening in on cocktail-party conversation again. Anyway, Parsons said the Communist Pathet Lao would win only two of fifteen contested seats, with the result that "the integrity and independence of Laos in the free world" would be preserved. Unfortunately, the votes were still to be counted. When they were, it was found that the Communists had won a crushing victory. They took nine seats and the neutralist Santiphab, aligned with the Pathet Lao, won three. Henceforth, the royal cabinet would have Communists helping it to spend the American taxpayers' capitalist dollars.

Souvanna Phouma, whom CIA had always distrusted, seemed to have further misgivings about the followers of his Red Prince brother. He resigned as premier, with a blast at the

Pathet Lao. On July 23, he was asked by the king to form a new cabinet, but the Assembly refused to accept his slate. Finally, on August 19, one Phoui Saninikone was named to head a government which excluded all Reds. CIA's politicking may not have been working well, but its dollars were. Souphanou Vong and many of his followers were arrested and charged with treason, but the situation was tinged with typical comic-opera overtones. Periodically, the government promised to bring them to trial, but it dared not do so, and during this time Souphanou Vong "escaped" at least once. From "retirement," Souvanna Phouma announced that if the king would reappoint him as premier he would exclude the Pathet Lao from his cabinet. "I will try to keep them out of cabinet posts because I have doubts about their political views," he said.

CIA apparently had little faith in this new government. despite its anti-Communist quality. For one thing, it lacked a "strong man." For another, it had too many lines of communication to Souvanna Phouma. Our cloak-and-dagger operatives set the wheels turning for the installation of an administration more to their liking. In their maneuverings in drawing rooms and back alleys, they encountered some resistance from the new American Ambassador, Horace H. Smith. Ambassador Smith charged that his operation was being crossed by CIA men attached to his embassy who were attempting to make United States policy in Laos.

Keyes Beech wrote in the *Saturday Evening Post* about these CIA operatives. "One of the more flamboyant," Beech wrote, "affected a cover that included a manufactured British accent, a luxuriant mustache, elaborately casual but expensive clothes, and a cane with a secret compartment that held—not a sword—but brandy."

Smith favored a conservative coalition government for Laos which would offer a little something to all factions. But the CIA was backing a group of militarists, naturally known as the "Young Turks." CIA's candidate for "strong man" was the forty-one-year-old Minister of Defense, General Phoumi Nosavan, a fervent anti-Communist with little or no political following.

Shortly, General Phoumi Nosavan organized and took over the leadership of an outfit called the Committee for the Defense of National Interest. Among others, it included Premier Phoui Saninikone's Ministers of Foreign Affairs and Information. Quietly and bloodlessly, the Committee overthrew Phoui Saninikone's government on January 1, 1960—Saninikone characteristically heard the news of his ouster over the radio after his usual afternoon siesta. Phoui Saninikone was succeeded by another royal prince, Tiao Somsonith, forty-seven, a northerner who had been an able provincial governor. But he was largely controlled by Phoumi Nosavan and was a doctrinaire anti-Communist. It was a regime too rigid for the blood of Laos' many dissidents, although it filled CIA's bill.

However, on the night of August 9, 1960, Tiao Somsonith in turn was overthrown in a revolt staged by two battalions of American-trained paratroopers led by one Captain Kong Le. This was a stunning blow to CIA, which had believed Kong Le was safely in the American camp. Quietly, a delegation was sent to confer with Kong Le, but he was intractable to the point where, before CIA could catch its breath, he had called back Prince Souvanna Phouma to take over as premier. This was considered serious enough to bring to the scene a visitor from Washington—former Ambassador Parsons, who had been promoted to the post of Assistant Secretary of State for Far Eastern Affairs. Parsons tried to talk Souvanna Phouma into joining the American camp, but since he and the prince had had little to do with each other in the past, the meeting was futile.

Meanwhile, Kong Le insisted he was not pro-Communist and Souvanna Phouma said he was wrapping around him "the mantle of real neutrality." To maintain this façade, Souvanna Phouma went so far, in mid-October, as to place Kong Le under fifteen days' "technical arrest" when Kong Le staged a reception for the new Soviet Ambassador, Aleksander N. Abramov. At that time, Souvanna Phouma denounced what he called "Communist ambitions in Laos." But Kong Le's arrest was so purely "technical" that he continued to roam about the city of Vientiane—and the first shipment of Soviet military supplies reached Vientiane by air on the same day Kong Le was reprimanded. Several days later, the United States sent funds to pay the restive Royal Laotian Army, including Kong Le's rebellious paratroopers, who were the best of a poor lot. This was attended to despite the fact that, a couple of days before, the capricious Souvanna Phouma had reversed himself and announced he would be "very happy" to receive Soviet aid in response to a "very generous offer" from Ambassador Abramov.

General Phoumi Nosavan soon was heard from in the southern area of Savannakhet where—with American assistance—he was organizing forces to drive Kong Le from Vientiane. He moved his pro-Western troops swiftly up to Vientiane and as Phoumi Nosavan approached the capital, Kong Le declared himself sole boss of the city. On December 9, Souvanna Phouma's loyal troops attacked Kong Le's men and gave them a sound beating. Kong Le was sacked as garrison commander. But on the same day, after conferring with both Kong Le and General Phoumi Nosavan, Souvanna Phouma flew with his family and a collection of neutralist government ministers to exile in Cambodia. It took more than a week of bitter fighting before Phoumi Nosavan's troops finally drove the remnants of Kong Le's forces out of Vientiane, and during the struggle the American Embassy was shelled and burned and hundreds of innocent civilians were killed or wounded.

On December 13, 1960, the National Assembly—or at least

a quorum of it—met at Savannakhet and named Prince Boum Oun Na Champassak as Prime Minister. Boum Oun is a fat and jolly playboy with no real interest in/or knowledge of government; it did not matter much, however, because General Phoumi Nosavan remained as the real power in the government. Unfortunately, the government still did not have enough power to keep the Communists away from its doorstep. Almost immediately the Pathet Lao mounted a powerful offensive apparently designed to conquer the entire country. General Phoumi Nosavan, having established himself as the boss, with his family in all the lucrative government jobs, seemed suddenly listless and unwilling to give the government forces the dynamic leadership the situation required. By May, 1961, the Communists had roared through Phoumi Nosavan's defenses until they held more than one-third of Laos and were within fifty miles of both capitals.

What then had happened to the 25,000-man army for which the American taxpayer had been picking up the tab for more than five years? Acting on information from CIA, the State Department had made the decision to build up an anti-Communist Laos by means of this unwieldy force despite all sound military advice. The number of foreign troops the United States will support are supposed to be established on the basis of the judgment of the Joint Chiefs of Staff. But in Laos, the Joint Chiefs flatly stated that "mutual security support of Laotian forces could not be recommended from the military point of view." They had agreed to such support only when "political considerations" became "overriding."

Moreover, intelligence failed almost completely, even after its mistakes became glaringly evident, in appraising the kind of people the Laotians were. The Pentagon, in a most unperceptive approach, was allowed to send to Laos a whole arsenal of weapons that many of the tiny Laotians could hardly lift, let alone use effectively. Heavy mortars and heavy machine guns were poured into the country, and ponderous vehicles like tanks that were useless in the kind of jungle fighting at which the Communist guerrillas excel. On his return from Laos in May, 1961, Roving Ambassador Averell Harriman reported to President Kennedy that in many cases the Royal Laotian units fought bravely and with considerable competence. But they were handicapped because they had been taught only how to use their weapons—how to fire them—but not how to deploy various weapon units in combat. The training of both officers and non-coms was so inadequate that it undermined the ability of the lower levels in the army to carry out commands in difficult situations.

The military must take a large share of the blame for this, but the fact remains that the one vital factor that was lacking in our maneuverings in Laos was proper information on the Laotians as people. It was CIA's duty to know that certain weapons were unsuitable for raw Laotian troops and that the Laotians were too peaceful and unwarlike to be capable of sustained and bitter fighting without properly trained leadership. Add to this the CIA's fetish for getting rid of Souvanna Phouma, and the United States never had a chance in Laos, for whatever Souvanna Phouma's tendencies toward opportunism and his inclination to work for both sides of the international street, he was the only leader in Laos who might have held some semblance of a government together with a fair range of support. And eventually, in October, 1961, the United States was forced to go along with a 14-nation conference in Geneva which decided on Souvanna Phouma as the only possible "neutralist" premier. So all of CIA's frantic maneuverings went down the drain.

CIA's failure in Laos, as an intelligence agency entrusted with the responsibility of knowing a country, is in startling contrast with the way the Communists operated in welding together the steel-strong Pathet Lao organization. In the little rice-growing villages, Communist agents treated the peasants with respect, spoke their local dialects, gave first aid, and offered to do simple household chores like carrying water.

It is, of course, more comfortable to make the rounds of the Vientiane cocktail circuit, and more exciting to gather with sophisticated and freshly bathed Army officers to plan a military coup. But unfortunately, there are more peasants in Laos than there are martini experts, and people with empty bellies far outnumber those in braid-encrusted uniforms and Paris creations. A nation like the United States, which collectively bridles at the thought of any ruling class within its own borders, looks particularly foolish when its CIA agents stubbornly refuse to acknowledge these facts of life.

Backing a "strong man" in Laos failed because the man was indolent and had no support from the people, and because CIA was lacking in ideas for combatting the Communist menace. In contrast, CIA backing of a strong man in the newly-born Congo nation succeeded because its Congo choice not only had popular support but controlled the armed forces and knew how to deal with the Reds.

Only the Pollyannas among the world's international experts fail to see this turbulent new nation as a regularly recurring problem for years to come. In the politically hectic atmosphere of the Congo, no government is safe and Communist imperialism always will lurk on the fringes, ready to take over. But on a short-range basis the United States, as represented by the Central Intelligence Agency, made a good start in those wild months of 1960-61 toward the containment of the Communist menace. It did so because in contrast to Laos, CIA came up with the right man at the right time and thereby started to bring a measure of stability to the new state.

The man's name was Joseph Mobutu, a onetime stringer for Agence France Press in Leopoldville and a former sergeant in the Force Publique under the Belgians. It seems safe to say that Mobutu was "discovered" by CIA. At any rate, he was not among those who sat above the salt when Congolese politicians celebrated their nation's achievement of independence on June 30, 1960.

Amidst the riots and general blood-letting which preceded independence, the principal political tug of war had been between two native leaders—Patrice Lumumba, president of Mouvement National Congolaise, and Joseph Kasavubu, president of the Abako Party. Walter Ganshof van der Meersch, the Belgian resident minister, originally had turned to Kasavubu as the more stable of the two; Kasavubu was inclined to be stodgy, while Lumumba was a fire-eater. However, a few days before independence, the Belgians were forced to withdraw their bid to Kasavubu and to turn to Lumumba, who had won a show of strength in the newly elected but not yet installed National Assembly. Accordingly, Lumumba was designated Premier of the new government and Kasavubu became chief of state, or president. The general assumption was that Kasavubu's post would be largely ceremonial, with Lumumba running the show.

Lumumba found a tough show to run. There was dissension and bloodshed among the savage tribes, a low literacy rate throughout the country, a serious lack of trained native leaders. The nation's economy had come to a jarring halt and its government structure was stumbling toward paralysis due to the wholesale exodus of the Belgians. There were mutinies in the Force Publique, which had become the Congolese Army, against the Belgian officers and Belgium rushed troops to the Congo to protect its nationals. Moise Tshombe's rich Katanga Province seceded on July 11, 1960, and in August a part of Kasai Province, under the former Lumumbist, Albert Ka-lonji, followed suit.

To cope with this situation, Lumumba took two steps which eventually would lead to a showdown between Communist influences and the West. He declared a state of emergency and, in effect if not in name, imposed martial law. And he asked the United Nations for assistance in reorganizing the Congolese armed forces. The UN Security Council promptly called upon Belgium to withdraw all troops from the Congo and within a few weeks 16,000 UN troops were patrolling Lumumba's domain.

But Lumumba soon proved his instability, if not his Communist leanings. Returning from a visit to New York and Washington—where he picked up an American credit of $5,000,000 through the UN—he found the political situation deteriorating to the point where he feared the UN was conspiring against him. He launched a series of attacks on UN Secretary General Dag Hammarskjold and, on August 19, demanded withdrawal of all white UN troops. Lumumba was joined in this assault on the UN by the Soviet Union and the United Arab Republic and, nearer home, by Ghana's Red-oriented President Kwame Nkrumah and Guinea's Communist boss Seku Toure.

In this hectic atmosphere, punctuated by rioting and pitched battles between Congolese and UN troops, CIA got into the act. It did so in bland fashion—by letting it be rumored that if President Kasavubu was uncertain about his constitutional powers there were American "officials" who would be glad to offer him counsel. Kasavubu undoubtedly knew what his powers were, but it was plain he wanted assurances of support in strong quarters. Thereupon he sat at the feet of the CIA men, who reminded him that it was within his realm of responsibility to depose Lumumba and form a new government. Kasavubu went home and on September 5 announced that he was ousting Lumumba as Premier and naming as his successor Joseph Ileo, president of the Congolese Senate.

Lumumba's reaction was typically flamboyant. He jumped into his black limousine and, with two military police guards, dashed to Radio Congo where he broadcast a fiery speech challenging the legality of the ouster, asserting that he was still in power and announcing that Kasavubu was no longer chief of state. Then he went back to the premier's mansion.

It was obvious that the indolent Kasavubu was no match for Lumumba, but CIA had the man to take charge in Kasavubu's name. He was, of course, Joseph Mobutu, the newspaperman and former Army sergeant who had served Lumumba briefly as Secretary of State without portfolio. Mobutu left his Cabinet post to return to the Army as a colonel and chief of staff to General Victor Lundula. Now—on September 14—Mobutu emerged as the Congo's military strong man. With Kasavubu's willing acquiescence, Mobutu took charge, ousting General Lundula and assuming the role of commander in chief of the Congo state.

Meanwhile, Kasavubu went through the motions of preserving civil authority. On September 30, still operating within the framework of constitutional authority, he assigned "administrative and executive authority" to a High Commissioners Council. This was a group of students and university graduates created to govern as caretakers by the military ten days earlier. Justice Bomboko, Lumumba's former Foreign Minister who had broken with him over the Communist issue, was named head of the Council. The United States' position was given, with straight face, by Ambassador Clare Timberlake: "I have always been accredited to President Kasavubu and that has not changed. But now we will have someone at government level to deal with."

By this time Patrice Lumumba's role as a potential puppet for the Kremlin in the Congo became clear. The High Commissioners Council, with CIA help, got its hands on a series of letters from Lumumba in which he had asked both Moscow and Peiping for "volunteers," arms, aircraft and cash. It was the feeling among Western observers that Lumumba had been deceived by certain of his aides that he was acting not as

a Marxist but as an African nationalist; there was evidence
the letters had been dictated by his pro-Communist Vice
Premier Antoine Gizenga and his Information Minister
Anicet Kashamura, both of whom had learned Communist
theory behind the Iron Curtain.

Communist China had sent Lumumba one million pounds
sterling. The Soviet Union furnished transport planes, Soviet
Air Force crews and army officers. Scores of Soviet "technicians" poured into Leopoldville and tons of Communist
literature were distributed. To the delight of his American
sponsors, one of Mobutu's first acts upon assuming power was
to throw these Russian technicians out of the country and
confiscate their literature. As the Soviet refugees flew off to
Accra, where Ghana's President Nkrumah waited with hand
outstretched, the Western world had cause for jubilation.
The Soviet's initial attempt to create a chaos out of which
a Communist regime could be imposed on the Congo had
failed.

Lumumba, however, remained a thorn in the side of the
Mobutu regime. On October 10, he made another of his
spectacular sorties from the prime minister's mansion, where
he was guarded by Ghanan troops representing the UN.
Lumumba went from bar to bar in Leopoldville, making
emotional speeches and announcing that he was assuming
power again. After this expedition, he returned to the mansion to await the rallying of the people behind him. The
rally never materialized, but Mobutu and Kasavubu decided
it was time to deal with Lumumba. They demanded that the
UN turn him over to the Congo government for trial. The
UN, under pressure from anti-Western elements, refused to
do so, whereupon there was a brief shooting war between
Congolese forces under Mobutu and UN troops in which
Mobutu's second in command was killed. Eventually the
Congolese withdrew and Lumumba remained in the protec-
tive custody of Red-loving Nkrumah's Ghanan soldiers.

The American friends of Mobutu and Kasavubu were worried about Lumumba, too, but for other reasons besides his attempts to regain power. The Congolese had whipped themselves up to a frenzy of hatred toward Lumumba, whom the Kasavubu-Mobutu regime naturally was tarring heavily with the Communist brush. It was feared that if Lumumba was turned over to the Congo government for justice it might develop into a case of shoot first and hold the trial afterwards. Or, Lumumba might fall into the hands of a mob. In either case, the prospect was not a happy one since, as a Kremlin puppet, Lumumba was a candidate for phony martyrdom if things got out of hand.

This uneasy impasse was ended by Lumumba on November 20 when he slipped away from his Ghanan guards at the premier's mansion and headed for Stanleyville in Eastern Province where, reports said, Antoine Gizenga was setting up an organization to seize the province. Gizenga had headed the pro-Lumumba delegation to the UN a couple of weeks before, and when the Kasavubu slate was seated, Gizenga had flown back to the Congo in a Soviet plane. Gizenga had been arrested by Mobutu's men in September when Mobutu charged that Gizenga and his henchmen twice had tried to assassinate him, but Mobutu later released him. Now Mobutu naturally feared that Gizenga and Lumumba would set up an independent regime in Eastern Province, which was strongly pro-Lumumba. The Congo strong man ordered that Lumumba be recaptured before he reached Stanleyville.

A few days later, Lumumba was recaptured by Moise Tshombe's troops at Port Francqui in northwest Kasai Province. There were reports at the time that CIA had helped track him down, but there is nothing on the record to confirm this. If CIA had any hand in the recapture it was only to counsel Mobutu to continue to treat Lumumba with at least legal consideration to avoid international repercussions. But either the Congolese got out of hand or Mobutu and Kasavubu turned a deaf ear to this counsel. Whatever the case, when Lumumba was returned to Leopoldville in a Congolese Army plane flown by a Belgian pilot he was forced to go through a brutal gauntlet. As he was being taken from the airport by truck, a cursing crowd fell upon him and he was kicked, beaten and spat upon. The prisoner was taken to Thysville, a former Belgian Army post eighty-six miles from Leopoldville. Reports of his mistreatment continued. They reached the UN Security Council, where Hammarskjold's personal representative in the Congo, the Indian Rajeshvar Dayal, gave the word that Lumumba was being held under "conditions reported to be inhumane." Dayal, a protégé of India's Defense Minister Khrishna Menon, was known for his pro-Communist sympathies but he apparently had Prime Minister Nehru's ear. Nehru told the press that Lumumba's fingers had been eaten off his hands, a gruesome fable that was proved untrue.

On January 18, Lumumba was shifted to Elizabethville, Tshombe's headquarters, where he was lodged in a maximum security jail. With him were Maurice Mpolo, his onetime Youth Minister, and Joseph Okito, vice president of the National Senate. Once again the mobs at the airport got out of hand and beat up the prisoners, and were joined by some African police while the white police turned away. After a short period in the Elizabethville jail, the prisoners were shifted again, but the Katanga government refused to say where they were held for fear they would be liberated. It was disturbing to Western observers that the prisoners were guarded by Tshombe's Belgian mercenaries, who were being paid $1000 a month and up per man.

Obviously the situation had to be resolved one way or another, and the Katanga government resolved it in definitive fashion—by Lumumba's death. On February 11, Radio Katanga announced that the three prisoners had escaped from prison in a small town in the northern part of Katanga Province by tricking their guards. This was seen as the usual prelude for announcing the prisoners' deaths, and three days later the announcement was made. Katanga Interior Minister Godefroid Munongo refused to name the village where the deaths occurred but the village was given the $8000 reward promised by the Katanga Cabinet for the capture, dead or alive, of the three men.

As foreseen by CIA, the world's reaction was violent. President Kennedy said he was "shocked," and other Western leaders expressed their outrage. The Soviet Union and its satellites made the expected propaganda field day of the affair. In Cairo, the Belgian Embassy was sacked and burned and the Belgian Embassy in Moscow was vandalized. Lumumba had won the martyrdom the Reds devoutly had wished for him because the Congo government would not listen to the friends who had assisted in its assumption of power.

Brutal as it was, however, there was no denying that Lumumba's death had cleared the air and contributed to an atmosphere where steps could be taken toward the unifying of the Congo. Even before Lumumba's death, on February 10, Kasavubu had ended military rule and formally installed Ileo as Premier, and a conference was called of all Congolese leaders to patch up their differences. All attended but Gizenga, who had proclaimed a rival regime in Stanleyville as Lumumba's political and spiritual heir. A second session was held in May, 1961, at which Tshombe rattled the rafters with his outbursts. He accused Kasavubu of selling out to the UN, which he had fought so long. He particularly was outraged at Mobutu's action in personally escorting back to the important supply port city of Matadi a replacement group of UN officers after an earlier UN garrison had been massacred and Congolese rule installed. Nobody answered Tshombe's questions, but as he attempted to board his plane at the airport he and his advisers were arrested. Mobutu showed up at the airport and genially greeted Tshombe with a "What goes on here?" Tshombe glowered at him, then turned away. After several hours, the Katanga chieftain was taken away and tossed into jail and Kasavubu announced that Tshombe would be tried for "high treason," including complicity in the death of Lumumba and counterfeiting—Katanga had its own currency.

Tshombe remained in custody for two months, while CIA operatives stewed about the danger of creating another "martyr" and made subtle representations to the Kasavubu government in Tshombe's behalf. Here, CIA's man Mobutu stepped in again with characteristic decisiveness. With or without consultation with Kasavubu, Mobutu, in June, ordered Tshombe released—three days after secret negotiations between Kasavubu and Gizenga ended in agreement to reconvene the elected Congolese Parliament in an attempt to reconcile the various factions in a new government.

Mobutu and Tshombe had made a deal, of course, and Mobutu fared very well; Tshombe agreed to turn over his Katanga army of 11,000 men to the command of Mobutu. Word also was passed that Mobutu was worried about Kasavubu's deal with the Red-oriented Gizenga; he and Tshombe presumably had entered into an alliance to block the Kasavubu government's implementation of its agreement with Gizenga and to resist Kasavubu's pledge to co-operate with the UN. Both Tshombe and Mobutu had reasons to sabotage the UN by that time; the UN pact had led to the expulsion of many of Tshombe's mercenaries and foreign advisers, and it had set up a plan for getting Mobutu's army out of politics.

Late in July, as the Congolese Parliament reconvened under UN protection on the campus of Lovanium University, twelve miles from Leopoldville, Gizenga's followers unexpectedly won victories which for a time seemed to strengthen Gizenga's bid for the premiership of a national coalition government. Gizenga's men won the presidency of the Chamber of Deputies, two vice presidencies and four top secretariat posts. But Kasavubu kept the upper hand by giving the Premier job to a pro-Western, anti-Communist labor leader named Cyrille Adoula, and then getting the appointment approved by the Parliament.

The rebel Tshombe had come out for Congolese unity and he had endorsed in principle the reconvening of the Parliament when he was released from his Leopoldville cell, but little credence was given to his words. Sure enough, when he returned to Katanga, Tshombe renounced the statements he said he made under duress, but curiously stuck by his pledge to put his Katanga army under the command of Mobutu. A few weeks later, Tshombe signed a treaty to that effect.

This materially strengthened Mobutu's hand as Kasavubu's strong man operating chief, and there were those who warned of a possible military takeover. But Mobutu repeatedly declared he had no political ambitions and Western observers generally were inclined to take him at his word that he would act only under President Kasavubu's direction.

What did happen might have been expected in the tug-of-war struggle between Tshombe and the central Congolese government. Aroused by the danger to their investments, British and European mining interests stepped in behind the scenes in Katanga and encouraged Tshombe to resist UN efforts to bring Katanga back into the fold. The shameless and bloody period which followed was climaxed by the death of UN Secretary General Dag Hammarskjold in a suspicious plane crash, while a new wave of bitterness swept the Congo.

Yet, what UN Correspondent William R. Frye has called the "rescue operation" in the Congo had worked well enough, considering everything. It had worked because it had strengthened a Congolese central government which at the outset had been a mere collection of quarrelling and bloodthirsty political precinct captains. It had worked because most of these Congolese leaders had been nursed to the point where they had been convinced that it was to their interest to fight with words rather than bullets and knives. Gizenga's Soviet-oriented principality in Stanleyville had been liquidated and Gizenga himself was in the official fold as vice premier of the central government—a Gizenga still distrusted by the West but at least momentarily contained.

And, in the back rooms and the back streets of diplomatic negotiations and in the skillful maneuvering for power, CIA had played an important role in the patient's sometimes irritable but continuing recuperation from overindulgence in the excesses of freedom.

16. *The Hollow Nickel*

HUMORISTS AMONG the segment of lower-echelon officialdom concerned with the so-called "Intelligence Community" are fond of speculating on the relationship between CIA and J. Edgar Hoover's FBI. One of the gags is that after a CIA man and an FBI agent shake hands each quickly counts his fingers.

Thus far no fingers have been found to be missing, but it is a fact that over the years the CIA and FBI have not always regarded each other with the warmth of kissing cousins. On one side, CIA men will tell you that the FBI still resents the fact that the establishment of CIA put Hoover's men out of the international espionage business. On the other, FBI men harbor the feeling that they could do CIA's job much better, and at wholesale prices.

This FBI attitude certainly is understandable. In 1940, when America's involvement in World War II seemed quite probable if not inevitable, President Roosevelt was seriously concerned about the problem of gathering foreign intelligence; he felt that the normal operations of Army and Navy intelligence services needed help, in view of the Axis' stepped-up campaign in the fields of spying and sabotage. After numerous discussions, it was decided to assign to the FBI the responsibility for cloak-and-dagger operations in the Western Hemisphere, excluding Panama, which remained a military

230

area. The Army and Navy retained responsibility for intelligence throughout the rest of the world.

Originally, the FBI was directed to collect only "non-
military" intelligence, but after Pearl Harbor there seemed
no official inclination to hold J. Edgar Hoover's men to the
letter of the directive. The Army and Navy shortly were
complaining that the FBI was infringing on their territory,
and later when the OSS was organized there was almost constant intramural warfare between that glamorous unit and
the FBI. The White House kept trying to define the FBI's
role as the collector of primarily civilian intelligence, but
frankly Roosevelt did not give a hoot who collected information as long as it was collected.

Even its critics admit the FBI did a resounding job, even
if it was a trifle sensitive about acknowledging its blunders.
A "Special Intelligence Service" was organized and a parade
of FBI agents shortly were showing up in South American
and Caribbean countries disguised as soap peddlers, stock
brokers, steel salesmen and booksellers. Other agents took up
residence in United States embassies and joined local and national police forces as "liaison officers." From these points of
vantage, the SIS put the finger on thousands of Axis spies
and managed to get a lot of them arrested. They located some
twenty-five clandestine Axis radio stations, discovered and
aided in the seizure of all kinds of contraband and otherwise
earned their keep as one of the guardians of national security.

Hoover was ready after World War II with a proposal to
retain this international arm of the FBI. He suggested that
the SIS continue to operate, but around the globe, as a kind
of central intelligence organization. In deference to the military, he proposed that SIS would concern itself only with
civilian intelligence, leaving the military spying in the hands
of the armed forces. But most of the influential voices in government felt that this was giving the FBI too much to do. It
was believed that the glamour of overseas operations might

cause the FBI to neglect its domestic responsibilities. At any rate, the CIA was born, as the Central Intelligence Group, and the FBI was ordered to withdraw from foreign intelligence operations, which it did with considerable sulkiness.

Today, the FBI is largely an agency concerned with domestic counterintelligence in the investigation of espionage, sabotage, treason and other crimes against internal security; CIA officials are always hastily explaining that they never meddle in any case limited to the continental boundaries of the United States. Meanwhile, however, the FBI still maintains liaison agents abroad as contacts with other intelligence and security agencies in cases which have overseas angles but which are properly matters for prosecution in the United States.

The FBI, of course, also remains a member of the United States Intelligence Board, which is an interdepartmental body representing the ten U. S. agencies which have intelligence responsibilities—CIA, Army, Navy, Air Force, State Department, Atomic Energy Commission, FBI, National Security Agency, and representatives of the Secretary of Defense and the Joint Chiefs of Staff. As such, the FBI works as closely with the CIA as personalities permit. Sometimes the two agencies have difficulty preserving the amenities, because each is inclined to accuse the other of meddling in its business. But when CIA and FBI do co-operate all the way down the line, the results are often spectacular, as they were in the case of Colonel Rudolf Ivanovich Abel. The Abel case was largely the FBI's baby, but CIA deserves a large share of the credit for the exposure and apprehension of this master spy.

Colonel Rudolf Ivanovich Abel, a spy for the Soviet Union's KGB, or Soviet State Security Service, was sentenced on November 15, 1957, to thirty years in prison for plying his trade in the United States. It was the climax of a brilliant piece of investigative work by J. Edgar Hoover's FBI, and yet Abel might still be at large, poking about in the nation's secret places, if it had not been for a CIA counterintelligence agent named John.

For it was John, operating in the quiet side streets of Paris, who discovered and bagged another Soviet spy who had become fainthearted about returning from the United States to Moscow. And it was this second spy, his brain well picked, who put the finger on Abel for the FBI and thereby also solved the Mystery of the Hollow Nickel.

In the Abel case, the CIA did not come on stage until May, 1957, but the story had its beginning on a sultry summer evening in 1953. On that evening, a delivery boy for the now defunct *Brooklyn Eagle* knocked on the door of an apartment at 3403 Foster Avenue in Brooklyn. He was collecting for the paper. A woman answered the door, asked the boy to wait a minute, then returned with a dollar bill. But the boy did not have enough money to make change, so he said he would ask the people across the hall if they could break the dollar bill.

Two women in the second apartment pooled their coins and between them managed to change the dollar bill. The boy left the apartment building jingling several coins in his hand. He noticed that one of the coins—a nickel—had a peculiar ring. He rested the coin on a finger; it felt lighter than an ordinary nickel. Then he dropped the coin on the floor and it fell apart. Inside was a tiny photograph, apparently a picture of a series of numbers.

Two days later, during a discussion of another investigation, a detective of the New York City Police Department casually remarked to an FBI agent that a kid in his neighborhood was showing off a strange nickel he had picked up on his collection route. The FBI man asked the detective if he could lay his hands on the coin, and the next day the cop called on the newsboy and traded him a real nickel for the trick coin. In turn, the cop turned over the nickel to the FBI agent.

In the FBI's New York office there was little doubt that the nickel somehow was involved in espionage work. The face of the coin was a 1948 Jefferson nickel. In the letter R of the word TRUST in the inscription IN GOD WE TRUST there was a tiny hole—obviously drilled there so that a fine needle or other sharp instrument could be inserted to force the nickel open. The reverse side of the coin had been made from another nickel, one minted sometime during the period from 1942 to 1945. It was composed of a copper-silver alloy, since there had been a shortage of nickel during World War II. The microphotograph inside the nickel appeared to show nothing but ten columns of typewritten numbers, with five digits in each number and twenty-one numbers in most columns. In Washington the experts went to work but were unable to decipher the message. Additionally, the agents were unable to identify the kind of typewriter used to type the message, an indication that the machine was of foreign make, since the FBI laboratory has a reference file on American-made typewriters. Several former Communist intelligence agents who had defected were called on, but they were no help.

Meanwhile, in New York, agents called on the two women who had given the boy the nickel. They remembered the boy, but not the nickel, and a thorough check convinced the FBI that they had no suspicious contacts. Proprietors of novelty stores and magic shops could not recall having seen such a nickel before. There was nothing to do but to keep checking, and the FBI did so—for four long years.

Then on that fortunate May day in Paris in 1957 the CIA's John ran into an old friend, a Finn named Eugene Nicolai Maki. CIA is not saying how John met Maki, nor how he had reached the conclusion that Maki was unhappy. But even before their encounter in Paris, there were indications that Maki was a man who had something to say and was trying to find somebody important enough to say it to. Over an apéritif in St. Germain, John and Maki chatted casually for a time. Then, suddenly, Maki blurted it out.

"I'm in trouble, John," he said. "I need your help. I'm an officer in the Soviet intelligence service and I'm on my way back to Moscow from America. My wife is still in the United States, and I don't want to go back to the Soviet Union. Can you send me to somebody?"

John certainly could. After all, every American Embassy has a CIA agent under its roof and John knew the Paris man would take very good care of Maki. He phoned the embassy, then came back to the table. "Come on, Gene," he said. "We're going to see some people."

At the Embassy Maki told his story. His real name was Reino Hayhanen, and he was not a Finn but a Russian, born thirty-seven years before in the village of Kaskisaari, near Leningrad. He had been a spy in the United States for five years, while working in an auto-body shop. He did not want to return to Moscow; and he was worried about his Finnish wife who did not even know he was in Paris.

Two days later, Hayhanen arrived in New York by plane and was met by Allen Dulles, who flew up from Washington to interrogate personally this latest Soviet defector.

Hayhanen's story revealed again for CIA how thorough is the system by which the Soviet Union buys, steals or borrows secrets all over the world. Hayhanen had started his career as a high-school teacher. He had studied the Finnish language and had become fluent in it, and two months after his assignment to a school in the village of Lipitzi he was conscripted by the NKVD, the Soviet's internal secret police. By that time, in the fall of 1939, the Finnish-Soviet war was on, and Hayhanen was assigned as an interpreter to an NKVD group and sent to the combat zone to translate captured documents and to interrogate prisoners.

At the end of that particular war, in 1940, Hayhanen was assigned to check the loyalty and reliability of Soviet workers in Finland and to develop informants and sources of information. His principal chore was to identify anti-Soviet elements among the intelligentsia. By 1943 Hayhanen was recognized as an expert in Finnish intelligence matters, and in May of that year he was accepted into membership in the Communist Party. After World War II, he rose to become a district leader in the MGB, once again charged with seeking out dissident elements among local populations.

In the summer of 1948, Hayhanen was called to Moscow by the MGB. The Soviet intelligence service had a new assignment for him—one which would require him to sever relations with his family, study the English language, and receive special training in photographing documents and in encoding and decoding messages. Reino Hayhanen was to become Eugene Nicolai Maki, a native of Enaville, Idaho, who had accompanied his Finnish-born father and American-born mother to Estonia in the mid-Twenties, when he was eight years old. Hayhanen was not told what had become of the real Eugene Nicolai Maki, but since the Maki family had written a number of complaining letters back to America after reaching Estonia he had a pretty good idea.

For a year Hayhanen matriculated in the MGB university for spies. Then in the summer of 1949 he entered Finland as Eugene Nicolai Maki, an American-born laborer. He lived in Turku for four years to establish his identity. During that period he had no contact with his Soviet superiors, who wanted to be sure the new Maki attracted no attention. But he did take a wife, Hanna Kurikka, who knew him only as Eugene Maki, a pretty fair plumber and a good dancer.

In July, 1951, Hayhanen visited the United States Legation in Helsinki where he displayed a birth certificate from the State of Idaho which showed he was born in Enaville on May 30, 1919. He said he wanted a passport so he could return to the United States with his wife. He got the passport about a year later, and on October 21, 1952, he arrived in

New York aboard the *Queen Mary*. His wife joined him four months later.

Several weeks before he left for America, Hayhanen was recalled to Moscow and introduced to a Soviet agent, "Mikhail," who was to be his espionage superior in the United States. To establish contact with Mikhail in the U. S., Hayhanen was instructed to go to the Tavern on the Green in New York's Central Park immediately upon his arrival and to look for a signpost near the tavern marked "Horse Carts." He was to let Mikhail know of his arrival by placing a red thumbtack in the signpost. If he suspected he was under surveillance he was to place a white thumbtack on the post.

Hayhanen worked with Mikhail from the fall of 1952 until early in 1954, when Mikhail was replaced by a man known to Hayhanen only as "Mark." Hayhanen and Mikhail met only when necessary, always in the Prospect Park subway station in Brooklyn. To exchange messages and intelligence data, they used "dead drops"—inconspicuous hiding places—in the New York area. One of these drops was an iron picket fence at the end of Seventh Avenue near the Macombs Bridge. Another was the base of a lamppost in Fort Tryon Park, a third a hole in a set of cement steps in Prospect Park.

As a matter of routine, the FBI checked these drops. Nothing was found until they reached Prospect Park, where they discovered the hole in the steps had been filled in with cement. Under Hayhanen's directions they cut another hole in the steps and came upon a bolt about two inches long and a quarter of an inch in diameter, with a hollowed-out center. In the center the agents found a piece of paper with the following typewritten message:

"Nobody came to meeting either 8 or 9th as I was advised he should. Why: Should he be inside or outside? Is time wrong? Place seems right. Please check."

Hayhanen laughed wryly. He had hidden the bolt in the

hole two years before, but apparently the hole had been filled up before Mikhail could get to it.

To the FBI, this was the kind of thing they had been looking for since the newsboy came up with that hollow nickel four long years before. Did the Soviet apparatus often use such gimmicks? "Oh sure," Hayhanen replied, "hollow bolts, pens, pencils, screws, batteries, and coins." He took the agents with him to his home in Peekskill and showed them a 50 Markkaa coin from Finland, obviously made from two separate coins. There was a small hole in the first A of the word TASAVALTA so that the coin could be opened with a needle.

Communist spies who defect are seldom told anything by the CIA or FBI except the time of day, but the moment had come to show Hayhanen the hollow nickel from Brooklyn. Hayhanen had never seen the nickel, but he recognized it as the kind of gimmick his spy apparatus employed. Moreover, he believed he could decipher the microphotograph. He could, and did, producing the following series of messages:

1. We congratulate you on a safe arrival. We confirm the receipt of your letter to the address V repeat V and the reading of letter number 1.

2. For organization of cover, we gave instructions to transmit to you three thousand in local currency. Consult with us prior to investing it in any kind of business, advising the character of this business.

3. According to your request, we will transmit the formula for the preparation of soft film and news separately, together with mother's letter.

4. It is too early to send you the gammas. Encipher short letters, but the longer ones make with insertions. All the data about yourself, place of work, address, etc., must not be transmitted in one cipher message. Transmit insertions separately.

5. The package was delivered to your wife personally. Everything is all right with the family. We wish you success.

Greetings from the comrades. Number 1, 3rd of December.

Hayhanen confirmed that the message apparently had been dispatched to him shortly after his arrival in this country, since it mentioned that his wife was still in Finland. Also, his superiors still were waiting for information about his "cover" and where he was living. He had no idea how the nickel had found its way to a Brooklyn apartment house, and neither did the FBI. Apparently, one of Hayhanen's colleagues had either lost the coin or spent it by accident.

At any rate, the CIA's tame Soviet agent had cracked a Communist spy code for the United States. Now he went about helping the FBI to track down the man who was using it. Since Mikhail had dropped out of sight, the probability was that he was safe in the Soviet Union, but Hayhanen furnished a description just in case. Mikhail, he said, was between forty and fifty years old, of medium build, with a long, thin nose and dark hair, and about five feet nine inches tall. The description was matched against those of Soviet representatives who had been in the United States between 1952 and 1954, and the FBI came up with a photograph of Mikhail Nikolaevich Svirin, former First Secretary of the Soviet United Nations Delegation in New York. Hayhanen merely glanced at the photo; Svirin was Mikhail, all right. Unfortunately, Svirin had left the United States a year earlier, but Hayhanen's identification of him added another name to the black list.

The man named "Mark" was still at large, however, as far as anyone knew. Hayhanen had never known where Mark lived, but he identified him as a colonel in the Soviet State Security Service who had slipped across the Canadian border illegally in 1948 or 1949. Hayhanen had met Mark at various rendezvous and from time to time Mark had sent Hayhanen on out-of-town trips on errands. One of these, Hayhanen recalled, was to locate an American Army sergeant formerly assigned to the United States Embassy in Moscow, where he had been recruited for Soviet intelligence work. The sergeant was known to Hayhanen only as "Quebec."

Here, Hayhanen's familiarity with the hollowed-out coin gimmick again proved valuable. He checked a piece of hollow steel, while agents looked over his shoulder, and came up with a piece of microfilm less than one inch square. The microfilm bore a typewritten message which identified "Quebec" as Army Sergeant Roy Rhodes. The FBI told the Army what it knew, and in due time Rhodes was court-martialed and sentenced to five years at hard labor.

Hayhanen also furnished a description of Mark—about 50 years old, five feet ten inches tall, thin gray hair, medium build. He recalled that Mark was an accomplished photographer and had once taken him to a storage room where he kept photo supplies in a building near Clark and Fulton Streets in Brooklyn. Seeking this storage room, agents discovered a photographer named Emil R. Goldfus living at 252 Fulton Street.

The FBI was told that Goldfus was out of town, and so a detail of agents was assigned to 24-hour surveillance of the building to await his return. Three tedious weeks later, Goldfus returned and when he left the building to take a subway train uptown, he was photographed with a camera one of the agents had inside his coat. Again Hayhanen was positive: "That's Mark," he said. "You've found him."

Colonel Rudolf Ivanovich Abel, alias Mark, alias Emil R. Goldfus, was arrested by the Immigration and Naturalization Service on an alien warrant based on his illegal entry into the United States and failure to register as an alien. He refused to co-operate except to admit that he was, in fact, a Russian citizen named Abel. But the government needed no help from Rudolf Ivanovich Abel. At his trial, in October, 1957, a short stocky man with light brown hair named Reino Hayhanen supplied all the testimony necessary to send Abel to prison for thirty years. When the trial ended, the CIA reclaimed Reino Hayhanen and found him and his wife a pleasant apartment "somewhere in the United States." In CIA's coy language, Hayhanen is being "taken care of until he can be absorbed into the economy"—which means the CIA has been supporting Hayhanen, for services rendered.

Members of the Intelligence community need no more examples than that of the Abel case to make them realize that they cannot afford to indulge in interservice jealousies and resentments. The FBI did a magnificent job of finding and jailing Colonel Abel. It might have done so without the help of the CIA. But the fact is that with CIA's help, the FBI got the job done faster. Every day there are new examples of the interdependence of the nation's intelligence agencies.

For instance, there is the National Intelligence Survey. This is a definitive wrap-up of an intelligence problem involving all or most of the agencies in the Intelligence Community. Producing a National Intelligence Survey starts with the National Intelligence Survey Committee, a subcommittee within CIA. This committee sets down what needs to be known and how that information is to be organized. If it is a survey that seeks a general picture, say, of Poland, the job is a community chore. The Army's Transportation Corps compiles the section dealing with highways, the Signal Corps does the section on telephones. CIA furnishes data on priorities and production schedules, the FBI chips in with a memo on suspected Polish Communist agents in the United States, the State Department with political and cultural data.

Allowing for the usual element of human error, here is a system that works. It is a system that makes use of the information and capabilities of every agency within the government that has something to contribute. Its results are not always as spectacular as in the Abel case, but it does achieve its purpose of laying on the President's desk as comprehensive an intelligence report as can be obtained. With this in mind, intelligence rivals may continue to count their fingers after handshakes, so long as they continue to shake hands.

17. *Catastrophe in Cuba*

THE SECOND GUESSERS who ply their opinions so vigorously among Washington's neoclassic temples of government are always in agreement on one point: the April, 1961, landing at the Bay of Pigs, Cuba, was one of the most poorly planned and executed military adventures in history.

President Kennedy is prone to dismiss any discussion of a scapegoat with the curt suggestion that "There's enough blame to go around." After all, he did not get much of a performance either from the Pentagon or from his close White House advisors. Nevertheless, the Central Intelligence Agency remains first in line for censure, for a variety of reasons. Chief among these is CIA's apparently traditional unwillingness to do business with any but the forces of the far right.

Because CIA insisted in maintaining that an invasion by 1400 men could seriously threaten a regime with a military force of upwards to 400,000, perhaps nothing could have saved the day. But at least the adventure would have had a better chance if Allen Dulles and his aides had availed themselves of a moderately liberal organization that not only had the most popular appeal among Cubans but also controlled the highly effective anti-Castro underground. There are sound military reasons to believe that with full use of this underground a good part of the invading forces might have been able to fight its way to the Fscambray Mountains where it could have mounted guerrilla raids and perhaps confronted Fidel Castro with a full-scale civil war. CIA now maintains that actually the invasion was designed exclusively for this purpose—the establishment of a guerrilla force in Cuba—but there is no record that Dulles explained it in this fashion to the President beforehand.

When the invasion was all over, a State Department White Paper implied, at the very least, that the American government was aware of the magnitude of Fidel Castro's military build-up. It now seems incredible that the invasion should have been attempted in the face of the frightening facts set forth in that document:

". . . It is important to understand the magnitude of the [Red] takeover. Since the middle of 1960 more than 30,000 tons of arms with an estimated value of $50 million have poured into Cuba. In January, 1961, an eight-hour military parade in Havana displayed Soviet JS-2 51-ton tanks, Soviet SU-100 assault guns, Soviet T-34 35-ton tanks, Soviet 76-mm. field guns, Soviet 85-mm. field guns, Soviet 122-mm. field guns . . . Soviet and Czech military advisors and technicians have accompanied the flow of arms . . .

"Cuba has the largest ground forces, 250,000 to 400,000 militia, in [Latin America]—ten times as large as Batista's former military establishment. On the basis of the lower figure, one out of every thirty Cubans is today in the armed forces, as against one in fifty in the Soviet Union and one in sixty in the United States . . ."

To understand all the blunders and military-politico nuances which went into the manufacture of the Cuban fiasco it is necessary to go back to the late spring of 1960 when the Eisenhower Administration decided to take a hand in the liquidation of the Castro regime. It was plain by that time that Fidel Castro had sold out to the Communists. CIA reported that eighty Cuban flyers had been sent to Czechoslovakia to learn to pilot Russian jets. Russian and Czech tanks and other heavy armaments were arriving in Cuba regularly. Certain construction projects using great quantities of concrete were springing up in Cuba and the word was that they looked a great deal like missile-launching sites. Castro had to go, and CIA was given the assignment of sending him on his way.

The first step was to try to make sense, and an organization, out of the various warring factions organized by Cuban exiles to regain power in their homeland. Foremost among these were two organizations: the Movement for Revolutionary Recovery (MRR), a moderately right-wing outfit composed of former Castro supporters and military officers and Cuban business and professional men, and Manolo Antonio Ray's People's Revolutionary Movement (MRP). Ray, who had been Castro's Minister of Public Works, a reward for sabotage work in Havana during the Fulgencio Batista regime, was the boss of the resistance movement inside Cuba. He had built up this organization of saboteurs during a precarious eight-month stay in Cuba after he broke with Castro, and it was a model of its kind. The network spanned the entire island, with a seven-man executive council in each province and lesser commands reaching down to the smallest villages.

But to CIA, Manolo Ray was an anathema almost from the start. He had escaped from Cuba with a program to retain many elements of the Castro revolution but without Castro. He favored continuation of land reforms and, in some cases, nationalization of industry. No other course, Ray said, was realistic in a country which had flocked to Fidel Castro because he promised uprooting of the old system—a system under which 85 per cent of Cuba's small farmers were tenants and more than half of the arable land was owned by foreigners. Ray plumped for a "mixed economy" of private enterprise and government ownership of utilities and monopolies.

In Miami, where the exile leaders spent their days in long-winded plotting, Ray became the target of reactionary Cuban businessmen and politicians, including the notorious Rolando Masferrer, who had been Batista's chief executioner in Oriente Province. The word was passed that Ray was dangerous, that he was a pronounced leftist who would maintain a Communist economy in Cuba, eliminating only Castro. CIA men in the field listened closely to these attacks; they knew the high command believed it dangerous to play ball with anyone too far to the left.

CIA did manage to get the exile factions united in something called the Revolutionary Democratic Front, which included Ray's effective and, among the people of Cuba, highly popular MRP. This was most necessary, since the MRR's popular appeal was limited, and the other groups were infested with *Batistianos*—brutal former cops from the Batista regime—and a number of greedy hangers-on whose only aim was to recover their confiscated properties in Cuba. Several isolated farms in Florida were leased or purchased and used as a training ground for recruits who flocked to the Liberation Army. CIA helped finance this training program and so did various Cuban and American corporations with Cuban interests. In overall command was CIA's Richard M. Bissell, Dulles' top deputy, and a former Yale economics instructor.

It was imperative that the United States stay as much in the background as possible. Therefore, the U. S. government worked out a secret agreement with Guatemala's President Miguel Ydigoras Fuentes shortly after he broke relations with the Castro government by which Guatemala furnished training fields for the Liberation Army. The first thirty-two recruits to arrive in Guatemala went to work building a training base on lush, junglelike acreage donated by a wealthy Guatemalan named Robert Alejos. Soon airstrips were built and American pilots in mufti arrived to train the rebels' flyers. Practically everybody in Central America knew about this training base and, of course, so did Fidel Castro.

The time was nearing when CIA had to pick a leader of

the invasion force. Despite Manolo Ray's pleas, CIA already had refused his MRP the financial aid and weapons it was giving to other anti-Castro organizations. MRP was being used, but only as cannon fodder. CIA's choice as the invasion boss was twenty-nine-year-old Manuel Artime Buesa, a one-time Castro soldier who had served Fidel briefly as an official in an Agrarian Reform Zone in Oriente. His military experience was inconsequential, but he was an accomplished orator and his political philosophy was basically conservative, although he clothed it in revolutionary slogans. Of perhaps equal importance, he had become known as "Bender's boy," the reference being to Frank Bender, chief CIA field man in Guatemala and an old guerrilla hand with the French underground during World War II.

By January, 1961, Captain Artime was ready to take over. He had not yet been given the top command—that would not come until ten days before the invasion and the appointment would be made without consultation with Manolo Ray. But Bissell and Bender used him in a move to shake up the Liberation Army and weed out "incompetents." After a series of high-blown speeches to the Freedom Fighters, Artime arbitrarily changed a number of the commanders. The troops were shocked, but all of the some 1500 went along with the persuasive Artime except for about 200 who refused to fight under their new commander, Captain Robert San Roman, because he had served as an officer under Batista.

The stubborn 200 were arrested and isolated from the rest of the troops, under guard. A few escaped, and some others were persuaded to rejoin their command. But there remained a hard core who refused to capitulate. Bender ordered them into his presence and told them their former commanding officer had been relieved of command for playing politics. Another CIA agent named "Bernie" accused the recalcitrants of being Communists. Still the troops remained obdurate, until Bernie agreed to receive a petition from them for submission to the Democratic Revolutionary Front. Then they agreed to resume training for five days while waiting for an answer.

When seven days passed and no word came from the Front, the troops went on strike again. CIA got tough. The soldiers were told they were mutineers and would be shot if they persisted in their tactics. Most of the soldiers then fell in line, except for a hard-nosed twenty. Eight of the men were imprisoned in a shed 15 by 30 feet, with a galvanized iron roof and a concrete floor, where they were confined for twelve days without being permitted to bathe or shave. When they were released, they and nine others were flown to a jungle prison in northern Guatemala, where they were kept for eleven weeks, or until the failure of the invasion. Then CIA let them out and flew them back to Miami, although the plan had been to turn the prisoners over to the new Cuban government for trial as mutineers had the invasion succeeded.

Although CIA's arrests of the dissident rebels undoubtedly were highhanded, they perhaps could be excused on the grounds that the soldiers technically were members of an army which was fighting a war and had no right to argue about anything. But there was no excuse for other stupid and careless errors committed by America's spy agency in the course of the Cuban adventure, many of them attributable to the fact that CIA permitted itself to be misled by right-wing Cubans with axes to grind.

Just before Dr. Jose Miro Cardona was named chairman of the Joint Cuban Revolutionary Council, for instance, CIA submitted to the Council a list of thirty-eight names of Cubans for the post. The list contained the names of twelve former Batista supporters. While preparations were going forward for the invasion, a group of several Cuban military leaders, all with experience in guerrilla warfare and all former captains in Castro's Army, were left languishing in their hotel rooms and took no part in the invasion. CIA also stopped its propaganda broadcasts to the Cuban people from Swan Island in the Caribbean fifteen days before the landing.

President Kennedy had issued an order excluding *Batistianos* from the Liberation Army, and in the last days of the preparation for the landing he ordered the Immigration and Naturalization Service to arrest Masferrer. But unknown to the President, CIA refused to put into effect Kennedy's *Batistiano* ban. Other former Batista officers, including the San Roman brothers, were given important commands because, as CIA explained it, they were experienced military men and, more important, *proven* anti-Communists. Manolo Ray demanded that the *Batistianos* be weeded out but although a representative of the Front signed a pact with Ray, accepting the latter's conditions, nothing was ever done about it. Meanwhile, Ray ordered his followers to report to the Guatemalan training camps, but they never got there. In Miami, 120 of them were detained by Front and CIA agents, along with some officers who had escaped from a Cuban prison in December, 1960.

Kennedy apparently was never informed of CIA's political maneuverings. All he was told was that the invasion looked like a fine idea and that the exile army was raring to go. Dulles and Bissell did not suggest that the Castro regime would topple the moment Artime's men hit the beach, but they did predict that there would be enough uprisings around the country so that the beachhead could be held and consolidated and so that the rebels could establish a government on Cuban soil which the United States then could recognize and support.

If the President had gone further afield for advice, he would have heard a different story. After a visit to Castro's Cuba in December, 1960, Senator-elect Claiborne Pell, Democrat of Rhode Island, suggested that the Cuban people were not so anxious to revolt as Dulles claimed. Pell, a former Foreign Service officer in World War II, reported in the *New*

York Herald Tribune that "The people of Cuba that I saw
and spoke to were not sullen or unhappy or dissatisfied."
About the same time, two other expert observers offered similar findings. They were General Hugh B. Hester (Retired),
a veteran of the Southwest Pacific campaign in World War II,
and Jesse Gordon, a public relations consultant. In "A New
Look at Cuba—The Challenge to Kennedy" for the *New
World Review,* Hester and Gordon wrote that 86 per cent of
the Cuban people supported Castro and that "if elections
were held tomorrow, Castro would be overwhelmingly returned to power." They added that if "the U. S. military high
command" went ahead with its plan to invade Cuba, "we fear
disaster will result."

But Dulles was almost overwhelmed with optimistic reports from this same Cuba. Almost every one of his operatives
inside Castro's dictatorship assured him that the Cuban people would rebel and support an invasion. CIA's plans were
reviewed by the Joint Chiefs of Staff, particularly General
Lyman Lemnitzer, Chairman of the Joint Chiefs, and Admiral Arleigh Burke, Chief of Naval Operations, and both of
these august military personages strongly endorsed them. They
did so on two conditions—that CIA was correct in its appraisal
of the political situation, and that the rebels would control
the air over the beachhead.

Kennedy could not be blamed if he felt he had to go along
with the decision. Some of his aides have said that he never
liked the looks of the operation because it smacked too much
of imperialistic intervention. But his experts recommended
it, and time was of the essence. The Guatemalan government
was threatening to throw the Freedom Fighters out of its
country. Soviet jet fighters were arriving in Cuba, and the
Czech-trained Cuban pilots were due back to fly the jets.
Moreover, the rebel army was growing restive; the troops
wanted to fight. Added to all this were the facts that the invasion plan had been initiated by a general named Eisenhower

and that the landing would liquidate a Communist regime only ninety miles off the American coast. The pressure on the youthful new President must have been tremendous.

Secretary of State Dean Rusk and McGeorge Bundy, Special Assistant to the President for National Security Affairs, had their doubts about the operation and so did Under Secretary of State Chester Bowles and White House Aide Arthur Schlesinger, Jr. But except for Bowles, who penned a strong memorandum to Rusk, none of them argued with any real vigor against the operation. At one tense meeting, Senator J. William Fulbright of Arkansas, Chairman of the Senate Foreign Relations Committee, denounced the operation with considerable eloquence as not only immoral but as the kind of thing the United States always did poorly. Fulbright's argument impressed Kennedy, and later influenced him to make two important changes in the plan which, to say the least, considerably weakened the effort.

As envisaged by Eisenhower, every effort was to have been made to avoid overt American intervention, except on a "contingency basis." That is, American planes would intervene if necessary to maintain control over the beachhead and prevent the destruction of the invaders. Kennedy did not like this idea at all; instead he proposed and had adopted a plan for air strikes against the Castro Air Force by Cuban pilots flying from Guatemalan bases. The sorties were to be advertised as the contributions of defectors from the Cuban Air Force. Then Kennedy ruled that *under no circumstances whatever* were American forces to become involved, and dispatched Schlesinger and his Latin American expert, Adolf Berle, to New York to so inform the Cuban leaders.

The Joint Chiefs advised Kennedy that without American air support the rebels might not be able to hold the beachhead. But in that case, they said, the invaders could make their way to the Escambray Mountains, fifty miles away, and form guerrilla bands to harass the Castro regime. Fifty miles is a far piece for defeated soldiers to travel, especially when hotly pursued. But this might have been possible had CIA not snubbed Manolo Ray's underground. For, although Dulles, Bissell and Company relented in the last two weeks and sent supplies of explosives to the resistance movement, neither Ray nor any other leader of the underground was told the exact date of the invasion. Consequently, the resistance movement was as surprised as Castro when the rebels hit the beach —possibly more so.

It would seem, too, that Allen Dulles and Richard Bissell might have been taken aback by the abandonment of the plan to offer American air support. Presumably, their optimistic predictions of uprisings by the Cuban people had been based in part on the people's probable reaction to a spectacular air show. But there is no record that they offered Kennedy a revision of their estimates. Surely both CIA and the Joint Chiefs had violated a cardinal principle of military planning, *i.e.*, that whenever a major change is made in the plans for a military operation that operation should be thoroughly reexamined to make sure it has not been materially weakened by the change.

Kennedy, on the other hand, seemed determined to weaken the plan even further. Five days before the invasion took place, he declared flatly at a press conference that the United States would never intervene with force in Cuba. It was good propaganda for world consumption, of course, but it did nothing to encourage the uprisings Dulles was predicting and must have caused that harassed gentleman considerable anguish. Second, Kennedy decided to call off the second air strike against the Castro Air Force, which was scheduled for just before the landing.

The President's reason for this might be called international embarrassment, complicated by Adlai Stevenson's congenital piety. The first air strike, in planes on which CIA had painted Cuban Air Force markings, and which were flown by Cubans, had taken place on April 15, two days before the invasion. Word from CIA was that there was every reason to believe the strike had crippled Castro's air power. Perhaps that is why Kennedy felt he could cancel the second one and thus offer some solace to Stevenson. Stevenson, of course, had been furious about the first air strike because he had not been told that the United States was involved and he had delivered an impassioned defense of his country at the United Nations, where the Cubans were charging American intervention. When Stevenson learned that the story about the strike being the work of Cuban Air Force defectors was a lie and that the American Ambassador to the UN had had his credibility impaired before the world, he hit the roof. He demanded of Kennedy that there be no more air strikes, and Rusk supported him. Thereupon, Kennedy canceled the second strike.

By this time, it was too late for any re-examination of the operation because the invading force was already at sea. Dulles since has claimed that the swampy coast of Cienaga de Zapata in the Bay of Pigs was an ideal landing place, since it had three airstrips and was difficult to approach because it had only three bad roads. CIA must have been confident, because there were no plans to blow any bridges or destroy a single railroad line to further hamper the movements of Castro's forces. This, of course, is the sort of chore the underground could have handled—if it had been informed of the date and place of the landing.

Manolo Ray's military leader, Colonel Ramon Barquin, had protested in vain the choice of the landing place. Barquin, an Army officer who had been imprisoned by Batista, was one of the most highly regarded military men among the exiles, and he knew Cuba as he knew his right hand. He pointed out that all three narrow roads leading inland from the Bay of Pigs were easily defended, and so was the railroad bed. He admitted the swamp offered the advantage that the invading force could not be flanked, but pointed out that

Castro would not have to bother with such maneuvers; all he had to do was concentrate his troops at the point where the roads entered the Central Cuban plain and destroy the rebels at will.

But by the time the troops took to their invasion ships, CIA was listening to nobody—and making sure that even the Cuban exile leaders would have nothing to do with the operation. On April 16, the day before the invasion, Dr. Jose Miro Cardona, president of the Revolutionary Council, and his colleagues received word in New York that they were to proceed to Philadelphia. There they were met and flown to Miami, where they were taken into custody and confined to a house on the outskirts of the city. No one was permitted to use a telephone or to communicate with anyone for any reason, and the only radio broadcasts they were permitted to hear were the reports on the progress of the landing.

Beginning at midnight, April 16, five Liberty ships chartered by dummy operators for CIA disgorged the invaders in the Bay of Pigs. When dawn came, some C-54 and C-46 transport planes from Guatemala and Nicaragua flew over the beachhead and dropped paratroopers. The air cover was provided by eight old B-26 bombers and a few obsolete P-51 Mustang fighter planes. Without opposition to speak of, units of the invaders marched forward, penetrating twenty miles inland. But this column was halted by a battalion of Castro militia and then forced to surrender by the arrival of heavy reinforcements.

CIA had informed the President that the Cuban Air Force had been rendered ineffective. The information was not quite accurate. Three American T-33 jet trainers, originally shipped to the Batista regime, suddenly appeared over the beachhead and went into action. The slow and awkward B-26's did not have a chance and were shot down like so many one-winged ducks. By noon of invasion day, the Castro planes had sunk the Liberty ship loaded with ammunition and a second one carrying all the communications equipment. Soviet tanks and heavy guns carried on trucks were transported over the roads which the underground had not been ordered to cut and wheeled into action to complete the debacle.

If Kennedy were to change his mind and permit American intervention, the time had come for action. On the night of Tuesday April 18, the President was called from a formal dinner and joined a White House meeting whose conferees included Dulles, Bissell, Bundy and White House Aide Walt Rostow. The men stayed up all night, trying to decide whether American forces should be sent to Cuba, but reached no conclusion. Next morning a similar meeting was held, and Kennedy decided to do nothing, largely because it was too late.

CIA, however, was still doing something. It was busy explaining, through a New York public relations firm hired by the Cuban exiles, that it was not really an invasion but merely a raid by a small force of two or three hundred men. The object, reporters were told, was to make contact with rebel forces in Cuba. Shortly Fidel Castro ruined that story by showing approximately 1200 captives on television, and telling the world from the mouths of the captives themselves that they had been duped by the Central Intelligence Agency of the United States.

Meanwhile, Castro was rounding up "subversives" in a nation-wide hunt designed to break up the underground forever. Estimates of those arrested rose as high as 100,000 men, women and children; it seems reasonable to assume that at least 50,000 were apprehended. In Miami, Manolo Ray took his MRP out of the Cuban Revolutionary Council in protest against what he called CIA's continued domination of the Cuban resistance movement, its meddling in Cuban politics and its continued romance with former Batista supporters. And Dr. Rodolfo Nodal Tarafa, a twenty-seven-year-old lawyer who had been one of the seventeen "mutineers" held for eleven weeks in a Guatemalan prison by CIA, organized a new Cuban movement known as the 17th of April organization.

"It's named after the invasion your CIA made us miss," said Dr. Nodal.

18. *AND NOW?*

ONCE THE IMMEDIATE EXCITEMENT over the Cuban invasion disaster had died down and the charges and countercharges had been hurled, most of the tougher-minded members of President Kennedy's inner circle began cautiously to suggest that, on a long-range basis, the Bay of Pigs humiliation would turn out to be a good thing. Their thought was that the Cuban adventure had emphasized the vital necessity for taking a hard look at CIA's operations and their relation to foreign policy.

Almost immediately that hard look was translated into action. Only a few weeks after the Bay of Pigs, the President took the first step to restore to the State Department *all* responsibility for the making and supervising of foreign policy. He wrote personal letters to all United States Ambassadors reminding them that theirs was the last word in their respective posts—that they were the chief and responsible American representatives doing business (either legitimate or otherwise) in their jurisdictions. Shortly Secretary of State Dean Rusk was telling the Foreign Service Institute that "We expect our ambassadors abroad to take charge of the relations of the United States with the country in which they are posted, and if necessary to take charge of all the officials who are there working with them."

Although brought on by the Cuban fiasco, this action was

257

largely aimed at the future avoidance of manipulations in-
dulged in by CIA in such countries as Laos and Iran. In those
countries, as in others, CIA either made policy or *gave the
impression* its activities were identical with policy. Too often
its operations were kept a secret from the ambassador who
supposedly was implementing that policy.

The official concern, then, was not so much that CIA had
bungled in the past, but that it either had been entrusted
with or had seized the broad responsibility for making policy
which belonged to the State Department. There were various
reasons for this, chief among them the fact that too few Foreign Service officers were prepared after World War II to
take over the vigorous leadership of foreign policy in a
changed world. CIA moved into this vacuum because it had
resources (up to $1 billion a year as compared with State's
1961 requested budget of less than $250 million), because the
Eisenhower Administration seemed to want it that way, and
because Allen Dulles was never a man to pass up a chance to
wear another hat.

Columnist Joseph Alsop summed up the case for CIA by
citing the Eisenhower Administration's insistence that the
agency take on so many chores. "It must be borne in mind
that a grossly excessive burden has been placed on CIA for a
very long time," Alsop wrote. "The CIA's operational branch
has in effect been used as a kind of general fire brigade, to
remedy all the results of a quite inadequate foreign policy
marked by grave failures of foresight. The CIA's intelligence
branch has been called upon to produce, not reasonable intelligence estimates in the normal sense of the phrase, but
micrometric measurements of Soviet progress which were
then used to justify dangerous economies in defense invest-
ment. These pernicious practices began under President Eisenhower and were continued by the new Administration."

Yet, Allen Dulles could not escape a large part of the
blame. Here was a man who loved his work, a man of monu-

mental dedication whose devotion to duty had a dangerous
blind spot: He hated to delegate responsibility and he could
not resist getting involved in matters that were none of CIA's
affair. As early as 1955, a Hoover Commission task force
headed by General Mark Clark reported that Dulles had
taken on too many burdensome duties and responsibilities,
but Dulles paid the report no heed. His friends have stated
that far from being burdened by his chores, Dulles was looking for more work, more challenges. Dulles enjoyed enough
status with President Eisenhower so that he should have declined unsuitable jobs assigned to CIA and himself. He could
have pointed out with absolute validity that mixing CIA in
certain matters violated the spirit of the statute which established CIA. But he did not; perhaps he was having too much
fun. Moreover, during most of Eisenhower's tenure, his Secretary of State was John Foster Dulles, and John Foster relied
much more heavily on brother Allen's estimates than he did
on the reports from his ambassadors. In effect, Brother John
Foster made of Brother Allen's CIA a kind of super Foreign
Service and apparently found nothing incongruous in the
fact that in some embassies CIA personnel outnumbered Foreign Service employees. It was small wonder that the average
citizen was confused, after Cuba, as to who was making foreign policy for the United States. Some top-drawer members
of the Washington diplomatic community were just as confused—because the White House and State Department have
always been so inextricably bound up with the information,
estimates and sharply drawn inferences of the Central Intelligence Agency.

Foreign policy in a large measure must be based on intelligence about other countries, including the friendly ones. But
the world has grown so complicated, and so many new bur-
dens have been placed on the Chief Executive that he no
longer has the time nor the resources to do his own evaluating of this intelligence. He has had to rely on CIA's own

estimate of the quality of its intelligence—and, since CIA officials are human, they are seldom inclined to downgrade the product of their labors. In Foggy Bottom, somebody is always complaining that CIA is not content merely to submit its intelligence, but must go the governmental rounds "selling its product."

Yet over the years there has been no other system for displaying these intelligence wares. The then Secretary of Defence, Charles E. Wilson, explained in a press conference in 1957 that he had no choice: "You see, what I get for my purpose is an agreed-on intelligence estimate . . . I have to take that, or I would have to bore through an enormous amount of detail myself to try to say that they were wrong or right . . . I accept what they say, and I can't go back of that from my time available."

Sometimes these estimates seem to play it safe by painting a darker picture than exists; sometimes they gravely underestimate the Cold War enemy's capacities and progress. Admiral Arthur W. Radford, former Chairman of the Joint Chiefs of Staff, always insisted that CIA normally overestimated Communist capabilities "in almost every respect . . . there has been an almost hysterical assumption of great capabilities on the part of the Communists, some of which, in my opinion, do not exist."

But the other side of the coin is illustrated by testimony before a Senate committee in 1956 by Lyle S. Garlock, Assistant Secretary of the Air Force. "Why are we so far behind?" demanded Senator Allen Ellender, Democrat of Louisiana. "There was too much of a letdown in the postwar period," replied Garlock.

"Do you charge that to faulty intelligence?" asked Ellender.

"I would say inadequate intelligence," replied Garlock. "It is fairly obvious that the [Soviet] development [in air force research and development] was faster than we anticipated."

AND NOW? 261

And in the same year Allen Dulles was constrained to compare Soviet missile progress with that of the United States during a television interview with Representative Harold C. Ostertag, Republican of New York. "I have no evidence that they are ahead of us," said Dulles.

Meanwhile, another post-Cuba development was a resolution introduced by Senator Eugene McCarthy, Democrat, of Minnesota, reviving earlier proposals for some kind of a Congressional watchdog over CIA. This would replace or augment the setup in operation since shortly after CIA's birth by which CIA regularly reports to four subcommittees of the Congress, made up of seventeen senior members of the House and Senate Armed Services and Appropriation Committees. McCarthy's proposal recalled the 1956 debate in the Senate over CIA's foreign-policy involvements when a similar resolution was introduced by Senator Mike Mansfield of Montana, who later would succeed Vice President Lyndon B. Johnson as Democratic Majority Leader.

During the debate, it was Mansfield's argument and that of other supporters of the resolution that CIA either was making policy or persuading foreign governments to believe that it was. The amiable Senator Leverett Saltonstall, Republican of Massachusetts, kept insisting that "CIA is not a policy-making body but that the policy-making body is the State Department," but his protestations seemed naïve even in that relatively less CIA-conscious day.

Mansfield's resolution ultimately was defeated by a 59 to 27 vote, but some of the points made by its proponents echoed with astringent validity during the Cuban debates. For instance, Oregon's Senator Wayne Morse, the Republican turned Democrat, noted acidly that "when we argue that CIA is not a policy-making body because under the administrative set-up it is not charged with making policy, it does not follow that it does not make policy . . . We should find out to what extent in fact—not in theory, but in fact—CIA is making policy . . . My suspicion is that it determines a great deal of policy. I happen to believe that we have the duty of finding out whether my suspicion . . . is warranted or not." Morse noted that CIA gathered information and made studies and, "On the basis of such studies and investigations and what it discloses to the executive arm of the Government, *and what it does not disclose,* someone in the Government must then make a determination."

In the custom of Senate debate, Morse had this question to ask of Mansfield: "Does the Senator agree with me that since CIA functions in any country in any part of the world where it may operate with the secrecy that surrounds it, so far as its relationship to the Congress is concerned, it is bound to *create the impression* upon the leaders of the foreign countries . . . that its activities represent the official foreign policy of the United States?"

Mansfield courteously, and predictably, replied: "I will say to the Senator from Oregon that that is a fairly sound assumption. The officials of CIA could be considered as agents of American foreign policy, and perhaps they are so considered in some countries."

Mansfield's argument was that the arrangement whereby CIA conferred from time to time with members of the House and Senate committees was at best a voluntary one, which resulted only in an extremely loose relationship between CIA and the Congress. He demanded a "black and white" arrangement, a provision that would give mandatory jurisdictional power to the Congress in its relations with CIA. To bolster his argument, he noted that during a recent twelve-month period, CIA representatives had met only twice with the Senate Armed Services subcommittee and only once with the Senate Appropriations subcommittee. That, said Mansfield, was not often enough.

Mansfield's premise that CIA should submit to frequent inspections by the Congress had been made the year before, in the Hoover Commission report of 1955, which was concerned lest a lack of proper Congressional surveillance lead to "the growth of license and abuses of power." The Hoover Commission also insisted that only by closer Congressional supervision could the public be assured of the "essential and trustworthy accomplishments of our Intelligence forces." This, said the Commission, logically would lead to "public support and participation in the Intelligence effort." Or, as one Commission member put it, "We'd like CIA to have the kind of public esteem enjoyed by the FBI."

CIA's public image always bothered Allen Dulles, and it was under him that tidbits of CIA's successful operations were leaked to friendly reporters for such journals as the *New York Times* and the *Christian Science Monitor*. "I am the head of the silent service and cannot advertise my wares," Dulles commented. "Sometimes, I admit, this is a bit irksome. Often we know a bit more about what is going on in the world than we are credited with, and we realize a little advertisement might improve our public relations. For major reasons of policy, however, public relations must be sacrificed to the security of our operations."

That was all very well, replied Mike Mansfield, but his chief concern was whether CIA was doing as good a job as it should—whether the quality of the intelligence produce compared favorably with, say, that of Great Britain's M-I 5. Closer Congressional surveillance, said Mansfield, would "compel even swifter and surer reform than could an executive committee."

The Mansfield resolution had considerable support around the country. The Scripps-Howard newspapers endorsed it and so did the *Wall Street Journal;* the *Journal* noted among its reasons for support one that would be heard often during the summer of 1961. It was that, while "Mr. Dulles may make no mistakes in assessing intelligence . . . he should not be the lone judge in matters that have to do with the intentions of other nations for war or peace." Hanson Baldwin, military expert for the *New York Times,* remarked crisply that "If war is too important to be left to the generals, it should be clear that intelligence is too important to be left unsupervised."

Yet it was because the Senate felt that CIA should be left generally *unsupervised* that the Mansfield resolution was defeated. The fight against the resolution was led by the respected Senator Richard B. Russell, Democrat of Georgia, who stated bluntly that the Congress had no business delving into CIA's secrets. Russell noted that the statement had been made on the floor that the Armed Services subcommittee of which he was a member had not revealed to the country what it had learned about CIA operations.

"No, Mr. President," Russell said, "we have not told the country, and I do not propose to tell the country in the future, because if there is anything in the United States which should be held sacred behind the curtain of classified matter, it is information regarding the activities of this agency . . . It would be better to abolish it out of hand than it would be to adopt a theory that such information should be spread and made available to every member of Congress and to the members of the staff of any committee."

Supporters of the resolution thereupon reminded Russell that the Joint Congressional Committee on Atomic Energy had never had a leak of AEC secrets, but Russell was not impressed. He said there was no comparison, that the Atomic Energy Commission's primary function was to "undertake to preserve secrecy within the United States," whereas CIA "functions outside the United States and its principal endeavor is to break secrecy and to obtain secrets."

But it was the minority support submitted by Senator Carl Hayden, Democrat of Arizona, which touched on the Executive Department's most pressing reason for protecting the secrets of CIA—to wit, the nation's relations with its allies.

That report noted that while atomic energy was a subject for general legislative consideration, intelligence activities were "peculiarly the prerogative of the Executive and intimately associated with the conduct of the foreign relations of the country." In the maneuvers behind the scenes, it was this argument that weighed most heavily against the Mansfield resolution. Closer Congressional scrutiny of CIA, it was said, would cause considerable anxiety among those allied intelligence services which work closely with CIA but which were resolutely opposed to sharing their own secrets with the United States Congress. A Congressional watchdog over CIA, Senators were warned, would make allied intelligence services wary about entrusting their information to CIA lest a Congressional leak whisper it to the world.

Russell and his colleagues also dwelt on the peculiar, dangerous delicacy of CIA's secrets, involving, as Russell said, "activities about which it almost chills the marrow of a man to hear." The point was made tellingly by Senator William F. Knowland, Republican of California, that the "slightest leakage of information regarding perhaps just one field of activity might result in the disclosure of all the agents who had been operating [in a given country] and might mean their death by hanging . . ."

These are the points that have always given Congress pause whenever it took up the question of setting a watchdog over CIA—that CIA's activities are so dangerous that as few people as possible should be informed of them. Yet, after Cuba, it was obvious that something had to be done to curb CIA's free-wheeling operations, especially in the political-military area. Due largely to CIA's enthusiastic intelligence estimates, President Kennedy had entrusted the nation's prestige to a little band of ill-trained Cuban revolutionists and when their adventure flopped it was the United States which lost face in the world. So Kennedy quickly reactivated the continuing Killian committee, which had been dormant under President

Eisenhower's last few years in office, and he ordered it to report periodically on CIA's activities. He instructed the committee, headed by General Maxwell Taylor, to unearth quickly CIA's most flagrant faults. And, after a decent interval, he replaced Allen Dulles with John Alex McCone, a California steel man and shipbuilder and a former chairman of the Atomic Energy Commission.

It was apparent that McCone's major role as CIA boss would be to tighten up the operation, to gather up those loose ends that have tended to get CIA in trouble abroad. As something of an engineering production genius, the fifty-nine-year-old McCone had earned a reputation as a hard-driving executive with a fetish for establishing firm lines of responsibility. But he also had learned, in Washington, some of the requisites of the diplomat—first as Harry Truman's Under Secretary of the Air Force in 1950-51, and later as Eisenhower's Atomic Energy chief from mid-1959 to January 20, 1961.

A lifelong Republican and, incidentally, a Roman Catholic like Kennedy, McCone made many friends among the Democrats during his tour of duty at the Pentagon. Legislators on Capitol Hill particularly liked the way in which he went about the job of increasing the production of military planes during the Korean War. And as chairman of the AEC he proved adept at patching up differences that had arisen between the Commission and the Democratic majority on the prerogative-jealous Joint Congressional Committee on Atomic Energy.

There was the usual criticism, when McCone's appointment was announced, that he knew nothing about intelligence work. That, of course, is not necessarily a handicap to an outstanding executive like McCone, who has spent a lifetime supervising other people. Moreover he has had official contact with Communist imperialism both at the Pentagon and at AEC, and his approach to the Cold War is hard-boiled, pragmatic and realistic. He has always insisted the United

States needed a greater "sense of urgency" to hold its own with the Soviet Union.

Besides, it would have been impossible to find a man who knew as much about intelligence work as Allen Dulles, whose career it has been. And since such was the case, President Kennedy's only alternative was to settle for a man like McCone, a proven executive familiar with the complex atmosphere of Washington.

Certainly the country was in the mood for a change. The Cuban disaster, with its reams of post-mortems, had reminded the citizens—or informed them for the first time—of the long list of intelligence-diplomatic-military failures which had accumulated over the postwar years. The man-in-the-street wanted the government to "do something about CIA." His irritation was kept in a raw state by CIA's critics, who kept harping on the list of failures. There was, for instance, CIA's downrating of the Soviet Union's atom-bomb program; a few years after the end of World War II CIA had estimated it would take Russia ten years to detonate its first A-bomb, and there were red faces in Foggy Bottom when the Soviets successfully tested the bomb in 1949. Then, in 1953, the Russians beat us to the first *workable* hydrogen bomb, and went on to produce Sputnik and a young man named Yuri Gagarin who became the first human being to spin into orbit around the earth.

Moreover, the Bay of Pigs adventure had not been merely a military disaster; it had enormously strengthened Fidel Castro's Communist regime. Within a few months after the invasion failure, at least thirty Soviet MIG-17 jet fighters had been delivered to Cuba and were in operation. Castro's armed forces—numbering at least 200,000—had gained confidence from the defeat of the invaders and defections had dropped to a trickle. Arms and other military equipment were arriving daily in Havana; the anti-Castro underground had been disheartened and disorganized. By the summer of 1961, nothing but a full-scale invasion by well-trained and heavily equipped troops could have overthrown Castro.

Still new and strange to the office of the Presidency, Kennedy had not displayed the effectiveness and cold acquaintance with facts that had been his campaign hallmark. He had been uncertain; instead of delivering clear-cut decisions he had tried to solve the conflicting opinions of his advisors by compromise. Nevertheless, his eyes and ears in that operation were the men of CIA, and CIA's information was incorrect. Furthermore, when the President canceled the second air strike, which all but doomed the landing, he gave CIA the right to appeal the decision with the assurance that he would listen to all arguments for a reversal of his decision. But Allen Dulles had not appealed, possibly because he was too wrapped up in his own optimistic intelligence estimates.

Under the new set-up, another Cuba presumably cannot happen again—at least to the hapless Central Intelligence Agency. But the argument still rages in White House offices concerning just what part the United States, officially and lawfully, should play in any similar undertaking. On one side are ranged those who insist that in any such operation use of United States armed forces is essential to insure success, and that, in a world which respects power, the United States could weather the disapproval of other nations. On the other side are those who insist, with Senator J. William Fulbright, the erudite Democrat from Arkansas, that a nation dedicated to morality and the rule of law cannot dispatch its soldiers and airmen to overthrow a foreign government, but may—in accordance with general international practice—give secret help to such an attempt by nationalists of the country in question.

The Central Intelligence Agency, which by its very nature cannot be overly concerned with questions of morality, apparently no longer will be permitted such wide influence on the decision between those two points of view. That decision, it now seems evident, will be made only in the office of the President of the United States—as directed by the Constitution.

INDEX

Abadan oil refinery, 92
Abel, Rudolf Ivanovich (Goldfus), 232, 233, 240, 241
Abendpost, Frankfurt, 29
Abramov, Aleksander N., 216
Abwehr, 41
Acheson, Dean G., 180
Adana, Turkey, 112, 122, 124
Adenauer, Konrad, 156, 158, 160, 166
Adoula, Cyrille, 228
Agent, CIA, qualifications of, 27-29
Ajodani, Ahmed, 97
Albania, 142, 151
Alejos, Robert, 246
Alfhem, 64, 65
Algeria, 44, 45-53 *passim*, 147
Alsop, Joseph, 258
Alsop, Stewart, 201
Alt-Glienicke, village of, 3, 4
Amin, Majid, 80, 81
Amini, Ali, 88, 98
Amoy, 201
Anderson, Vernice, 184
Anglo-Iranian Oil Company, 90, 91, 93
Arab Legion, 83
Aref, Rafiq, 77, 81
Argentina, Nixon's trip to, 70
Armas, Carlos Castillo, 60, 62, 65, 66
Asanuma, Inejiro, 71
Ashraf, Princess, 93
Aswan Dam, 101, 108
Attaturk, Mustapha Kemal, 56, 57
"Authentication," 28

Baghdad Pact, 75, 76, 79, 80
Baldwin, Hanson, 264
Baraduc, Pierre, 50, 51
Barquin, Ramon, 253
Batista, Fulgencio, 245, 246
Baughman, U. E., 72
Bayer, Celal, 56
Beech, Keyes, 214
Bender, Frank, 247
Benjamin, Hildegarde, 163

Beria, Lavrenti P., 150
Berle, Adolf, 251
Berlin, East, *see* East Berlin
Berlin, Obert, 29, 30
Berlin, West, 3, 4
Berlin tunnel, built by CIA, 3-7
Berman, Jacob, 174
Berry, Frank, 146
Bissell, Richard M., Jr., 52, 246, 247, 249, 252, 255
"Black Chamber," disbanded by Stimson, 16
"Black" CIA employees, 24, 27
Black Lady of Espionage, 115; *see also* U-2 flight(s)
Boer War, Dulles' book on, 36, 38
Bonney, Walt, 124, 125
Boum Oun Na Champassak, 217
Bowles, Chester, 251
Bradley, Omar, 183, 184, 193, 194
Brooklyn Eagle, 233
Buesa, Manuel Artime, 247, 249
Bulganin, Nikolai A., 111, 175
Bundy, McGeorge, 251, 255
Burke, Arleigh, 14, 250
Burma, 196, 197, 198
Burns, Eugene, 78
Byrnes, James F., 9

Cairo, Egypt, 102, 104, 105
Cambodia, 210, 216
Cardona, Jose Miro, 248, 254
Carney, Robert, 203
Castro, Fidel, 244, 246; Cuban invasion defeated by, 254-55; popular support of, 250; strengthened by failure of invasion, 267; *see also* Cuba
Central Intelligence Agency, and Algerian crisis, 45-53 *passim*, 147; Berlin tunnel built by, 3-7; budget of, 15; in Burma, 198; and Chiang Kai-shek, 199, 200, 201, 202, 204, 205, 206; and coat hanger analysis, 20-21; Communism fought by, 44,

269

Tiao Somsonith, 215
Timberlake, Clare, 222
Time magazine, 37
Tito, Josip B., 175
Titoism, 174
Todd, Clover, 37-38
Toure, Seku, 221
Trans-Jordan, 82
Trudeau, Arthur Gilbert, 160
Truman, Harry S., 9, 10, 31, 35, 42,
  179, 199, 200, 266; and Korean
  War, 180, 181, 182, 183, 190, 191,
  192; meeting with MacArthur, 183-
  84, 185
Tshombe, Moise, 220, 224, 225, 226,
  227, 228
Tudeh, 92
Tunnel, Berlin, built by CIA, 3-7
Turkey, generals' revolt in, 55-58;
  Incirlik Air Base in, 114, 115, 121,
  122
Twining, Nathan, 203

U Nu, 198
U-2 flight(s), 112-15; and Eisenhower,
  113, 123, 125, 126, 127-28, 129, 130,
  131; evaluated by Soviet officials,
  132-34; and Khrushchev, 113, 120,
  122-23, 124, 126, 129-30, 131, 132-
  33; by Powers, 115-19
United Nations, 87, 111, 253; in
  Congo, 221, 223, 226, 227; in Korean War, 181, 183, 192; Security
  Council of, 180
United States Intelligence Board, 232
*United States News and World Re-
  port,* 163
Uruguay, Nixon's trip to, 70

Vandenberg, Hoyt S., 10
Venezuela, Nixon's trip to, 69

Versailles peace conference, 37
Vershinin, Marshal, 120
Vientiane, Laos, 210, 216, 219
Vietminh, 208, 209, 210
Vietnam, 208, 210, 211
Voice of America, 166

Wafd Party, 102, 103
Wall Street Journal, 263
Walsingham, Francis, 8
Washington Post, 109, 110
Washington Post and Times-Herald,
  122
Washington Star, 48
Washington Times-Herald, 30
Western Enterprises, Inc., 201, 202
White, Lincoln, 124, 125, 127
White, Michael, 78
White, Sam, 50, 51
"White" CIA employees, 24, 25, 27,
  155
Wiley, Alexander, 132, 166, 183
Willoughby, C. A., 169, 185, 186, 187,
  188, 193
Wilson, Charles E., 260
Wilson, Woodrow, 36
Witaszewski, Kazimierz, 177
Wolff, Karl, 42
Wood, George, 42
World Peace Council, 46, 154
World War I, 16, 34, 35
World War II, 2, 34, 39 ff., 54, 156-57,
  230, 231, 258
Wyszynski, Stefan Cardinal, 177

Yaffi, Abdullah, 85

Zahedi, Fazlollah, 94, 96
Zaisser, Wilhelm, 163
Zhukov, Georgi, 151, 175